Of BOOKS
and MEN

Of BOOKS *and* MEN

By JOSEPH J. REILLY

Author of *Dear Prue's Husband, Newman as a Man of Letters*, etc.

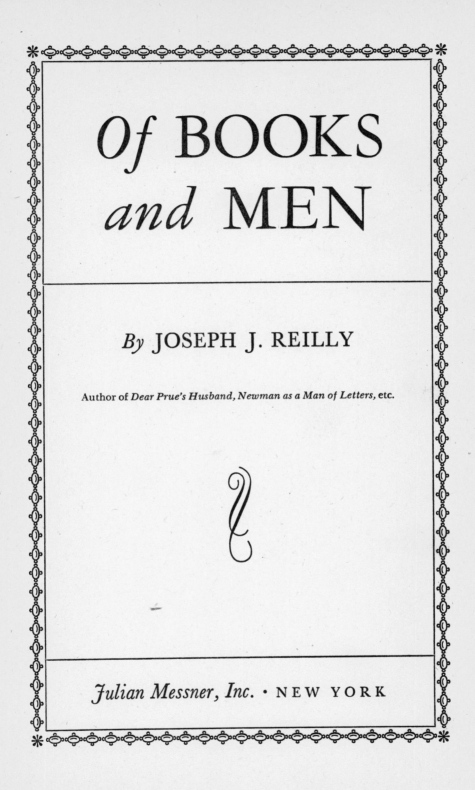

Julian Messner, Inc. · NEW YORK

PUBLISHED BY JULIAN MESSNER, INC.
8 WEST 40TH STREET, NEW YORK

PRINTED IN THE UNITED STATES OF AMERICA
BY MONTAUK BOOK MANUFACTURING CORP.

FOR
Ellie and *Kathie*

Contents

Acknowledgments

WHILE THIS BOOK WAS IN THE MAKING, CERTAIN INTERESTED FRIENDS offered timely suggestions, among them Dr. George N. Shuster, President of Hunter College. Others generously read the proofs: Mrs. Edith Donovan, Miss Eleanor Downing, Miss Margaret Grant Plumb, Dr. Claire McGlinchee, and Miss Renata Remy. It is a pleasure to acknowledge these debts and offer thanks.

For permission to use copyright material I am grateful to Dodd Mead & Co.: *The Collected Poems of G. K. Chesterton;* Henry Holt & Co.: *The Poetry of A. E. Housman;* Houghton Mifflin Co.: Louise Imogen Guiney, *Happy Ending;* The Incorporated Society of Authors, Playwrights, and Composers, Briarlea House, Mortimer, Berkshire, England: A. E. Housman, *Easter Hymn;* Miss Willa Cather, author, and Alfred A. Knopf, Inc., publisher, of *April Twilights;* Charles Scribner's Sons: John Finley, *Poems;* Yale University Press: *The Letters of Charles and Mary Lamb.*

JOSEPH J. REILLY

Hunter College of the City of New York
1942

Some of These Moderns

The Poetry of A. E. Housman

WITHIN THE PAST SEVEN YEARS, FOUR ENGLISH POETS HAVE CEASED to sing and their voices have sunk into silence. Although none challenged the princes of English song, all added something beautiful and distinctive to what is the most magnificent body of poetry in the world. In William Watson poetry and criticism met in exquisite union. Kipling reclaimed the ballad from brilliant artificers and gave it back to the spontaneous uses of the people. Chesterton took that same ballad and without despoiling it of spontaneity endowed it with gorgeous color and an almost epic grandeur. A. E. Housman, latest of the four to die, had his distinctive place and made his unique contribution no less than these others. Just where is his place and what was his contribution?

In 1896 a slim volume of verse appeared called *A Shropshire Lad,* whereupon Louise Imogen Guiney wrote a friend:

> They fired me, as new-discovered things in art do. The book's best is genuine, full of conscious literary power, exquisitely and negligently carried. It has taken me prodigiously.

So too it took the world, achieving a popularity exceeded only by FitzGerald's *Rubaiyat.* Miss Guiney lived for a quarter of a century longer, but was in her grave before the author of *A Shropshire Lad* broke into song again, this time with *Last Poems* (September, 1922) which he prefaced with a brief but revealing foreword.

3

I publish these poems, few though they are, because it is not likely
that I shall ever be impelled to write much more. I can no longer
expect to be revisited by the continuous excitement under which
in the early months of 1895 I wrote the greater part of my other
book, nor indeed could I well sustain it if it came.

Housman did not change his mind; he published no more
verse but on his death in May, 1936, it was discovered that he had
sanctioned a posthumous volume, intrusting it to his brother
Laurence and charging him to include in it nothing which seemed
inferior to the average of the two earlier collections. The result
was *More Poems* (October, 1936) which contained forty-eight
lyrics. As virtually all these were in existence when *A Shropshire
Lad* and *Last Poems* appeared, it seems clear that their author's
fastidious taste had judged them inferior. I think he was right.
But to call them inferior is not to dispraise them but to say
that with all their virtues—and they are the virtues of a great
poet—they miss, sometimes by a hairbreadth, the glamour, the
poignancy, and the enchantment of the others.

Just who was this mysterious person who published an epoch-
making volume at thirty-seven, was silent for twenty-six years, and
then at the age of sixty-three published another, even more
slender than the first, with the laconic remark that this was all?
Alfred Edward Housman, born March 26, 1859, was an Oxford
graduate, who from 1882 for a decade was a clerk in the Patent
Office and from 1892 till his death Professor of Latin first at University College, London, and later at Cambridge. Though he
ranked as one of the greatest classical scholars of his time he was
so reticent, shy, and withdrawn that long before his death he had
become a legendary figure to the typical undergraduate. Only
once since the publication of *Last Poems* did he reappear: on
May 9, 1933, he delivered the most famous lecture of the twentieth century, entitled "The Name and Nature of Poetry," which
has proved enormously provocative and bids fair to achieve a place
with such classic pronouncements on poetry by poets as those of
Sidney, Shelley, and Leigh Hunt.

Housman's range is not wide; the fundamental ideas with which
he concerns himself are few. He tells us that death is certain; that
the joys of life are casual, its sorrows sure; that a dead man's
friends soon forget him and his sweetheart finds ready consolation

in another's arms; that Nature, though beautiful, is indifferent or even unkind; that when the drums beat it is to a conflict without reason, a struggle without hope. In all this there is nothing new; the newness is in the way it is said and said again and yet again, each time from a fresh point of view and with terse and startling beauty.

> With rue my heart is laden
>   For golden friends I had,
> For many a rose-lipt maiden
>   And many a lightfoot lad.
>
> By brooks too broad for leaping
>   The lightfoot boys are laid;
> The rose-lipt girls are sleeping
>   In fields where roses fade.

Here is the same thought, more crisply put, its tempo heightened, the note of regret veiled but unmistakable, like the faint moan of a distant sea:

> From far, from eve and morning
>   And yon twelve-winded sky,
> The stuff of life to knit me
>   Blew hither: here am I.
>
> Now—for a breath I tarry
>   Nor yet disperse apart—
> Take my hand quick and tell me,
>   What have you in your heart.
>
> Speak now, and I will answer;
>   How shall I help you, say;
> Ere to the wind's twelve quarters
>   I take my endless way.

It is not Housman's preoccupation with death that marks him as a pessimist, but his conviction that the grave is the end of all things and life its unwanted, dull, and futile prelude. Men rise with the sun, till their fields, endure rain and cold, seek the meager respite of sleep, and so on endlessly till the night comes that has no dawn. Others will follow, born to the same toil, the same delusive hopes, the same dreamless and unending sleep at the last. What shall man do who peoples so profitless a world? If he turns to Nature, to the loveliness of the cherry trees "living with bloom along the bough," his joy withers at the thought that a day will dawn when he will behold it no more; if "beyond the moor and mountain crest" he turns to the sunset, he incurs the poet's caution:

> Comrade, look not on the west:
> 'Twill have the heart out of your breast;
> 'Twill take your thoughts and sink them far,
> Leagues beyond the sunset bar.

All thought is torment, says Housman, for it leads to emptiness and despair. Men may banish it, taking refuge in liquor, love, or fights, but not for long:

> But men at whiles are sober
> And think by fits and starts,
> And if they think, they fasten
> Their hands upon their hearts.

Then death is better than life? Yes. But does not death hold its own terrors? Beyond life, says the poet, lurk no shapes of evil, only silence and darkness:

> Now hollow fires burn out to black,
> And lights are guttering low:
> Square your shoulders, lift your pack,
> And leave your friends and go.

> Oh never fear, man, nought's to dread,
> Look not left nor right:
> In all the endless road you tread
> There's nothing but the night.

Since our joys are delusive, nature in her beauty a monitress of the inevitable end, and thought a ghost that rises for our torment and despair, what shall we do?

Housman gives the answer under many guises, sometimes as a direct admonition as in "Epilogue" and in "The Chestnut casts his flambeaux"; sometimes indirectly as in "On the idle hill of summer" and the mordant "Epitaph on an Army of Mercenaries"; sometimes by insinuating it with cool impersonality as in "The Oracles," "Lancer," and "Grenadier." The mood in which he speaks varies from languor born of despair to a rare and bitter defiance like that in which his fellow pessimist Hardy wrote "New Year's Eve" and brought *Tess of the D'Urbervilles* to a close. Says Housman:

> The troubles of our proud and angry dust
> Are from eternity and shall not fail.
> Bear them we can, and if we can we must.
> Shoulder the sky, my lad, and drink your ale.

Usually Housman's belief that stoical endurance is the only course is exemplified in the soldier. The Spartan, whose oracle can tell him only that against the Persian host

[whose] fighters drink the river up, whose shafts benight the air

he and his fellows will "die for nought," remains unperturbed:

The Spartans in the sea-wet rock sat down and combed their hair.

Even the hired soldiers of old time, the riff-raff of the world, those nameless and forgotten men, played their stoical part without heroics, without self-pity:

> These, in the day when heaven was falling,
> The hour when earth's foundations fled,
> Followed their mercenary calling
> And took their wages and are dead.

It has been said that Housman has no English forbears; that as poet he stands alone. To a degree that is true but he is not without a kinship with other poets: with Landor in his crispness and brevity; with the ballads in homeliness of setting and unabashed simplicity of treatment; with Arnold in his stoicism; with James Thomson in his sense of the vanity and nothingness of things; with Thomas Hardy, his closest spiritual brother, in intensity of feeling, in his conception of nature as a seductive but malign enchantress, in pessimism as an inescapable but joyless conviction, and in pity for humankind. James Thomson's great poem is like a mass of masonry alternately plucked out of the dark by lightning and plunged back into its depths again. Housman's poems are like cameos, cut by an exquisite and unerring hand. Thomson's verse echoes the cry of a soul in torment; Housman's is always measured, crisp, with a deceptive coolness veiling its fires. Curiously enough both Hardy and Housman once broke through their inflexible pessimism, once at least felt their unfaith trouble them, Hardy in his longing to find a ray of hope, whether beside the Manger on Christmas Eve or in the ecstasies of a carolling thrush; Housman in the first poem of his posthumous collection, a passionate thing, haunting in its beauty and its anguish:

EASTER HYMN

If in that Syrian garden, ages slain,
You sleep, and know not you are dead in vain,
Nor even in dreams behold how dark and bright
Ascends in smoke and fire by day and night
The hate you died to quench and could but fan,
Sleep well and see no morning, son of man.

But if, the grave rent and the stone rolled by,
At the right hand of majesty on high
You sit, and sitting so remember yet
Your tears, your agony and bloody sweat,
Your cross and passion and the life you gave,
Bow hither out of heaven and see and save.

Both Hardy and Housman have written unforgettable lyrics but Housman is the finer artist. Indeed he is one of the great lyric artists in English who in some miraculous way achieves the perfect expression of his thought by means which seem elementary and outworn. His diction is as simple as that of the ballads which Wordsworth hallowed by praise and use; his metrical patterns are limited and traditional; his imagery is gathered from no far domains or scarce-known usages; his metaphors are rarely bold. Just as he expounds no novel views so he reveals no novel technique. His favorite devices are few and simple: colliteration, assonance, unlooked for pauses and shifts of stress, the occasional substitution of a trochee or an anapest for an iamb. True he handles them with such skill and grace that they seem casual but skill and grace go only a short way to explain his art. Looking further we find that his rhymes are always handmaids of his thought and have the air of being in their inevitable places. Again, we note in the midst of the everyday diction he employs—as with Wordsworth at his best—the unexpected (never the *precious*) word that surprises and delights us:

> And our football on the track
> Fetched the *daunting* echo back.

> But the city *dusk* and *mute*
> Slept and there was no pursuit.

With such slender resources, from such common things as dawn and ships, with common words in common molds comes this transfiguration, this thing of startling beauty:

> Wake: the silver dusk returning
>   Up the beach of darkness brims,
> And the ship of sunrise burning
>   Strands upon the eastern rims.

The ultimate secret of Housman (and of every other poet) must remain impenetrable, but a nearer approach to it may be found in the varied and mournful cadences that dwell beneath the flow of his lines like "the moan of Thessalian seas." The tears of things known of all men are in them and weigh upon the heart as words alone can never do. "Poetry," he said in his famous lecture, "is not the thing but the way of saying it," and again, "Meaning is of the intellect, poetry is not," and however one may disagree it is clear that Housman, true to his pronouncement, seeks primarily a certain emotional response from the reader and that he has mastered those metrical subtleties which unfailingly evoke it. Some of his most perfect poems do little more than induce a vague sadness, a not unpleasing melancholy, as if the wraith of some remote, half-forgotten experience, too tenuous to sustain thought, had been awakened. They are "unsubstantial fairy things" but they are hard to forget, as witness that haunting four-stanzaed lyric which begins

> White in the moon the long road lies,
>   The moon stands blank above;
> White in the moon the long road lies
>   That leads me from my love.

"O Sancta Simplicitas!" cried Louise Guiney, and small wonder. Did ever poet do more with less? Here is a handful of commonplace monosyllables, versed without tropes, the third line repeating the first, and each substituting an initial trochee for an iamb. But by some miracle they sing, they awaken the imagination, their cadence sighs like a mournful undertone into one's heart and lo! a thing of beauty in which live the magic of all moons, the sadness of all parted lovers!

It is Housman's poetry not his pessimism that is meant for mankind and that seems to promise him enduring fame. Though much of it was written in the decadent nineties it was untouched by either the sensual or the perverse, and its reading of life, though without hope, reveals sincerity, heroism, and a strength that neither strives nor cries. Housman yearned for the infinite and it was his inability to believe it attainable that quenched his sun as it quenched Lucretius'.

Does his reading of life offend me? Except in three or four of his lyrics (and those not the best), No. His spell is upon me. I too regret those "blue remembered hills" in "the land of lost content," the "early laurelled head" now in the dust, the once glad voices that now cry "down the sighing wind in vain." I too love "the star-filled seas," the "light-leaved spring," the flowers that "stream from the hawthorn on the wind away," the shadows of night that "drown in the golden deluge of the morn." I too know the bitterness of disillusionment, the irony of circumstance, the need for sheer courage, the sweetness of life, and the chilling thought of death. And when Housman touches these themes in lyrics of such subtly cadenced and austere and poignant beauty as English verse has rarely equalled, I give him thanks. It is when he finds the life they bear upon a dark riddle whose only answer is death that we part company; for as he bids me mark the sinking sun that

> drinks away
> From air and land the lees of day

the "eternal thoughts" that steal upon us from across "the gulf of evening" only desolate his soul, but mine, chastened and enriched, they fill with peace.

The Novels of Maurice Baring

THE WRITINGS OF BELLOC AND OF THE LATE GILBERT CHESTERTON
have overshadowed those of Maurice Baring, the third member
of that extraordinary fellowship. Everybody knows that *Lepanto*
is one of the most gorgeous poems in the language and that *Marie
Antoinette* ranks among the memorable biographies of our time,
but few are aware that Baring is equally many-sided and that his
beauty of style, deep human sympathies, and psychological penetration help to make him one of the most important of contemporary British novelists. He has been many things, diplomat,
journalist, soldier, critic, and poet, and won distinction in every
role. In 1909 he became a Catholic, "the only action of my life,"
he wrote, "which I am quite certain I have never regretted." It is
necessary to know this in order to understand his outlook on life
as it is revealed in his novels.

Baring selects his characters, settings, and incidents from the
life he knows best. Most of his people have means and culture,
they recruit the diplomatic service and the civil professions, and
they are equally at home at great country houses, embassy dinners,
and continental watering places. His men are decent, intelligent,
unspiritual, and, all told, undistinguished. His chief concern is
with women and he draws them with delicacy, sureness of touch,
and extraordinary insight. Here are dowagers, (the Princess Julia,
in *Cat's Cradle*, Guido's mother, cool and masterful, to whom
her daughter-in-law is not a human soul but something between

11

an ornament and a chattel, is unforgettable); aunts in the late
autumn of their years who always have worldly wisdom and sometimes fortunes to bestow on favorite nephews; widows of retired
diplomats or army officers whose sole thought is to hold their social
places and marry off their daughters to the "right" men; the
daughters themselves who obediently acquiesce in the parental
plans even though, as sometimes happens, their hearts are
elsewhere.

In all but one of Baring's most important novels it is a woman
who plays the leading part. Why? Because in Baring's view women
are more interesting. Why that? Because morally they are more
self-sufficient, their emotions are subtler, deeper, and more enduring, and finally because they have a certain spirituality at the core
and a greater capacity for self-dedication and sacrifice. If they do
not inspire men to great achievements they are capable of banishing emptiness from their lives and bringing harmony to their
souls; should they fail, the fault is less with them than with their
stars or with the instability or blindness of the men.

Baring pictures them as lovely and gracious with a light in their
eyes when young, a thinly veiled sadness when mature, and always
a distinction elusive but unmistakable. Here is Madame D'Alberg
(*The Coat Without Seam*) as Christopher Trevenen first sees her:
"She was pale, remote, and still, with the stillness of deep waters;
no longer young, but not yet middle-aged. She had not lost her
youthfulness of line and figure. She had ripples of dark hair, and
her face in repose was sad. Christopher thought he had never seen
a sadder face. It was a young face, and the sadness in it seemed
inappropriate and ill-allotted, an unfair, unmerited load. But
then there were her eyes . . . her eyes . . . with their long lashes;
what colour were they? Brown or blue? or black? When she smiled
an elfin gleam lit up her face, which gave one the idea that at
some time or other her spirits had been, and perhaps even now
were at moments wild. There was twilight in her eyes but it gave
hints every now and then of some radiant dawn. They were like
some curious precious stone, that is dark in the daytime, and has
strange golden lights at night."

It is the social not the business side of life to which we are
introduced; not offices or shops or surging crowds, but concerts,
exhibitions, dinner parties, varied by week-ends at shooting lodges

in Scotland or holidays in Cornwall or along the upper Thames
or on the Continent. Does this sound like a restricted world, a
Henry James world? Perhaps, but whose world is not restricted?
The important point is that beneath the well-bred restraint of
Baring's people burn the fires of those passions which are in all
the children of men; the same temptations, the same divided
loyalties, the same ills of mind and spirit are their equal heritage.
If Baring's interests center in the Colonel's Lady rather than in
Judy O'Grady, he knows that every hunger of heart, every impulse
which Judy experiences is shared by her more highly placed sister-
under-the-skin. Kranitzky, the clever Russian *(Daphne Adeane)*,
says to Fanny Choyce, wife of a member of Parliament and mother
of two children: "You take life as it comes . . . you feel safe, serene,
and secure. But if one day . . . well, if one day there should be a
careless Brangäne who should leave a *philtre* lying about, and
you were to mistake it for wine and drink it . . . Then you would
be mad . . . you would love like a tigress and like a *grisette*,
comme une . . . well—bêtement."

To marry and to be given in marriage is, as a social fact, the
world's primary business, and the endless complications pre- and
post- provide the stuff of virtually all fiction; the infinite variety
of its treatment is what proves the novelist. To the incurable
romantic the climax of courtship made dramatic by numerous
obstacles is a happy marriage; to the realist, as Thackeray observed, marriage does not end but ushers in the most interesting
phase of life. With this of course Baring agrees for though he is
at heart a lyric poet, he has been in close contact with life too long
to ignore its facts.

In the typical Baring novel a young girl marries at eighteen
or twenty. She is fresh, unspoiled, and docile. If she has had an
early love affair, it is usually with a romantic young man who cares
deeply but whose lack of money or prospects provides older heads
with a reason for interfering and preaching with ultimate success
the superior wisdom of marrying the man of their choice. (Baring
treats these youthful affairs with understanding and reverence and
he provides for their culminating episode a setting whose loveliness recalls the fourteenth chapter of *Richard Feverel.*) In any
case she has had little experience with life, and when a man of
means and position, usually her senior by ten or twelve years, is

attracted by her youth and beauty, her elders manage matters with "sense" and the marriage occurs with "everybody" present. There is a honeymoon in the country, a return to London, the opening of the town house—and then the real story is ready to unfold.

The society which the bride glimpsed before but becomes a part of now is composed of people with whom restraint and good breeding are essential and the ultimate condemnation is to behave badly. It is a sophisticated society like Henry James's and Galsworthy's, half pagan and inwardly restive, which lives by its own code, prizing a pledged word more than continence and demanding that its members, in deference to the outer decencies, affect to believe that their spouses, however notorious their "affairs," are above suspicion. To find consolation for a husband's or a wife's infidelity is general and, according to the code, so natural that the opposite course arouses comment.

The typical Baring heroine does not yield herself to the semi-paganism in which this society is steeped, for within her is an unconscious and saving grace. Besides, she finds satisfaction in a fine home, a husband universally deemed desirable, and the novelty of a situation never experienced before. Soon, sometimes tragically soon, she comes to realize that what counts most is none of these things but her relations with her husband. That realization reacts in different ways but it leads in every case to one discovery, the discovery that love complete, reciprocal, absorbing, love as the grand passion beside which all else in life shrinks to nothingness is wanting. It is this passion, a noble and transcendent thing, which Baring's heroines crave and to which they are capable of sacrificing every lesser good. It is this passion, let me repeat, which fails to find fulfilment in their marriage. Therein lie the seeds of tragedy. Fanny Choyce, loving her husband dearly, finds him giving her everything but the one thing necessary; Princess Blanche (*Cat's Cradle*) and Madame D'Alberg, unable to meet their husbands' passion on equal terms, see it in the one case (with vain self-reproach) bestowed elsewhere, and in the other, turn to something deadlier than hate; Daphne Adeane strives to give her husband the all which his love deserves, but with an unsuccess of which his ignorance makes the result no less tragic; Zita Harmer (*The Lonely Lady of Dulwich*) and Mrs. Housman (*Passing By*) give everything only to meet with neglect and infidelity. Where love or jealousy is awakened Baring's women and most of his men are extraordinarily perceptive. They do not need anything so gross as an affirmation or a denial, an unearthed letter or a warning from a meddler. As with Henry James's women the intonation of a voice, a moment's silence, a look meaningless to all the world else, tells everything.

Thus what follows belongs in each case to the hidden drama of life; on the surface little happens, but in the relations of husband and wife certain imperceptible but subtle changes occur sensed by each in turn but overtly unacknowledged. The rift steadily widens until at last the woman is oppressed by a sense of the emptiness of life or of her personal isolation and moral loneliness. Wealth, social success, even children, serve less to mitigate this feeling than to accentuate the absence of the one essential thing. Then one day a man comes into her life, subtly different from all the others, who gradually fills its emptiness and re-establishes her sense of participation in life and the joy of it. And so at last the high moment comes, love awakens love, the grand passion is born, and the woman's heart (the ultimate center, let me repeat, of Baring's interest) comes into its own. Now at last its thirst is to be quenched, its hunger satisfied; after long wanderings in the desert it reaches the City of Delight. The mutual revelation of the lovers' passion is pictured in Baring's novels as in his poetry as a transcendent experience. Francis Greene tells Fanny Choyce he loves her. A moment later "she was in his arms, and his first kiss seemed to last for ever. And for her and for him the world stood still. They were far away in another world, beyond the stars, above the skies, under the seas, east of the sun and west of the moon. . . . Fanny felt that she was dying of happiness, that she had died, not one but many deaths, and had been born again, and that she was living and soaring through aeons of bliss, exploring new circles of Paradise that seemed to open and unfold like the petals of a rose of fire."

In this hour of rapture all the operations of life seem suspended; it is as if the lovers were beyond the reach of man and fate.

But our days are not lived thus. The insistent and inescapable claims of life pluck us back to reality, to loyalties transformed to duties by long service, to innumerable nameless things akin to these, *imponderabilia* light as air that weigh us down, to conscience scotched but already quickening. For a while the lovers give hostages to fate, establish a kind of *modus vivendi* whereby, on the surface, things remain as before. Sometimes this is not hard to do, as for Dr. Greene and Fanny Choyce whose husband is away at the front, sometimes it is difficult, as for Blanche Roccapalumba *(Cat's Cradle)* whose husband's jealousy seems armed with a hundred eyes.

But the significant thing is that apprehension dogs the lovers' steps; the man's mind, the woman's conscience, find no rest; something will happen, *must* happen; they feel (the woman more acutely) that they are living beneath a suspended sword or are drifting downstream to a whirlpool. Then one day—a matter of months, a matter of years—the sword falls: the forces of Fate (or Destiny, if you prefer, or Providence), temporarily halted, resume their imperious march; the evasion of the inevitable comes to an end, and, for the woman, "Duty and inclination," in Stevenson's fine phrase, "come nobly to the grapple." Sometimes, as with Madame D'Alberg, Hyacinth Wake *(Daphne Adeane)*, and Mrs. Housman *(Passing By)*, we are not permitted to see that duel but merely to surmise its intensity from the character of the woman and the aftermath; sometimes, as with Princess Blanche and more especially Fanny Choyce, we are given the struggle in full view and then Baring's treatment is admirable for its firmness and delicacy.

Let me bring Fanny's case into focus. At twenty she marries Michael Choyce, thirty-three, whose political career is promising. He admires her, she adores him; but though children come and her life is full and interesting, she knows she has missed love. When her husband's admiration for her is finally transformed to passion it is too late. At the outbreak of the World War he enlists, she takes up nursing and in the course of her work meets a brilliant specialist, Dr. Francis Greene. They fall passionately in love and for three years the relationship continues. Meanwhile Michael is reported missing; exhaustive inquiries continuing throughout the war yield nothing more. At last, just as Fanny and Greene are completing arrangements for their marriage, word comes that Michael has been found in an obscure corner of Belgium, that the amnesia from which he suffered for over two years has cleared up and that he will be home within thirty-six hours. Fanny resolves to meet Michael with a brief statement of the facts: she refuses to give up Francis; she cannot resume the old life with Michael for this, as she sees it, is to live a lie. . . By chance she meets Father Rendall, an acquaintance of earlier years, and though she is not a Catholic but "a Pagan who believes in Fate and Law but not in a future life or a personal God," she presents her case and hears in return of the necessity for sacrifice in a scene reminiscent of that immortal one wherein Savonarola, encountering the disillusioned Romola fleeing from Florence and her husband, reminds her of the undying claims of duty. Fanny is rebellious. . . . Back in her house, full of memories, "She sat down and thought over the situation. The tremendous, the unexpected, the inevitable had happened. She could hardly realize it yet. She was still stunned by the blow. The inevitable—the end had come—what she had feared—what [she and her lover] had both feared—had happened. Fate or Providence had stepped in as surely and suddenly, as irrevocably, as in Greek tragedy, and had separated her and Francis once and for all, and for ever."

It would be a mistake to suppose that all Baring's novels follow an identical pattern. The pattern varies in many details and in accordance with the character of the woman who plays the chief part. Yielding to a great passion does not always result in a *liaison* as with Fanny and Greene. Mrs. Housman, a Catholic, worn down by her husband's infidelities, resolves to elope and leaves a farewell note in his desk. In London, on her way to the rendezvous in Paris, she receives a telegram that her husband has just died of a heart-attack. Only she and the dead man could have known the contents of that fateful letter. She returns at once, yields him burial, and a fortnight later enters a convent in Italy. Zita Harmer, on discovering that her husband has guessed her intention to go to Algiers with the poet Bossis, is overwhelmed with shame and gives up the plan. Princess Blanche agrees to elope with Alfredo Chiaramonte, not because she is in love but because she seeks an escape from a marriage no longer endurable. The sudden collapse of her husband intervenes, she abandons her plan, and remains to nurse him. Hyacinth Wake and Daphne Adeane, both Catholics, meet the challenge of the grand passion, Daphne by resistance, Hyacinth by surrender first, then by renunciation, and each pays the price in health and life. Mme. D'Alberg, unhappily married, accepts the attentions of Carlo Altamura and, while not going to extremes, permits him to sacrifice to her both his home and his career.

Let us look further into these cases. In all but Daphne Adeane's, the woman acts against her conscience, however much passion or marital unhappiness may seem a justification. In one form or other each pays the price for her lapse. Mrs. Housman gives up the man who adores her and the world for which she seemed born. Zita Harmer's great passion, not for Bossis but years later for Walter Price, is tragically misplaced, and the publicity she risks to advance Price's career results in breaking up her home and bringing her to a lonely old age. Mme. D'Alberg's hour comes when she finds herself in love with Christopher Trevenen, but a sense of obligation to Altamura, now that his wife's death removes the sole obstacle to marriage, stands in her way. The case of Blanche Roccapalumba has its individual aspects. Into the weary months of her self-sacrifice to her stricken husband which follow her abandoned elopement, comes Bernard Lacy, protesting his love and awakening her whole soul for the first time. When at last her husband's death leaves her free to marry Bernard, he is in love with Rose Mary Clifford, her niece, and though Blanche knows it she interprets as her own a proposal intended for her younger rival. "[Bernard and Blanche] remained a long time silent. He held her hand, and they looked into each other's eyes, and Blanche said to herself: 'Oh, my God! if I have done wrong I will make it up by loving him in a way nobody has ever loved any one. This can't be wrong. I have a right to him. I love him more than any one else can or could love him. He is mine, mine, mine . . . for ever, till death, and beyond, and no one can take him away from me . . .' "

Blanche and Bernard are married but the satisfaction she sought eludes her. The shadow of Rose Mary darkens her path; the certainty that Bernard, though outwardly devoted, really loves the younger woman, more than ever embitters her days. "The Nemesis is in your acts," thought Blanche. "Every sin avenges itself, carries its vengeance with it, just as a seed carries its fruit . . . And even those who do not admit this have to submit to it . . . They cannot avoid their retribution although they may call it by some other name . . . The mistake was marrying Guido. I knew it 'was wrong at the time, and I did it; everything else proceeded directly from that, nothing wiped out that first blunder."

But the first blunder of Baring's women is not a deliberate piece of wrong-doing: it is a mistake in judgment, in entering upon a marriage in deference to the wishes of a parent or without understanding (how can a girl of eighteen or twenty understand?) the innumerable compromises and delicate adjustments involved in the most fundamental and hazardous of life's relationships and the unpredictable reactions which make or mar it. Having taken that first step she cannot turn back or free herself from the new obligations in which she has become enmeshed. It is when she tries that she finds herself inviting the counterstroke of Fate (or Providence); it is when she persists that its weight falls. Is this realism? Of the most essential kind. Do we find it upsetting? Tragically so. Can we change it? No, says Baring, and Thomas Hardy would agree with him. Why not? Because life is like that, full of imperfect understanding and innocent hopes defeated and moral waste so vast and seemingly so purposeless. Whence comes all this tragedy inexplicable because counter to the instincts of human justice? From the malicious Overlord, says Hardy, ("President of the Immortals," he calls him in *Tess*), who toys with his creatures as a cat with a mouse, and, suddenly wearying of the sport, destroys them with a blow. Baring disagrees. Our individual tragedies, he says in his most moving novel, *The Coat Without Seam,* are like the patches and stains on the wrong side of a perfectly woven garment. The disfigurements come from our faulty vision, our awkward fingers; the perfection of its seamless beauty from One whose eyes can see all things, even men's secret thoughts, and whose hands can shape all things, even their broken hearts, to a nobler destiny than they dare to dream. It is this faith which Baring won by the step he has "never regretted," and which Hardy desired in vain. How shall we face life and live it through? With stoicism, says Hardy, in which there is no hope. With resignation, says Baring, which alone brings healing and peace.

Baring's ideal woman is Daphne Adeane, a Catholic, "a will of steel in a frail body," whose name is given to a novel in which she never appears, since like Tom Outland in Willa Cather's *Professor's House,* she has died before the story opens. But, again like Outland, she is a living influence throughout and is the most

effective of the characters because morally the strongest, spiritually the most valiant. Three men loved her passionately, her husband and two others. To the love of one of those two her heart
responded in what she knew to be the great passion of her life.
She resisted it and, though the struggle wore her out and finally
killed her, she never once by word or overt act betrayed her secret.
Her pretence of light-heartedness never failed, her guard was
never down, and the man who watched for a sign that she returned
his adoration watched in vain. To the little clan that knew her
intimately she underwent after death a kind of canonization: to
resemble her in looks or manner was to be adored, to deviate from
her standards of conduct was ultimately to undermine the very
love which prompted the deviation.

Baring is never directly didactic. His Catholics, even his priests,
explain the teachings of their faith only when asked, and confess
that life poses to them as to non-believers questions which evade
all logic but that of faith. Baring is too good an artist and too
honest an observer to imply that people who inherit or accept
Catholicism escape devastating temptations or always defeat them.
Much is given them, but the final effort, the will to victory, as
with Hyacinth Wake, only they themselves can supply. Mrs. Lacy
(Cat's Cradle), a devout Catholic, muses thus over her son Bernard:
"He will have to go to the school of life like every one else. There
was no escape—no escape from life, no escape from sorrow, misery,
and pain; or, rather, man confined in those dungeons is forced to
make his own rope-ladder, to climb the spiked walls, and with
scarred hands and bleeding feet to reach 'lasting freedoms.' "

Of Baring's novels Cat's Cradle is the most ambitious, The Coat
Without Seam the most deeply felt, The Lonely Lady of Dulwich
the most deftly done, Friday's Business the most satiric, A Triangle
the subtlest, Daphne Adeane all told the finest. Long after one is
finished with Baring's novels scenes from them cling to the
memory: the pleasure party on the Thames in Robert Peckham,
with the song of the revellers and the serenity of a summer afternoon stilling for a little hour and for the last time the tumult in
Robert's heart; the final chapter of Friday's Business, marked by
Hardy's irony of circumstance and Maupassant's detachment; the
love scene in Cat's Cradle between Blanche and Bernard, where
the semi-darkness of the vast reception room seems alive with

hostile eyes and the whisper of accusing voices, to which all at once Guido enters bearing a lamp, his voice cold like steel, his eyes smouldering with hate; the evening in *Daphne Adeane* before Michael's departure for the front, when all his lately-born love for his wife finds words but no commensurate response, and both are left with the poignant thought that their great moment has gone forever; in *The Coat Without Seam*, the idyllic summer days at Sorrento, which give to Madame D'Alberg and Christopher the one perfect interlude they would ever know; and the closing chapter, where Baring reveals his infinite pity for Christopher— for all us other bunglers—his sense of life flowing on undeterred by death, of death as the herald of peace, of peace as the final desire of men's hearts.

Baring's literary relationships are numerous. Like Browning he believes in love at first sight, not because it is a vulgar passion easily aroused but because it is the mutual recognition of the kinship of two souls, which comes with the swiftness of light and the suddenness of a revelation. Thus it is one of the transcendent realities of life and, whether charged with weal or woe, one of the most transforming of human experiences. Again like Browning he is acutely aware of that hidden place where the motive-forces of every man dwell, a place of mystery and unsoundable depths. Unlike Browning he has never sought to penetrate its final and darker secrets—he has for instance written nothing comparable to "My Last Duchess" or "Any Wife to Any Husband"—but he points the way for the imaginative reader with a subtlety so extraordinary that it often goes unnoticed. The device by which Browning in *The Ring and the Book* exposed to full view the limitations of human insight (by presenting the opinions of "one half Rome, the other half Rome, and the Tertium Quid") Baring has successfully adopted in narrower compass when treating Blanche's departure from her husband's home and Daphne Adeane's secret, and throughout two shorter novels, *A Triangle* and *Overlooked*.

Baring's concern with men and women of the leisure class and his interest in the psychological effects of action rather than in action itself, recall Henry James. But Henry James got to the point where he placed art above life—a pitfall Browning escaped—as if people existed to be studied under the microscope and to be meticulously reported on, after tortuous explorations of their souls and minds. To do this he slowed his tempo until it lost step with life and the reader gave up in despair, convinced he was dealing with a clinician in the guise of a novelist. With Baring art is a means not an end; it exists to present life; the sense of time with him as with Tolstoi is never lost. Indeed it is a part of Baring's purpose to keep us aware of its onward march as of the footsteps of an unseen monitor who whispers that the night cometh when no man shall work—or play or marry or give in marriage.

As a contemporary portrayer of English society prior to the World War Baring challenges comparison with Galsworthy. Each presents men and women of some culture but scant faith, a society which took its pleasures furtively before 1914 and flauntingly thereafter. Both men are keen, sensitive, deeply sympathetic; each is a romantic, honestly facing reality and striving to picture it faithfully. Baring is a cosmopolitan who has seen life on many fronts and is free from Galsworthy's insularity. Baring is more objective in treatment and creates sympathy for his characters without betraying his personal partiality. Thus one cannot be sure what he thinks of Rose Mary Clifford *(Cat's Cradle)*, a woman hard at the core, but Galsworthy's liking for the self-righteous Irene *(Forsyte Saga)*—one of the most unloveable women in modern fiction—is transparent.

A chief source of Baring's power is his rich and inexhaustible sentiment; Galsworthy's primary weakness is his sentimentalism (sentiment over-ripe and touched with decay) which permits him to believe that "love" (meaning physical passion) is its own justification, that "Spring in the blood" excuses a flirtation with fatal consequences, and that an embezzler who commits suicide deserves our sympathy if he prepares for the deed like an Epicurean and consummates it like a Stoic. In those two terms is expressed Galsworthy's philosophy of life. Baffled by what he sees, unable to appraise conduct by spiritual standards, eager that men may attain their desires in an unsatisfactory world, he says as an Epicurean, "You have the right to be happy," and admonishes as a Stoic, "Do not lose your form."

If on rare occasions Baring's men strive and cry or fail to keep their form, his women never do. Except for Mrs. Bucknell in *C* (Baring's Becky Sharp) they know the difference between love and its counterfeit, they have a moral sense, and sooner or later they learn the wisdom of renunciation whose ways alone are peace. In all Baring's novels there is a sense of the pathos of life, the tears of things. Why then are they not depressing? Because they present reality without bitterness and with infinite compassion and unfailing beauty.

Agnes Repplier:

"Age Cannot Wither Her"

MISS AGNES REPPLIER DID US ALL A SERVICE WHEN SHE SELECTED sixteen essays from her many books and published them with the title *Eight Decades*. (That title, be it said, proclaims what her powers deny—her age.) Here are many old favorites: "The Grocer's Cat" (cats have always been one of Agnes Repplier's adorations), "Allegra," the beautifully told story of Byron's natural daughter, an early revelation of her interest in biography, "When Lalla Rookh was Young" (her knowledge of literary history and its fashions is astonishing), "The Condescension of Borrowers," which the author of "The Two Races of Man" would have read with delight, "The Headsman," an excursion among the curiosities of history with which she has an endless intimacy, and "Horace," which reminds us that the great figures of literature have been her inseparable companions all her long life. To read the volume through makes it clear that first and foremost Agnes Repplier is a social critic.

The beau ideal of social critics is Addison, cultured, traveled, reasonable, possessed of an air of amused and slightly ironic detachment. His chief concern was with the foibles and follies of his day and occasionally with those aspects of manners which touch upon morality.

But "the eighteenth century moralized, the nineteenth preached." In the wake of the French Revolution old standards, old ideas, and old interests were engulfed. Social criticism took

24

on a new significance. It was deepened and broadened enormously,
fed and finally transformed by a new interest in political and
economic problems and the needs of the masses. With Carlyle and
Ruskin moral indignation awoke, detachment vanished, irony was
converted from a bodkin to a sword and humor into a ridicule
that seared like a flame. Addison spoke to the town, not to the
nation; his appeal was to reason, not to the conscience; his voice
was modulated to the intimacies of the breakfast table, not charged
with the thunder of prophecy. Social criticism in the Addisonian
sense survived in the irony and urbane restraint of Newman and
Arnold, but beneath them burned the passionate earnestness of
the new dispensation whose shibboleth was "social justice." Social
criticism in the Addisonian sense is virtually a lost art: manners
as deviations from good sense are left to Dame Chance; manners
as colored by morality to the Churches. Social criticism has become a leaden-footed vagrant whose proper domain has been
usurped by economics, sociology, science, and a type of ethics so
highly personal that sanctions and standards know it no longer.

The collapse of Addisonian social criticism has left us immeasurably poorer in good breeding without, I suspect, improv-
ing us in those inner attitudes of mind of which good manners
are the evidence. The Addisonian type has its place, a place that
has nothing directly to do with economics, sociology, politics, or
religion but a great deal to do with good sense, consideration for
others, and personal dignity. Granted the revolutionary changes
in social attitudes in the nineteenth century, social criticism may
properly be said to include such things as our reactions to movie
sentimentalism, our herd-mindedness, our indifference to those
cultural sources that lie under our very eyes. If the field be further
widened, if the Addisonian type of social criticism be conceived
of as embracing those forgotten indices of civilization, tolerance,
abnegation, and restraint (for Addison in his moments could be
"a parson in a tie-wig"), the critic who is true to the tradition must
substitute reason for emotion and either avoid open didacticism
or, in Addison's phrase, "temper it with wit."

To follow Addison, to write in his tradition, is not easy; on the
contrary it is enormously difficult, like swimming against a powerful current. It means keeping within a given domain, preserving
a point of view, employing reasoned and tested standards, holding

fast to urbanity, maintaining at least the appearance of detachment, rejecting scorn, abuse, exhortation, and ridicule as weapons and employing a humor that is never wry, an irony that is never bitter, a tolerance that never degenerates into indifference.

That the Addisonian tradition of social criticism has survived in America is originally due to a small volume, *Books and Men,* which appeared in 1892. Among its seven essays were such alluring titles as "The Benefits of Superstition," "The Decay of Sentiment," and "Children Past and Present." They revealed more intellect than emotion, more penetration than charm; they were a little angular and self-conscious but they were distinctly unusual. What made them unusual was not only their ironic touches, gleams of humor, shrewd sense, and the presence of a keen and balanced mind, but their method. That method at its typical best consisted of presenting from the history and literature of the past many aspects of the subject under discussion, and then, by brief comments along the way or a quotation from a contemporary authority or a challenging question at the end, bringing home to the reader the absurdity, hypocrisy, or danger implied in present-day practice. Thus the humor and tragedy of the superstitions of the past point to the insolence which mingles with the scientific knowledge of the present; the emotional outbreaks of our great-grandparents, induced by deep feeling, evoke the question whether our emotions are under better control or our feelings shallower; the stern and often brutal treatment to which children were subjected in the name of education and good manners sharpens the question, "Where will the indulgence of today lead?" This method was full of difficulties. But behind the method and the triumphant use of it was a real person. That person was Agnes Repplier.

As Miss Repplier went on writing essay after essay it became clear that she had found her vein from the start. Her tone became more assured, her handling of her themes more deft, her irony more incisive, her humorous touches more frequent, and her knowledge of the history and literature of the past more breathtaking. As for her vein it proved as inexhaustible as the absurdities, vagaries, and follies of contemporary American life, and such titles as "The Discomforts of Luxury," "In Behalf of Parents," and "The Chill of Enthusiasm," while intriguing to the reader, revealed the nature of her interests and her humorously ironic approach. As time went on some of her essays convicted Miss Repplier of a serious purpose (but Addison, remember, also had a serious purpose), and of being often openly didactic—as Addison seldom was. But (to risk a repetition) social criticism has never been so light-hearted since the Victorian prophets breathed moral indignation into its veins, though it can—and in Miss Repplier's hands does—find in wit and irony relishes that make didacticism palatable and even savorsome.

It was impossible that the World War with its threats to modern civilization both here and abroad should fail to stir to the depths so penetrating, thoughtful, and responsive a social critic as Agnes Repplier. Her European traditions, her American loyalties, her convictions that are as the breath of life, were vitally engaged by things said and done on both sides of the Atlantic, and the essays in *Counter Currents* (1916) revealed the drift of her interest from the sphere of American social aberrations to disputed aspects of the tragedy which darkened the world. Temporarily the war took its toll: it quenched her humor, sharpened her irony into acerbity, and kindled a scorn and indignation which consumed restraint. To say this is not to condemn Miss Repplier but to record that among the evils of war is that of enticing the Muses into the train of Mars, of burdening Mary with the tasks of Martha. Miss Repplier realized this herself for as late as 1931 she wrote: "The protracted pain of those four years [of war] is an ever-present memory; and there are many of us who have failed to regain the lightness of heart which seemed a normal condition before this horror came."

Perhaps Miss Repplier's excursions into the field of biography were prompted not only by a talent already revealed in such early essays as "Scanderbeg," but by a desire to escape for a time from a bewildered and exhausted world to an earlier and simpler one where romance and compassion were fellows and conquest meant new frontiers for the Kingdom of God.

Gradually Miss Repplier returned to her role of social critic, her wit recaptured, her irony purged, her method of revitalizing the past as a norm for evaluating the present resumed again, and her concern restored in the social shortcomings of the day. There is a didacticism in the post-war collections, *Points of Friction*

(1920), *Under Dispute* (1924), and *Times and Tendencies* (1931), toward which she was tending earlier and which is apparent in two of the finest essays she ever wrote, "The Virtuous Victorian" and "Living in History." It was not until *To Think of Tea* in 1932 that Miss Repplier completely returned to the more leisurely approach, the less didactic manner, and the more oblique treatment which marked her finest pre-war essays. With *In Pursuit of Laughter* five years later she happily followed suit.

A social critic without a philosophy of life is impossible; he is a guide without sight, a warrior without arms, an exhorter without a voice. Agnes Repplier has a philosophy which stands revealed to the attentive reader of any half dozen of her essays. He learns of the things she honors, of those she despises, of those she cleaves to as the moral and spiritual fundamentals which give life its meaning. She confesses somewhere to being old-fashioned, and she is in the sense that her philosophy of life is based upon such faith and such sustaining virtues as have always been held in honor among civilized men. She hates sentimentality and pretense in all its protean forms. She detests cowardice and loves courage, physical as well as moral. She reveres fortitude, restraint, and abnegation as her forbears revered them in the days of chivalry, and though she is too brave for fear, she is full of apprehension as to the depths to which life must sink should these things cease to weigh with men. She deems patriotism a universal virtue to whose making many others go, a noble sentiment, a democratic impulse, a *lingua franca* understood of right-thinking men everywhere. She loves laughter and often voices her impatience with those who subtract from it by one iota. Finally, she believes life immensely worth living but insists that there is something worse than death and something "better than human life and love." "Life is neither a pleasure nor a calamity. 'It is a grave affair with which we are charged and which we must conduct and terminate with honour.' " Are these hard sayings? Beyond question, but they are implicit in Agnes Repplier's philosophy from the beginning and she never feared or evaded its logic.

Her enormous reading in the field of history did more than satisfy her romantic interests and her endless intellectual curiosity; it gave her a knowledge of the past as extraordinary as it is rare and enriched by an unexampled acquaintance with biography, memoirs, and letters. (Has anything in print escaped the eye of this astonishing woman?) As a result she knows that history began before 1918 and even before 1900; that man has always faced under various guises difficulties similar to ours; that to meet and conquer them then he required the same qualities he requires now; and that the thing called honor and that other called sacrifice were and still are, sacred. History stirs her as it stirred Henry James and Carlyle before him "more than the most thrilling and passionate fiction." Why? Because it is alive with man's heroism and ennobled by his ideals. It has its deathless admonitions, for we are not "able to disentangle life from history, to sever the inseverable" and the symptoms of today's diseases are there to see. "The magnifying of small things, the belitting of great ones indicate mental exhaustion." The weight of history oppresses little minds and irks those who would escape its authority. Ignorance of it, she constantly insists, "impairs our understanding by depriving us of standards, of the power to contrast and the right to estimate. . . . The book of the world is full of knowledge we need to acquire, of lessons we need to learn, of wisdom we need to assimilate."

As a lover of biography she has no patience with those who would debunk the survivors of oblivion. She recalls not merely that Pericles made an address in the cemetery at Athens but that he uttered wisdom which the lip-servers of democracy forget. Nearly a quarter of a century ago she quoted to us a brief sentence of Polybius, "In Carthage no one is blamed, however he may have gained his wealth," and she commented: "A pleasant place, no doubt, for business enterprise; a place where young men were taught how to get on, and extravagance kept pace with shrewd finance. A self-satisfied, self-confident, money-getting, women-loving people, honoring success and hugging their fancied security, while in far-off Rome Cato pronounced their doom." Only those blind to the events of the past decade and a half can miss the point. When Agnes Repplier wrote *A Happy Half Century* she evoked the ghosts of many literary "immortals." Where are our own immortals of ten or twenty years ago? Where are the snows of yester-year? Will Dreiser outlast Hawthorne, and John Dewey Aristotle? Are our "discoveries," so solemnly pronounced, new? Are we the original proclaimers of the economic basis of history? "Trade," said a Lombard banker to the Duke of Burgundy, "finds its way everywhere and rules the world." But the truth goes deeper than that, how much deeper Miss Repplier tells in "Living in History," one of the wisest and most eloquent essays written in our time. When you have finished it you will agree with her that "it is with the help of history that we balance our mental accounts."

Agnes Repplier's own mental accounts have always been balanced, not only because she knows history but because from her French forbears she inherited the precision which marks her style and the clarity of thought which, for half a century, has been a beacon in what has seemed at times our intellectual fog. She has never split hairs or softened a hard saying; she has not trafficked in ambiguities or compromised a principle to justify a violation because it wore a sentimental aura. She has always dealt in reasoned convictions and shares Renan's hatred of vagueness of thought. To a feminine penetration she joins a vigor and directness of mind which are essentially masculine. This explains three interesting facts: that she never cloys, that her emotions (deep-seated and sometimes eloquently voiced) color but never dominate her thinking, and that there is a steady brightness about her essays which wearies the eye of none but the mentally apathetic.

Unlike Chesterton Agnes Repplier never juggles with a thought; she has no flair for paradox, even paradox alluringly—and Chestertonianly—described as "truth standing on its head." There is a Celtic strain in Chesterton's wit, a Gallic strain in Agnes Repplier's. At heart he is a poet and hence sees truth in high moments and clothed in metaphor; essentially Agnes Repplier is an intellectual in whose processes of thought, imagination and emotion hold a secondary place. That does not mean that they are stifled; actually, they lend warmth and illumination to her convictions for Agnes Repplier has a lively imagination and responsive emotions, loves fiction and poetry, and thrills to the great English ballads which evoke for her no problems of peace and pacifism but stir her heart—as they stirred Sidney's and Addison's—as with a trumpet. But when she comes to the lawful matters of social criticism, her instinct is to convince rather than to persuade and thus her appeal is to a cultivated and, in consequence, a limited public.

Wisdom, alack! can be dull and too often is, but Agnes Repplier knows how to make hers sparkle. In fifty years she has proved herself mistress of the brilliant phrase, the arresting sentence; a book of them would make a *vade mecum* for believers in a sane life. This is for those who put more faith in rhetoric than in work: "If by demonstrating the injuriousness of evil we could insure the acceptance of good a little logic would redeem mankind." This is for those teachers who forget that their profession is an art and not a science: "The by-products of education are the things that count." This is for the purveyor of nostrums (may his tribe decrease!): "History cannot accommodate itself unreservedly to theories; it cannot be stripped of things evidenced in favor of things surmised." This is for today, harrowed by international contentions: "A sense of humor is the peacemaker of the world." This is for the Lilliputians who forget (in Newman's phrase) that a dwarf perched on a giant's shoulders may see farther than the giant: "It is a liberal education to recognize and to endeavor to understand any form of evidence which the records of mankind reveal." This is for all of us: "Without the vast compelling presence of God, the activities of men grow feverish."

Miss Repplier's power to make brilliant points in favor of her convictions is matched by her skill in using irony to weaken or destroy a false position. She has intimate acquaintance with the lords of irony and has studied them as assiduously as Lytton Strachey, employing what she learned with a quite un-Stracheyan passion for tolerance and intellectual honesty. Her irony swings a wide circle: it can be as sly as Addison's, as gentle as Lamb's, as sharp as Voltaire's, as cruel as La Rochefoucauld's, as indirectly dealt as Gibbon's. It can be as innocent as in "Lectures are transient things, forgiven as soon as forgotten," as caustic as when she describes a woman (she has no special tenderness for her own sex) as "brightening up wonderfully under the beneficent influence of other people's misfortunes." La Rochefoucauld might have written: "Next to the joy of the egotist is the joy of the detractor." Less bland than Arnold she knows, like him, how to point her irony with "Gallic malice," as when she writes of Gladstone:

"There are evidences that under the benign influence of tea he betrayed now and then signs and tokens of fallibility." Gibbon would have chuckled over, "Reformatory measures are hailed as cure-alls by people who have a happy confidence in the perfectibility of human nature and no discouraging acquaintance with history to dim it."

As proof that Miss Repplier's energies have remained untouched we have the amazing fact that in the past ten years she has published some of her finest things. At seventy-four, with *To Think of Tea,* she returned completely, as I have already said, to the manner and treatment which marked most of her social criticism before the first World War and belong to the Addisonian tradition. A volume centering about a single topic was not unique with Miss Repplier, for in 1901 she wrote *The Fireside Sphinx,* a book rich in information and delight and dedicated to the memory of her beloved cat Agrippina. It could have been entitled *To Think of Cats* and might have been described by a solemn cataloguer as "A study of certain aspects of the evolution of society from the earliest times in the light of its attitude to the *species felina.*"

As one might suspect, *To Think of Tea* is not exclusively devoted to the most humanizing and solacing of beverages. Our cataloguer might describe it as "presenting something about tea, interspersed with anecdotes about the great, the near great, and the unknown, the whole intended to illustrate the lighter side of social life in England from Sir Walter Raleigh to W. E. Gladstone." Here in the company of great poets and men of letters, stout smugglers, adroit politicians, complacent bluestockings, and intriguing little-knowns and unknowns (strangers to all the moderns but her) she is back to her earlier allegiance—to the old friends whom her love and imagination invest with life, to irony with bite but without bitterness, to salty humor, and to the graciousness of the Addisonian tradition.

Her method in *To Think of Tea* permits no end of minor and diverting revelations for it is as diffusive as the steam of her tea-urn; it responds to the faintest breath, the lightest cross-current, of a fresh interest. If tea was a pet object of contraband, she recalls that Charles Lamb favored the smuggled variety, that most other celebrities of his day shared his penchant, that once his whimsical lawlessness led him to bring Henry Robinson a waistcoat from Paris without benefit of customs, and that, like the innocent in their first fall everywhere, he was caught in the act. Criticisms of the contemporary scene abound in *To Think of Tea,* but are often implied or obliquely conveyed in a parenthesis, a modestly subordinated clause, the turn of a sentence, a demure comment, and to the vigilant reader who already knows Miss Repplier's views, their understatement speaks eloquently. Godwin liked green tea and hated black, whereupon Miss Repplier is moved to remark: "Godwin was also poor but his habit of living on his friends robbed poverty of its sting."

A Victorian member of Parliament, we read, "affirmed that 'tea ennobled the graceful weakness of women'" to which Miss Repplier appends the demure parenthesis, "This was before the days of female athleticism." Birth-control, ignored hitherto, is treated here with a humorous but deadly brevity which flashes out from its parenthesis like a sharp-shooter from behind a wall. "An occasional contributor to the *Spectator* was Pierre Motteaux who came to England after the revocation of the Edict of Nantes. He had twenty-two children, and was mysteriously murdered (perhaps by an advocate of birth-control) in a London slum."

In Pursuit of Laughter follows a similar but less discursive technique and its serious purpose is more apparent. True laughter implies the power of honest self-appraisal (for which Burns uttered his famous prayer) and is an index of tolerance, humility, and a faith in what Stevenson called "the ultimate decencies" and in the high purpose which alone makes them significant. Thus laughter becomes a measuring rod of the good life, a norm of civilization; our solemn cataloguer might describe the book as "A record of certain readings of the social barometer from the Middle Ages to the present time." In the Middle Ages laughter was universal; it needed no pursuing. But with the religious revolt certain things happened, and the sixteenth century found itself striving robustly to encourage the laughter which the thirteenth century had striven to subdue. The pursuit has gone on ever since. Charles II, the merrie monarch, headed the chase in his day and closed his tired eyes forever without having overtaken it. The eighteenth century came nearer than any other to the Comic Spirit, but went its way, and the "boisterous high spirits of the early nineteenth century drooped and were lost in measureless confusion before it closed."

Miss Repplier makes no concessions to our day but looks the foes of laughter in the face and closes her book with a challenge which upsets our complacency as she has been upsetting our complacency for the last fifty years. "Today we make scant pretense of cheerfulness; and absurdities, when recognized, seem insurmountable to some and inspirational to others. Strange coercive drives pursue us relentlessly and leave us drained of purpose. And ever and always the ill-organized pursuit goes on:

> I cry a reward for a Yesterday
> Now lost or stolen, or gone astray
> With all the laughter of Yesterday."

If I were forced to a choice of Miss Repplier's work I should take (after a prayer for guidance) *To Think of Tea* and three essays, "Living in History," "The Virtuous Victorian," and "Horace." A Cabinet Minister with authority over higher education might well require those three essays to be mastered as a prerequisite for a degree, for then at least he might be sure that the departing neophytes from our temples of learning had grasped certain fundamentals of social wisdom: the windows of the mind should be flung wide to the past; our ancestors, in Lamb's phrase, should "not be set down in the gross for fools"; the first wisdom was Adam's but the last is not today's; without intellectual humility higher education is a failure and culture a mere phrase.

"Horace" is Miss Repplier's finest piece of prose and the most satisfying example of her gifts in miniature. It is perfect in its serene dignity, unhurried in tempo, played upon by alternate light and shadow like those alluring nooks to which Horace retreated to his day dreams. "If he missed the Fountain of Bandusia, that leaping cascade which he was wont to climb so far to see, and to whose guardian deity he sacrificed a flower-decked kid, he had in its stead the falling waters of the Anio; the Cascata Grande, not then the torrent it is now, and the lovely Cascatelle streaming down the hillside in broken threads of silver. The orchards of Tibur were wet with spray, and the Tiburtive Sybil delivered her oracles to the sound of many waters. Even Italy had nothing better to give. Small wonder that Horace wrote with a sigh of content, 'May Tibur, founded by Argive wanderers, be the home of my old age and my final goal.' "

Miss Repplier breathes life into the Roman poet, transforming him from a name into a man, one unembittered by disillusionment but made tender instead, the gayness of his temper resisting the sadness of his heart; who loved his liberty more than luxury and pleasure; whom the world has cherished these many centuries as "the persuasive exponent of a reasonable life, the clear, sad thinker who led no man astray." In this essay she points no deliberate moral but with an artist's (not a preacher's) skill vindicates the social virtues anew.

Sainte-Beuve, paying tribute to Mme. de Sévigné, wrote: "She had a knowledge of the world and of men, a lively and acute appreciation both of the becoming and the absurd." Of Agnes Repplier he might have added: She has championed those ideals of thought and conduct by which the dignity and grace of life are maintained and its inalienable values reaffirmed.

The Poems of a Great American

MANY YEARS AGO WHEN A COLLEGE UNDERGRADUATE I CAME UPON A brief poem in a current magazine which delighted me and has remained in memory ever since. The poet's name was only vaguely familiar but, ironically enough, I was to find myself six years later on the English staff of the college to whose presidency he was named in the interval. This is the poem which won me:

On the Way to the Bourne

I'd have the driving rain upon my face,—
  Not pelting its blunt arrows at my back,
  Goading with blame along its ruthless track,
But flinging me defiance in the race.

And I would go at such an eager gait
  That whatsoe'er may fall from heaven of woe
  Shall not pursue me as some coward foe,
But challenge me—that I may face my fate.

There is revealed the courage of Henley's famous "Invictus" without the swaggering self-confidence which evoked the gibe of James Whitcomb Riley. "I am the captain of my fate" sang the boastful Henley. "The devil you are," retorted the irreverent Hoosier.

The more modest poet of whom I write was endowed with enormous energies and many talents: he was internationally

36

known as an educator, a journalist, an administrator, and an historian, and his name is associated with the City College of New York, the *New York Times, The French in the Heart of America* (a fine study crowned by the Académie Française), and the International Red Cross in whose service he went to Palestine in 1918 as Commissioner for the Near East. He traveled widely throughout the United States, and as Professor Phelps of Yale came to be an apostle of culture he was recognized as an ambassador of good will. Wherever his countrymen foregathered in the interest of civic or educational betterment, he was in demand as a speaker, and his words, uttered with infallible tact, endowed graciousness, hope, and mutual understanding with fresh reality.

He was a great American and in the best sense a citizen of the world. Because his mind was always open to beauty, his heart responsive to the hopes and aspirations of men, and his imagination capable of transmuting the commonplace into the significant, seeing the stars in wayside pools and "heaven in a wild flower," he was a poet. His name? John Finley.

His *Poems,* published in a handsome volume last year, covers the long period from his late twenties (one suspects that he suppressed considerable earlier verse for he was modest and his standards exacting) until 1940, the year of his death, and reveals a man singularly true to himself. He had time for nature but not for pessimism, keen eyes for beauty but not for ugliness. Like Hazlitt and Thoreau he loved long walks, finding companionship in his own thoughts, in the beauty of wayside flowers, in clouds that drifted lazily across the sky, in the shifting shadow patterns on the hills, in the fragrance of the tilled earth, and in the prospect of a friendly hearth at the end of the day. He had a talent for friendship and an instinct for kindred souls to the secret of whose powers he penetrated unerringly. Professor Phelps paid him the perfect tribute: "He had the mind of a scholar and the heart of a boy."

From first to last he loved children, not with easy sentimentalism but with tenderness and understanding. His humor was neither boisterous nor bitter but always warm and often fanciful. Though he was keenly sensitive to the pathos of life dejection found no lodging place with him, for it vanished in the face of his optimism, his buoyant faith, and the serenity which like Wordsworth he drew from Nature.

John Finley was not only many-sided but his spiritual and intellectual roots were deep and far-reaching. In his blood were the independence of his Scotch ancestry, their sense of duty and acceptance of discipline, and so too was his love of literature, which ranged from the Greek classics to the best of his contemporaries in prose and verse. The late George B. McClellan, long professor of History at Princeton, never ended his most crowded day even when mayor of New York without reading a page or two from Macaulay. I suspect that John Finley budgeted his hours in similar fashion, deeming no day complete that denied him communion, however brief, with some great master of the written word. His own prose was unfailingly touched with poetry whether it were in a formal address, an after-dinner toast, or an editorial in the *Times* where, behind the veil of anonymity, it glowed like a jewel. Like the man in his poem "Duoviri," he confessed to two personalities, one the dreamer of dreams to whom wind, sea, and stars had secrets to tell; the other the practical man, one of those

> who habit towns,
> Who fashion, barter, carry, and control.

Mingling, bound in a single being,

> They
> Tried each with each to do their double best
> 'Twixt dream and deed—poet and pragmatist,
> Mystic and potent manager of men.

His poems form the eloquent record of that side of him which was hidden from the multitudes who knew only of his achievements in the world of affairs.

John Finley's travels in Palestine combined with his deep religious sense to inspire a sheaf of poems touched by beauty and profound emotion. As with Chesterton not only were his thoughts and feelings fresh as spring flowers but they were possible only to a man whose spirit was no stranger to the Holy City. What had long been a reality to his imagination became at last a reality to his eager eyes. Vigor and the deep joy of hope fulfilled are in "Armageddon"; a sense of the worthlessness of life without immortality and of immortality without love in "Ain Karim"; in "I Walked One Night in the Shepherd's Field," a solemn and consoling conviction which brings inward peace even in the midst of war. Perhaps the most poignant of all the poems in this group is

The First Knight of the Holy Cross

"And as they lead Him away, they laid hold upon one Simon, a Cyrenian, a countryman, and on him they laid the cross that he might bear it after Jesus."

> A countryman he was from far away
> Who happened in the Holy Town that day,
> Swarthy from hot Cyrene's sun, and strong
> To bear the fresh-hewn fragrant tree along
> The dolorous way that led to Calvary,—
> The first cross-bearer of humanity.
>
> .   .   .
>
> O Knight of Christ, compelled to lift the load
> For Him! What radiance fell upon thy road
> When He but looked to thee in gratitude
> And made of those crossed beams the Holy Rood!
> What swift, sweet passion filled thy giant frame
> When He said, "Follow Me," and spoke thy name!

The revelation of John Finley's religious sense was not confined to his visit to the Holy Land in 1918-19 but appears in many other poems both before and after that experience, such as "Matins," "The Sepulchre in the Garden," "My Rosary," and "The Time of Evening Sacrifice," one of the most distinguished of his poems, which recalls Henley's "Margaritae Sorori" in its serenity and Francis Thompson in its imagery and its tone of exalted reverence.

A hundred years ago the question whether the progress of science would hamper poetry was considered by critics and poets and answered affirmatively by Keats, Hazlitt, and Tennyson and negatively by Wordsworth and Leigh Hunt. "If the labors of men of science," wrote Wordsworth in his celebrated Preface to the *Lyrical Ballads,* "should ever create any material revolution . . . in our condition, and in the impressions which we habitually receive, the poet will sleep then no more than at present; he will be ready to follow the steps of the man of science [whose] remotest discoveries . . . will be as proper objects of the poet's art as any upon which it can be employed. . . . If the time should ever come when what is now called science . . . shall be ready to put on, as it were, a form of flesh and blood, the poet will lend his divine spirit to aid the transfiguration, and will welcome the being thus produced, as a dear and genuine inmate of the household of man." Wordsworth's vision, so eloquently revealed in that prediction, comes to mind as one reads the poems of John Finley which celebrate the airplane in exultant and glowing words. Here is a stanza from "Via Dei," the phrase meaning "the thousand ways that led from palace and from cell toward the Holy Land."

> But with the wings of morning I
> A "Via Dei" of the sky
> Have found, amid the paths of light
> Where airmen make their pilgrim flight
> High in the Heav'ns—the ways ne'er trod
> Save by the glowing feet of God
> Above The Holy Land. . . .

> And then I saw Jerusalem
> Lying an opalescent gem,
> Or breastplate, 'mid the ephod's blue
> And gold and purple ambient hue,—
> A city from the skies let down
> To be henceforth the whole earth's crown
> Set 'mid The Holy Land.

If John Finley felt exultation over the vast conquests of the airplane he was stirred to wonder and awe by the achievements of the radio and the wireless telephone and led to indulge in hopes whose realization only a handful of mystics might dare to claim. His poem is called "My Hut" and its final lines are these:

> Last night I heard one say how on the deep
> He called his brother, leagues of dark away,
> Roused him from sleep and quick got his reply
> Of that far continent toward whose shores
> Himself was sailing, seeking some new world;
> And, hearing this known miracle, I prayed
> Out of new faith, our spirits might be tuned
> That each the other's cry might hear, and each

The other's need might know, though it were night,
Though mountains lay between, or seas, or days,
Though dark or distance intervened—or death.

John Finley's loves did not cease with friends and home and books and Nature in all her manifestations. As Dickens loved London he loved the imperial city of the West where, in contrast to the ancient antagonisms of the old world, many races center and "Forget long hates in one consummate faith." He loved his native land with a fervor which ennobles his sonnet "Like Castles Stand the Bastioned Walls of France," wherein he sees in every American youth a symbol and a pledge of the greatness of this country's future. Finally, he loved his fellowmen and, overleaping all bars of time and place and creed, proclaimed himself "of one soul and clay" with them.

To read these poems is to commune with a lofty spirit. For it is to feel one's mind cleared, the bonds of human compassion strengthened, devotion to all things that are lovely and of good report rekindled, one's faith restored. In these days when nations struggle beneath their cross and darkness descends upon their children, what praise can be higher?

A Singing Novelist

SEVERAL YEARS AGO, ON A BOSTON BOOKSTALL WHICH OFFERED THE passer-by his choice at a price too grotesquely low to name, I chanced upon a slender brown volume. It contained thirty-six poems, all brief, and bore the copyright date, 1903, below the words: "Boston, Richard G. Badger, The Gorham Press." I had already made the acquaintance of the author in *Troll Garden,* a collection of little-known short stories, distinguished by so rare a touch and so keen a flavor of life that I at once predicted great things of her future. To meet her thus in the guise of a poet, came with a shock of surprise. I had not dreamed of that gift of song.

To chance upon this stranger volume was a delight, but to discover it on a bargain shelf, its fortunes so sadly fallen, brought a sigh. Today I sigh no more, for its fortunes have risen mightily. Cinderella has shaken the dust of the chimney-corner from her feet and is numbered among the elect. That slender volume now occupies a place in special catalogues which are devoted to rare items and first editions.

What is this little treasure-trove? A paper label (with orange-colored decorations) pasted to its modest brown cover bears the legend, *"April Twilights,* by Willa Sibert Cather."

April Twilights is to be found in current booklists and in modern garb. Twenty years after the appearance of the Gorham Press volume a new edition was issued with, however, certain changes: a dozen of the earlier poems were dropped and an equal number of new ones substituted. A second printing of this new issue occurred in 1924. It is now in its fourth edition.

In the warmth, flexibility, and vivid exactness of her prose, Miss Cather is so often revealed as a poet that her ventures into verse were inevitable; the surprising thing is that they were not more frequent. Distinction marks *April Twilights* no less than *A Lost Lady* and *Death Comes for the Archbishop*. It clings to these poems like a fragrance. It is in such single lines as that which calls a melody at night "Tender as dawn, insistent as the tide," or that which marks the "golden silence" of autumn when "Sunk in honeyed sleep the garden lies"; but in the finest of these poems it is all pervasive. Here is a typical instance in which breathe the yearning of all lovers, their sense, inextricably mingled, of love's beatitude and life's impermanence:

EVENING SONG

Dear love, what thing of all the things that be
Is ever worth one thought from you or me,
    Save only Love,
    Save only Love?

The days so short, the nights so quick to flee,
The world so wide, so deep and dark the sea,
    So dark the sea;

So far the suns and every listless star,
Beyond their light—Ah! dear, who knows how far,
    Who knows how far?

One thing of all dim things I know is true,
The heart within me knows, and tells it you,
    And tells it you.

So blind is life, so long at last is sleep,
And none but Love to bid us laugh or weep,
    And none but Love,
    And none but Love.

If you seek a more outspoken passion than is expressed here you will scarcely find it, for passion in these poems is never hectic or unrestrained, never overreaches itself or leaves one with a

sense of exhausted emotions. It is not that the love *motif* is rare in
April Twilights, but that love with Willa Cather the poet is (as
Mrs. Craigie once said it always was with the Celt) a sentiment
rather than a passion. The note is low, not insistent; it is reminiscent of the spirit rather than of the body; it is acquainted little
with triumph, much with tears. In "The Hawthorn Tree" is the
note of joy; in "Thou Art the Pearl," the rare note of triumph,
but softened in tone to give one a sense of the lover's awe, kneel-
ing and adoring, in the presence of beauty and its mystery:

> I read of knights who laid their armor down,
>   And left the tourney's prize for other hands,
> And clad them in a pilgrim's somber gown,
>   To seek a holy cup in desert lands.
> For them no more the torch of victory;
>   For them lone vigils and the starlight pale,
> So they in dreams the Blessed Cup may see—
>   Thou art the Grail!
>
> An Eastern king once smelled a rose in sleep,
>   And on the morrow laid his scepter down.
> His heir his titles and his land might keep—
>   The rose was sweeter wearing than the crown.
> Nor cared he that its life was but an hour,
>   A breath that from the crimson summer blows,
> Who gladly paid a kingdom for a flower—
>   Thou art the Rose!
>
> A merchant man, who knew the worth of things,
>   Beheld a pearl more priceless than a star;
> And straight returning, all he hath he brings
>   And goes upon his way, ah, richer far!
> Laughter of merchant of the market-place,
>   Nor taunting gibe nor scornful lips that curl,
> Can ever cloud the rapture on his face—
>   Thou art the Pearl!

In mentioning the Celt (so sensitive, so melancholy, so sensuous) and his love as a sentiment rather than a passion, I do not
mean to imply that there is a Celtic strain in Miss Cather, al-

though these poems encourage the conjecture.[1] For often the Celtic note appears, elusive enough in all truth and yet not to be missed. Listen for it in "In Media Vita" whose first two stanzas run thus:

> Streams of the spring a-singing,
>   Winds o' the May that blow,
> Birds from the Southland winging,
>   Buds in the grasses below.
> Clouds that speed hurrying over,
>   And the climbing rose by the wall,
> Singing of bees in the clover,
>   And the dead, under all!
>
> Lads and their sweethearts lying
>   In the cleft of the windy hill;
> Hearts that are hushed of their sighing,
>   Lips that are tender and still.
> Stars in the purple gloaming,
>   Flowers that suffuse and fall,
> Twitter of bird-mates homing,
>   And the dead, under all!

It is that last line which does it, coming like sudden tears after laughter, and revealing memories too poignant to be banished for long.

Here is another instance, thoroughly Celtic in tone, expression, and sentiment, and clearly in the ballad tradition:

Grandmither, gie me your still, white hands, that lie upon your breast,
For mine do beat the dark all night and never find me rest;
They grope among the shadows an' they beat the cold black air,
They go seekin' in the darkness, an' they never find him there,
    An' they never find him there.

Grandmither, gie me your sightless eyes, that I may never see
His own a-burnin' full o' love that must not shine for me.
Grandmither, gie me your peaceful lips, white as the kirkyard snow,
For mine be red wi' burnin' thirst, an' he must never know.

[1] As a matter of fact the surmise is correct. The Cathers though long settled in Virginia were Irish.

Grandmither, gie me your clay-stopped ears, that I may never hear
My lad a-singin' in the night when I am sick wi' fear;
A-singin' when the moonlight over a' the land is white—
Aw God! I'll up an' go to him a-singin' in the night,
     A-callin' in the night.

Grandmither, gie me your clay-cold heart that has forgot to ache,
For mine be fire within my breast and yet it cannot break.
It beats an' throbs forever for the things that must not be,—
An' can ye not let me creep in an' rest awhile by ye?
A little lass afeard o' dark slept by ye years agone—
Ah, she has found what night can hold 'twixt sunset an' the dawn!
So when I plant the rose an' rue above your grave for ye,
Ye'll know it's under rue an' rose that I would like to be,
     That I would like to be.

Lacrimae rerum! In nearly all the poems in this slender volume
the tears of things are near. The "sad earnestness" which Newman
found in Horace flows like an undercurrent through lyrics that
are only too aware of life and summer, of roses and love. "Oh death
in life, the days that are no more!" Sometimes this sadness is
mingled with languor, as if tears had left the singer no strength
for rebellion or had brought her to acquiescence at the last. Sometimes it is touched with hopelessness, as if aspirations and bright
dreams had perished beyond the power of any magic to restore
them. Sometimes it is wedded to a yearning tenderness that goes as
deep as any passion, as in "The Swedish Mother," "Song," and
"The Poor Minstrel."

    Christ hath stars to light thy porch,
      Silence after fevered song;—
    I had but a minstrel's torch
      And the way was wet and long.
    Sleep. No more on winter nights,
      Harping at some castle gate,
    Thou must see the revel lights
      Stream upon our cold estate.
    Bitter was the bread of song
      While you tarried in my tent,
    And the jeering of the throng
      Hurt you, as it came and went.

When you slept upon my breast
   Grief had wed me long ago:
Christ hath his perpetual rest
   For thy weariness. But oh!
When I sleep beside the road,
   Thanking God thou liest not so,
Brother to the owl and toad,
   Could'st thou, Dear, but let me know,
Does the darkness cradle thee
Than mine arms more tenderly?

Sometimes the note of sadness springs from a piercing sense of the soul's loneliness. This is a dominant note with certain rare individuals even as unlike as Newman and Joseph Conrad, and Browning has one of his lovers voice it unforgettably in "Two in the Campagna." For all of us, whether we will or no, the hour strikes when we find ourselves alone, in spirit even more utterly than in body. There are recesses of the soul where none may follow and where not even Love's self may find the way. It is in such an hour as this that "L'Envoi" was written:

Where are the loves that we have loved before
When once we are alone, and shut the door?
No matter whose the arms that held me fast,
The arms of Darkness hold me at the last.
No matter down what primrose path I tend,
I kiss the lips of Silence in the end.
No matter on what heart I found delight,
I come again unto the breast of Night.
No matter when or how love did befall,
'Tis Loneliness that loves me best of all,
And in the end she claims me, and I know
That she will stay, though all the rest may go.
No matter whose the eyes that I would keep
Near in the dark, 'tis in the eyes of Sleep
That I must look and look forever more,
When once I am alone, and shut the door.

At least two of Miss Cather's poems are colored by an irony more sad than bitter whose implications go deep. In "Paradox" the night is made beautiful by a song; surely, such melody flows from the lips of Ariel, "proud prince of minstrelsy." In its witchery

> The heart of night and summer stood confessed.
> I rose aglow and flung the lattice wide—
> Ah, jest of art, what mockery and pang!
> Alack, it was poor Caliban who sang.

In "The Encore" a poet is praised for a song. But the praise is belated; it was withheld from him in the day when he sought it and deserved it most, in the hour of his first fine careless rapture; it is yielded to him now when his golden note is fled and his glad confident morning gone forever. The song they laud today was "done lang syne and was its own delight":

> When I came piping through the land,
>   One morning in the spring,
> With cockle-burs upon my coat,
>   'Twas then I was a king:
> A mullein scepter in my hand,
>   My order daisies three,
> With song's first freshness on my lips—
>   And then ye pitied me!

In all her poems Miss Cather avoids subtleties, symbols, abstractions. She has the true poet's eye for the concrete and the true novelist's interest in men and women. It is the heart which lures her, its yearning, its tears, its dreams of dear but unforgotten yesterdays, its revolt against blindness to beauty, its sense of the inescapable loneliness of life. She buys a silver cup in a mean Venetian shop, "the only bright, the only gracious object" there; it becomes for her, as it would for Browning, eloquent of the hopes and heartaches of its quondam owners. When she gazes on the bust of some patrician of old Rome she sees there the revelation of a soul empty of joy, a prey of lassitude, as if the living features had hardened into stone.

ANTINOUS

> With attributes of gods they sculptured him,
>   Hermes, Osiris, but were never wise

To lift the level, frowning brow of him
　Or dull the mortal misery in his eyes,
The scornful weariness of every limb,
　The dust-begotten doubt that never dies,
Antinous, beneath thy lids though dim,
The curling smoke of altars rose to thee,
Conjuring thee to comfort and content.
　An emperor sent his galleys wide and far
To seek thy healing for thee. Yea, and spent
　Honour and treasure and red fruits of war
　To lift thy heaviness, lest thou should'st mar
The head that was an empire's glory, bent
A little, as the heavy poppies are.
　Did the perfection of thy beauty pain
Thy limbs to bear it? Did it ache to be,
　As song hath ached in men, or passion vain?
Or lay it like some heavy robe on thee?
　Was thy sick soul drawn from thee like the rain,
Or drunk up as the dead are drunk each hour
To feed the colour of some tulip flower?

Even in the two poems of nature presented in *April Twilights*
it is the human note, expressed in "Poppies on Ludlow Castle"
(with its echo of Louise Guiney) and reserved for the last line of
"Prairie Dawn," that gives to each its poignancy.

PRAIRIE DAWN

A crimson fire that vanquishes the stars;
A pungent odor from the dusty sage;
A sudden stirring of the huddled herds:
A breaking of the distant table-lands
Through purple mists ascending and the flare
Of water ditches silver in the light;
A swift, bright lance hurled low across the world;
A sudden sickness for the hills of home.

Miss Cather's fame as a novelist has eclipsed her celebrity as a
poet. It is possible that comparatively few of the countless readers
of *My Antonia* and *Death Comes for the Archbishop* are even

aware of *April Twilights*. Be that as it may, novels and lyrics are a flowering from the one stem, nourished by the same love of beauty, the same awareness of the pathos of life, the same keen and sensitive powers of penetration, the same swift responsiveness to those things which are the stuff of normal emotions everywhere.

"Billy" Phelps of Yale

NINE YEARS AGO LAST JUNE, AT SIXTY-EIGHT, BILLY PHELPS RETIRED from the faculty at Yale. Today at seventy-seven he is busier than ever, writing, lecturing, contributing monthly reviews of books to two outstanding periodicals, giving sermons and commence-ment addresses, preaching in great churches and university chapels, championing still, in all these ways, the things of the mind and the spirit. "My idea of happiness," he told me once, "is to be chronically overworked at what one loves to do." That remark is a perfect revelation of the man.

On a Monday noon in late September, 1910, one hundred and fifty of us graduate students and privileged seniors were assembled in a huge class room of Lampson Hall at Yale. As the chimes of Battell Chapel struck 12:30 a man in grey flannels entered, walked quickly to the desk, swept the group with a kind but appraising glance, and began to talk.

I missed those opening remarks, for I was too interested regis-tering the speaker's physical appearance. He was tall with good shoulders, slightly marked by the scholar's stoop, and a finely poised head. The tanned face revealed the lover of outdoor life. The forehead, crowned with thick iron-grey hair, was that of a man of swift thought and ready though unhurried utterance; the eyes were keen and penetrating and seemed always twinkling behind his glasses. The nose and chin were an index of an inde-pendent thinker who had the courage of his convictions. The mouth I purposely noted last. It was generous and finely shaped with upturned corners, such as men have who accomplish big things seemingly without effort, who are tolerant and enjoy laughter, whom life loves because they love life and refuse to let it weigh too heavily on mind or heart. This was my first sight of Billy Phelps.

As he was one of the magnets that drew me to Yale I knew something of his career. He was of seventeenth century Connecticut stock, a minister's son, New Haven born, and a graduate of Yale in the class of '87. He had taught and studied at Harvard and taken his Ph.D. at Yale on whose faculty he was beginning his nineteenth year of service. As a lad he loved literature and history and hated mathematics. At twelve he was on intimate terms with Shakespeare's plays and shed tears over the downfall of the Athenian expedition to Syracuse, but he remained deaf and blind to mathematics in college no less than in high school. Once in a course given by the great Sumner, he was confronted with a set of figures designed to show the financial condition of a bank. Billy scanned it carefully and pronounced the institution in perfect shape. "Perfect shape!" echoed the astounded Sumner; "why, on such a showing the examiners would close that bank within twenty-four hours."

That first class with Billy Phelps was unforgettable. For sixty minutes we listened. Not a chair creaked; not a man coughed; not a pair of eyes left that keen, kindly face. Every word spoken registered. It was a revelation of great teaching and a great teacher. What did he talk about? About the origins of the drama, though, to be frank, I should have to delve into my well-stocked notebooks (still treasured) to recover details. But my unaided memory recalls that the lecture was scholarly, touched with occasional wit and frequent humor, and brilliant with those penetrating flashes that cast light into dark corners, illumine dim by-paths, and point the way to realms of gold where the mind finds knowledge and the spirit refreshment.

Every Monday before that 12:30 class one hundred and fifty papers were slipped through a slot in Billy Phelps's office door, representing one hundred and fifty reactions to the plays assigned for the week. On the following Monday they were returned, having been read and graded by the indefatigable professor in person. If you have ever read and graded papers you know what that means. If you have not, be assured that it is the deadliest phase of the teaching profession. To perform it by choice was nothing short of heroic. Of course Billy might have avoided it; he might have turned it over to his assistant. But he chose this way of keeping close to his students, of estimating them directly for himself, and of giving them the satisfaction (greater than most professors realize) of knowing that they were appraised not by an understudy but by the "Chief" himself. If Billy Phelps's self-imposed weekly task was heroic it was climaxed in February and June, for he passed on the mid-year and final examinations personally and, when the strain began to tell, he would lie out on the couch in his library, his pipe well filled, while his assistant read the papers to him and recorded his judgments. Possibly such devotion to the grind of teaching was folly, but if so it was that divine folly which characterizes all great teachers. They spend themselves beyond need but they are repaid by an enthusiastic devotion on the part of their students which smiles at time.

"I love to teach," said Billy Phelps once, "as a painter loves to paint, as a musician loves to play, as a singer loves to sing, as a strong man rejoices to run a race." Of course there were weak brothers among his students but if they had wit they stood more than half redeemed. One of his pet stories concerns a lazy lad who summed up his knowledge of Browning's life thus: "Browning died in 1889. In that same year I was born. What a shameful exchange!"

Let it be said here and now that above all things else Billy Phelps is a great teacher. And let it be added that a great teacher is *rarissima avis*. The student who encounters *one* between kindergarten and his doctor's degree is fortunate; the college which can boast of two is justified in translating its good luck into seven figures; the university to which a benignant Fate or a wise president has attracted three is not perhaps to be found this side of Utopia. As truly as the poet, the great teacher is born, not made. If great, he is a scholar, an interpreter, and a stimulator, all three. One of the most distinguished scholars under whom I ever sat was an unfailing soporific; his powers as interpreter were slight, as a stimulator, nil. Interpreters are not always scholars; and most college and university presidents, when trying to make a decision between a scholar and a stimulator, are torn by conflicting emotions.

Personally I have had my share of great teachers but the crowning stroke of my good fortune was to sit under Billy Phelps. He revealed the three-fold gift, so admirably balanced that with him scholarship ceased to be a leaden-footed plodder, and, transformed, went "sounding on its way" full of buoyancy and zest. In spite of his years of research, the dry bones of Elizabethan drama lived again in his lectures. Under his magic touch a heroine of Beaumont and Fletcher became as radiantly alive as yesterday's debutante; a villain of Ford or Massinger as real as the bad man in a current movie.

Billy Phelps has never held literature at arm's length. At Yale he did not invest it with the curious pseudo-reverence which attends so much college teaching of English, as if one were veritably in the presence of the dead. He sees all great literature as a living thing, as vital as the humanity it reflects, wherein the tears, laughter, and yearning of unnumbered yesterdays are one with the passions of today. To him Ottima, Beatrix Esmond, and Ruth "standing amid the alien corn," Malvolio, Uncle Toby, and Huckleberry Finn are our contemporaries. He is what Hazlitt would call an "onlooker" at life first, a professor of literature afterwards. He is enthusiastic about books but more enthusiastic about humanity; that is his greatest secret. He puts both in the right perspective and keeps them there. He and Pedantry have not even a bowing acquaintance. If you know his books you agree at once; if you do not, read for a start his *Browning*, full of insight and enthusiasm and, incidentally, the best introduction to the great Victorian ever written.

His enormous popularity as a lecturer runs back for many years. In my Graduate School days I always knew when Billy's public course was in progress, for on Tuesdays at three a cordon of automobiles encircled the campus. His audience overflowed the largest lecture hall at the University and moved into the Congregational church on the Green opposite the campus.

Rest assured that the people who throng to hear him once or a score of times are not intellectual drones who attend because it is the smart thing to do. Billy Phelps is the hardest working man I have ever known; he has no interest in drones nor they in him.

To enjoy him you must bring to his public lectures what his best students always brought to his classes, an alert, well-stocked mind, a love of truth and beauty, and—by no means least—a keen sense of humor. The more you know of literature the more you will enjoy him; if in addition you know life you will appreciate him most of all.

His taste is extraordinarily catholic. He has written on eighteenth century romanticism, on the novel, contemporary drama, and latter-day poetry; has edited several plays of Shakespeare as well as volumes by Gray, Thackeray, Stevenson, and Chapman, the glorious old poet whose translation of Homer stirred Keats to the soul; he is the foremost living authority on Browning; and he has written books on the Bible which reveal not only deep faith and insight but an amazing familiarity with both the Old and the New Testaments. His interests do not stop there. He delights in good plays, clever essays, stimulating criticism, a vivid biography, and fine poetry, lectures on them and writes about them with endless enthusiasm. He has a weakness for "thrillers," considers Henry James' *Turn of the Screw* the very best of the brand, and confesses that after reading it he was afraid to go upstairs to bed.

Billy Phelps's enthusiasm points to another of his secrets. He stirs people to see good plays, to read good books, to think about them, and to understand why they are good, which is a way of saying that he has a gift for making his enthusiasm contagious. The gift becomes genius when one considers that his following is recruited from every class, type, and profession which still refuses to believe that matter counts more than mind. It is not surprising to find undergraduates, alumnal associations, commencement throngs, and book lovers among his army of readers and audiences, but it is amazing to see that army widen out to include the idle rich and the overworked poor, complacent Rotarians, busy mothers, harassed school teachers, and tired business men.

Billy Phelps has other secrets, among them the fact that he is an optimist, outspoken and unashamed. The pessimism of conviction he can understand as he proved when he wrote with insight and comprehension of the archpessimist Hardy. But the pessimism of pose and of jaded nerves he ridicules, sometimes with irony but mostly by the eloquence of his sanity and frank joy in life. True he was once accused of being a "Rotarian optimist" but as the charge was made by a Rotarian pessimist it was promptly laughed out of court. As a matter of fact Billy Phelps's optimism goes deeper than preserving his serenity in the face of poor train connections, unexpected showers, a lost golf match, the snarling of anti-punsters, and even the criticism of professional pessimists. It is an optimism which has grappled with the hard facts of life and floored its adversaries. It is built to stay for it is based on faith in all things that are lovely and of good report. It stands the test of a rigorous examination and does not break down when put to trial. It asks nothing of your digestion, your purse, or your vanity; it asks a great deal of your will-power and your common sense. Billy Phelps does not regard life as a Sunday school picnic and he knows—and says—that contentment and happiness are such precious things that you must fight hard to get them and fight even harder to keep them. He is that kind of fighter himself. If you doubt it, take a good look at his mouth and chin.

There is nothing parochial about Billy Phelps. His interests overflow all academic bounds. He frequently slips down to New York for first nights and never misses those occasional revivals of drama classics by which Manhattan seeks to save the artistic soul of America. He loves grand opera, worships Wagner, and after valiantly aiding the effort to establish a symphony orchestra in New Haven, he became president (and is now president emeritus) of the flourishing Association which supports it. He is deeply interested in the civic theatre movement and with voice, pen, and purse has backed it gallantly. Between wars he keeps in touch with the new literary and dramatic developments at Paris, Berlin, and London, knows personally the leaders in both arts at all three centers, and somehow finds time to alternate internationally in the roles of host and guest.

Though a citizen of the world he loves New Haven as Lamb and Dickens loved London and O. Henry loved New York. He would like to live there, he says, for the next five hundred years and after a short interval of rest somewhere else return for five hundred years more. To outstrip Methuselah holds no horrors for him for he believes with Rabbi Ben Ezra that old age is the best part of life.

There is nothing warped about Billy Phelps. He thinks straight, talks straight, and looks you straight in the eye, albeit there is often a twinkle in his own. When the pseudointelligentsia has laid sole claim to the terms "artistic," "candid," and "true to life" and has affixed to its opponents the epithets "puritanical," "narrow," and "pharisaical," Billy Phelps has not raised his voice in protest. He has let the pseudointelligentsia go smugly on its way and he has gone quietly—and effectively—on his. It is only when some of its professed apostles have claimed the honors of literary canonization for their idols that he has shown any concern, and then he has not hesitated to debunk them with a phrase.

Billy Phelps has still other secrets which help to explain his wide appeal. One is his human quality which is felt in all his lectures and writings and is a delight to everyone who knows him personally. It reveals itself in a variety of ways. In his teaching years he did not oppress his students with irrelevant details nor plume himself on the number of hours he could immure them in the library. His teaching instinct convinced him that once you got a student fascinated with his work you would not need to drive him and you could not hold him back. He appreciated highly a certain old adage known to fame and would not have Jack a dull boy (or Billy either) for want of recreation. He is an early riser but his busiest day seldom closes without a round of golf or tennis. In his prep-school teaching days he coached baseball, football, tennis, and hockey, still loves sports, and never fails to attend a Harvard-Yale game. He is no academic onlooker, glorying in his neutrality, but like all red-blooded men is an avowed partisan. When he was once asked which he would rather do, discover a beautiful poem or see Yale defeat Harvard on the gridiron, he answered: "I never smashed my hat over a beautiful poem."

The human side of Billy Phelps explains many things: why for decades he was the most popular professor at Yale; why as Commencement Orator he so humanized the frigid formulas of introduction that they became news; why he was as thrilled on discovering Gene Tunney's delight in Shakespeare as an astronomer on discovering a new star; why he invited the then world's champion boxer to address his Shakespeare class.

That affair was news of the kind that made millions of citizens gasp. What could a professional boxer have to say about Shakespeare? Wasn't Shakespeare a kind of literary cadaver to be dissected before college classes down to the last muscle and most obscure nerve-center? And wasn't this dissecting job the type of thing typical professors of English were hired to do?

Of course there should have been nothing startling in the news from New Haven. In the first place Billy Phelps was never typical, and in the second place the typical professors had been having their chance for generations; why shouldn't some "mere man" of admitted intelligence who had taken his Shakespeare "straight" put in a word on his own account? That the professor who loves life invited the boxer who loves books to do this very thing throws light upon his eager interest in the point of views of others, his unstinted sympathies, and his appreciation of what is fine in men whose primary interests may be poles apart from his own.

To examine into Billy Phelps's "secrets" is to understand how and why he has become a guide and philosopher to a country-wide audience whose members have never heard him lecture in New Haven, at the Town Hall in Manhattan, or anywhere else (although he has lectured in every state in the Union) but whose acquaintance is based on his magazine articles, his critical and familiar essays (charmingly done in the Lamb tradition), or his talks on the radio. His wit and humor delight them, his sound sense wins their confidence, his instinct for the vital things in books and plays is a stimulus, his enthusiasm for life and litera-ture an inspiration, and his optimism a bulwark against the forces of cynicism, bitterness, and spiritual defeat.

He has, however, done more than that: he has achieved a rare triumph, for the members of his vast audience have come to regard him as an intimate friend. Why? The explanation is to be found in Billy Phelps's personality which pervades whatever he does or says and charms everyone. Former Governor Cross of Connecticut, his colleague at Yale for many years, said finely of him, "He is in love with all the world, and all the world is in love with him." When as a cub instructor he summered abroad, he had no difficulty in persuading staid old professors to sit up talking books with him till three in the morning. If he dines alone in some hotel remote from New Haven strangers who once heard him lecture seek him out to pay their respects. If he is a passenger on a branch train in the Grand Canyon the locomotive fireman on a day off joins him for a chat. Distinguished foreign writers lecturing at Yale (Chesterton, Galsworthy, A.E., to name but a few and of a former day) have always found his home their Mecca, while the after-dinner guests that crowd his library to share in the rich talk are recruited from eager—and envied—undergraduate members of the Elizabethan Club. Let him give a lecture anywhere from Boston to San Francisco and he is besieged by people with requests for his autograph, with invitations to luncheon or dinner, or with messages from old friends and former students.

The appeal of Billy Phelps's personality does not depend on his presence. It reaches out through the written word revealing a generous and ardent spirit, full of charm and rich in kindliness and wisdom, who looks upon the multifarious concerns of humanity with the gusto and the intellectual curiosity of the men of the Renaissance.

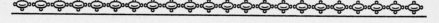

Chesterton as Poet

CHESTERTON HAD THE DISTINCTION OF BEING THE MOST VERSATILE and brilliant English writer of his day. He was novelist, biographer, critic, essayist, editor, and poet, and in every field he has left his mark. His audience was enormous, his devotees legion. Warned by literary history, however, one asks certain questions: Does his versatility presage a lack of lasting distinction in any one field? Does his amazing popularity imply a merely ephemeral appeal? Would it be better for his enduring fame as a poet if like A. E. Housman he confined himself strictly to poetry and within that realm to a handful of brief lyrics? Would his reputation be more secure in the keeping of a little clan of worshippers than in the careless hands of the multitude? Will a man be forgotten whose full-throated melody in the market-place halts the passers-by and sends them on again with a new light in their eyes and a firmer tread? Will a man be remembered whose songs are kept for the few, are sung in a language that only the initiate understand, and are given utterance in some secret penetralia amid exotic odors, dim and curious lights, and sounds subdued to mystery? Who shall say!

The wise men who have pondered over poets and their secrets tell us that what the poet reveals to us is his particular vision of life. It may be a bizarre vision like Poe's or James Thomson's, a vision darkened by evil chance like Hardy's or chill with futility like Housman's, or gorgeous with apocalyptical splendors like

Francis Thompson's, or dim with tears of resignation like Christina Rossetti's, or, as in Chesterton's case, it may be unlike all these but an arresting vision none the less and to many of us the most satisfying of all.

"The question, *how to live*," says Matthew Arnold, "is the question which most interests every man, and with which, in some way or other, he is perpetually occupied," and he goes on to insist that it is the business of poetry to attempt to answer it. Conceiving of poetry thus Arnold calls it "a criticism of life," a definition to which Saintsbury would prefer "an interpretation of life" and Professor Phelps "an illumination of life." But whatever the defects of Arnold's definition his thought remains clear: poetry to endure must treat of moral ideas, must face the question *how to live*. Let us now consider how Chesterton's poetry meets that test.

In his buoyancy and explosive energy and in his interest in the world of men Chesterton reminds one of Browning. But what fascinated Browning were the hidden and subtle processes of thought which precede action; what fascinated Chesterton was rather action itself. To say this is not to imply that Chesterton's interests stopped there. No contemporary British writer, as a matter of fact, was more vitally concerned with ideas or with the moral qualities which affect them when at length they are translated into action. But in the world as he saw it hostile philosophies cannot always be confined to books or to the polished periods of orators in debate. Sometimes rivalries of opinion grow hot in antagonism and take fire in men's minds until shibboleths become holy things like faith, freedom, justice, patriotism, for which they are willing to cast sloth aside. Chesterton comprehended this as a thinker; he visioned it as a poet. In great crises men must not merely weigh and will but *do,* and it is in action, in the collision of opposing forces, even of armies dreadful with banners, that his conception of life is most dramatically, most poetically, most satisfyingly realized.

To him as to Browning and Carlyle inaction was unthinkable; men are not merely contemplative philosophers; they think in order to do; they do greatly only when they possess certain moral qualities, call them virtues, gifts, endowments, as you will. Sustained by these, even unheroic men act decently always, gloriously sometimes, and Chesterton was immensely interested in having the world run always decently and sometimes gloriously. It was because of his interest in the first that he wrote prose; it was because his interest in the second stirred his imagination and his emotions that he wrote poetry. It is because his imagination was alert, his emotions responsive, and his convictions vital that Chesterton won his place as a poet. It is because beneath his ringing verse, his gorgeous color, and his originality of theme and treatment there are moral ideas, an answer to the question *how to live* (to re-invoke Arnold's phrase) that Chesterton has a chance to endure. It is not merely that he was an optimist in a day of pessimism: he went farther and offered enduring substance. At his worst by preachment, at his best under the conditions required by poetic beauty and poetic truth, he proclaimed his conviction that the things by which men live are four—courage, love of truth, laughter, and humility. Let us see.

In his longest and most ambitious poem, "The Ballad of the White Horse," Chesterton glorified courage in ways that belong to the great ballad tradition of England. It was the courtly and elegant Sidney who confessed that "The Hunting of the Cheviot" with its smashing tale of gore and valor "stirred his heart as with a trumpet," and Chesterton's tale of Alfred's triumph over the invading Danes, rich in color, bitter with the scent of blood, sweet with the fragrance of flowers, quiet under the midnight stars, thunderous with the tumult of war, tender with the pity of death, sets even modern pulses galloping and sometimes brings a mist to the eyes.

A throneless king, Alfred secretly summons to his aid his three bravest thanes, Eldred with the "great and foolish heart"; Mark, "a man from Italy," bronzed and lean, with the eyes of a hawk; Colan of Caerleon, a Celt who, true to the madness which God laid upon the Gaels, was "gay when he held the sword" and "sad when he held the harp." When the king's forces foregather, Alfred exhorts them with an eloquence which was to live again with Henry V on the eve of Agincourt. Each king in his great hour is the true democrat, leal brother of his men, fashioned from similar clay, warmed by similar blood, nurtured in the same land, sworn to the same cause.

"Up on the old white road, brothers,
    Up on the Roman walls!
For this is the night of the drawing of swords,
And the tainted tower of the heathen hordes
Leans to our hammers, fires and cords,
    Leans a little and falls.

"Follow the star that lives and leaps,
    Follow the sword that sings,
For we go gathering heathen men,
A terrible harvest, ten by ten,
As the wrath of the last red autumn—then
    When Christ reaps down the kings.

"Follow a light that leaps and spins,
    Follow the fire unfurled!
For riseth up against realm and rod,
A thing forgotten, a thing downtrod,
The last lost giant, even God,
    Is risen against the world."

The progress of the battle joined that day is followed with Homeric attention to the duels of the opposing chiefs and with Chestertonian gusto and magnificence of imagery. Eldred, another Ajax, moves through the press of battle like "the tall white devil of the Plague" or "a locust-tower" darkening "purple and peacock skies" or "like tawny sand-winds tall and dry" blowing death "out of Araby," but at last he is smitten to the heart whereat terror seizes the soldiers. But

"Stand like an oak," cried Marcus,
    "Stand like a Roman wall!
Eldred the Good is fallen—
    Are you too good to fall? . . .

"The lamps are dying in your homes,
    The fruits upon your bough;
Even now your old thatch smoulders, Gurth,
Now is the judgment of the earth,
    Now is the death-grip, now!"

Marcus, for all his eloquence, met his doom

> Fell in the sea of agony,
> And died without a sound.

Alfred and Colan the Celt fight on but are repulsed and separated. Amid the gathering darkness and the clash of arms Colan falls, and "the last cry of the Gael" comes dimly across the hill to the ears of the defeated but still battling King. Refusing to despair and while

> ...a yellow star
> Hung over thorn and hill

Alfred blew a blast which reached the ears of his flying soldiers,

> And they all abode like statues—
>   One sitting on the stone,
> One half-way through the thorn-hedge tall,
> One with a leg across the wall,
> And one looked backwards, very small,
>   Far up the road alone.

(That stanza is a perfect instance not only of Chesterton's picture-making power but of his unique skill in suddenly shifting attention from great to little things thereby enhancing the reader's sense of the immediacy of the scene and the reality of the action.) The troops, heartened by that gallant blast, re-form about the king and to the consternation of the Danes go cheering up the road for a last charge. The fate of Christian England hangs in the balance, but Heaven itself sets its benediction on human courage. Suddenly

> The king looked up and what he saw
>   Was a great light like death,
> For Our Lady stood on the standards rent,
> As lonely and as innocent
> As when between white walls she went
>   And the lilies of Nazareth.

Alfred's forces, exalted to superhuman courage by the Vision, perform miracles of valor, the very peasants fight like Paladins, and Christianity triumphs in its great duel with Heathendom. Verily, as the poet sings,

Life is mean to the mean of heart and only brave to the brave.

Chesterton loved truth like Newman, he hated its opposite, in all its guises, like Carlyle. Sham, cant, hypocrisy, intellectual posing, pretentiousness, and self-deception—all these drew his attack and evoked a gift for satire that ran from jovial parody to bitter irony. When he bantered pseudohumanitarians, when he deflated Dean Inge with the question

Damns he the day whereon his body and soul
Escaped the vigilance of Birth-Control?

when in "Race-Memory" he chuckled at the pretensions of pseudo-science, in verse which loses nothing by its reminiscence of Thomas Hood, he was not wasting time on passing fads and follies but, with deeper purpose, was satirizing that tendency to shape truth to his own image and likeness, to which, in every age and in ever-changing fashions, man is impelled by his vanity, knavery, or lack of spiritual vision. Thus in "Dolores Replies to Swinburne," the affectation of passion breaks like a spent bubble, and a bit of wisdom as old as Adam peers out from behind the jovial ridicule of the parodist:

I am sorry, old dear, if I hurt you,
    No doubt it is all very nice
With the lilies and languors of virtue
    And the raptures and roses of vice.
But the notion impels me to anger,
    That vice is all rapture for me,
And if you think virtue is languor
                    Just try it and see.

Thus when he wrote that blandest of satires "A Ballad of Suicide" he was not only poking fun at *Weltschmerz*, that affectation of our sad young men, but proclaiming a favorite conviction that the world has its fun, its sanities, and its beauty for those who have eyes to see.

Chesterton the satirist was not always bland or jovial and in his serious mood his scorn was bitter. In the typical politician he saw a betrayer of truth who sets Mammon above honor and deals covert wounds to the popular liberties he professes to defend. Read "Antichrist," whose lash must have made F. E. Smith wince even beneath the thick robes of his pharisaism; read "Sonnet with the Compliments of the Season," the intense feeling of whose sestet scalds as with tears; read "In Memoriam P.D." where he paid his respects to "small statesmen" who

> . . . climb and climb, and cannot sink
> So deep as death and honour.

Read "The Dead Hero," where only by invoking the grotesque could he charge his climax with the full measure of his contempt. Read "The Secret People," in which he wondered if the long-silent English masses might not some day match "God's scorn for all men governing."

Lytton Strachey in the "new biography" led a revolt against the custom of suppressing the faults of the distinguished dead and endowing them with imaginary virtues. Chesterton's protest against that same violation of truth was made in one of his most striking and carefully wrought poems, "A Man and His Image," which might be Browning's in conception but in treatment could be Chesterton's alone. It tells of a dead man canonized by universal esteem, whose statue, raised by reverent hands, wins endless worshipers. One strange night the dead man rises and utters his protest to the statue:

> "You make me perfect, public, colourless;
>   You make my virtues sit at ease—you lie!
> For mine were never easy—lost or saved,
>   I had a soul—I was. And where am I?
>
> "Where is my good? the little real hoard,
>   The secret tears, the sudden chivalries;
> The tragic love, the futile triumph—where?
>   Thief, dog, and son of devils—where are these?" . . .

Wordsworth in noble lines declared that the stars keep to their courses because obedient to Duty; Chesterton in "Behind," whose mingled wisdom and naiveté recall Blake's "Songs of Innocence and Experience," proclaimed that the world goes round because it is ever seeking God. Tennyson, feeling that the flower in the crannied wall held in its mystery the greater mysteries of man and God, betrayed the sadness of one whose vision of truth was imperfect and who was halted on the threshold of the sanctuary. But Chesterton felt no such doubt: behind the veil is Truth Itself; confident and content he asked no more.

THE HOLY OF HOLIES

"Elder father, though thine eyes
   Shine with hoary mysteries,
   Canst thou tell me what in the heart
   Of a cowslip blossom lies?

"Smaller than all lives that be,
   Secret as the deepest sea,
   Stands a little house of seeds,
   Like an elfin's granary.

"Speller of the stones and weeds,
   Skilled in Nature's crafts and creeds,
   Tell me what is in the heart
   Of the smallest of the seeds."

"God Almighty, and with Him
   Cherubim and Seraphim,
   Filling all eternity—
   Adonai Elohim."

Laughter, to Chesterton as to Carlyle, "if it come from the heart, is a heavenly thing." It is never the crackling of thorns under a pot but always an explosion of joy. It is joy in such diverse things as a good joke, the exhilaration of a fight for a great cause, the sight of moral loveliness, some revelation of Nature not as destroyer but as the handmaid of God. It blows across men's souls like a spring wind and leaves refreshment in its wake. Genuine laughter is impossible to the mean, the stupid, the mentally warped. It is no casual gift, no secondary virtue, but a cardinal attribute which comes from no source but Divinity itself, the source of all good things.

> I know there can be laughter
> On the secret face of God.

To possess it implies the possession of other things—vision, a sense of proportion, some share of the genius "to see life steadily and see it whole" including in "life" that mysterious microcosm, our own selves. In its perfection it bears an intimate relation to courage, love of truth, and humility. The coward cannot laugh for Fear dwells upon his lips; Chestertonian laughter rings out even in the teeth of Death. The desecrator of Truth cannot laugh for the fountain of genuine joy is dry within him. The proud man cannot laugh for he is incapable of laughter's ultimate victory, the power to see a joke on himself. Alfred, Chesterton's ideal hero, has it in perfection. When the good wife whose cakes he lets burn boxes his royal ears he goes hot with fury—as becomes a King, but suddenly bursts into a roar of laughter—as becomes a great man. It was the laughter of one who sees himself as others see him, a wholesome, brave, unaffected outburst, impossible without true humility:

> And the beasts of the earth and the birds looked down,
> In a wild solemnity,
> On a stranger sight than a sylph or elf,
> On one man laughing at himself
> Under the greenwood tree.

When Colan, matching his skill against the Danish Harold in battle, bursts into laughter, Harold answers in kind—a foeman (the poet implies) worthy of the Gael's prowess. In that ringing poem, "The Last Hero," a man beset by foes whose dull eyes and passionless hearts have never perceived the beauty of life will oppose their spears and die,

> As merry as the ancient sun and fighting like the flowers.

He is no creature of mere brawn, this hero; he is a true poet, therefore the possessor of the tetrad of great virtues. He has found life a succession of splendors, and without tears or terror but with laughter he will greet the Ultimate Experience:

> To see this fair earth as it is to me alone was given,
> The blow that breaks my brow tonight shall break the dome of
>   heaven . . .
> One sound shall sunder all the spears and break the trumpet's
>   breath:
> You never laughed in all your life as I shall laugh in death.

The eyes of the man who is willing to swing from a gibbet to provide the vultures a feast are "full of lovely mirth"; the skeleton lying among the flowers by the water-side is merry, since Death is no tragedy but "the good King's jest"; earth and sun, gazing on a simple faith we are too blind to see, shake with

> An everlasting laughter
> Too loud for us to hear,

and the first rain on the parched Chiltern Hills is like "falling laughter," typifying the joy which the drooping spirit of England needs. The miracle of Christmas has inspired some of Chesterton's most beautiful poems: he pictures it as greeted neither by awed silence nor by ravishing music:

> Hark! Laughter like a lion wakes
>   To roar to the resounding plain,
> And the whole heaven shouts and shakes
> For God Himself is born again.

The fourth virtue which sustained Chesterton's world is outlawed by modernity; it has no place in our contemporary design for living. To him, however, it was the ultimate virtue, the crown of all; it saves courage from grossness, laughter from mockery, and love of truth from complacence. The lack of it in Shaw, Wells, and Kipling (to name no other "prophets") explains their failure to escape their inherent provincialism. What is this virtue, so essential, so potent? As every Chestertonian knows it is humility.

In "The Ballad of the White Horse," which Chesterton intended to be his poetic *magnum opus,* his four heroes, King

Alfred and his Thanes, possess it though in different degrees. In the tense moment before "the high folly of the fight" begins, all but Marcus open their hearts in turn and perform that act of perfect humility—the public confession of their faults. It is the king whose cup is the most bitter, but he utters the mighty *mea culpa* possible only to greatness, for he publicly proclaims no clouded heritage like Colan's, no generous follies like Eldred's, but such a secret act of lust and murder as David wrought against Uriah the Hittite.

Kipling in his "Recessional" drew Chesterton's fire for "boasting that he did not boast" and, unwittingly, inspired "A Hymn for the Church Militant" which has caught the stately measure of the Kipling masterpiece and tacitly indicts its arrogance by pleading for humility:

> Great God, that bowest sky and star,
>   Bow down our towering thoughts to Thee,
> And grant us in a faltering war
>   The firm feet of humility.
>
> Lord, we that snatch the swords of flame,
>   Lord, we that cry about Thy car,
> We too are weak with pride and shame,
>   We too are as our foemen are. . . .
>
> Cleanse us from ire of creed or class
>   The anger of the idle kings;
> Sow in our souls, like living grass,
>   The laughter of all lowly things.

Christmas fills the poet with joy but brings him to his knees for he deems its primary lesson not happiness, peace, or love, but humility:

> Light Thou Thy censer to Thyself, for all our fires are dim,
> Stamp Thou Thine image on our coins, for Caesar's face grows
>   grim,
> And a dumb devil of pride and greed has taken hold of him.
> We bring Thee back great Christendom, churches and towns and
>   towers,

And if our hands are glad, O God, to cast them down like flowers,
'Tis not that they enrich Thy hands, but they are saved from ours.

"The Wise Men," with lines marked by Tabb's simplicity and
Louise Guiney's tenderness, is an admonition to spiritual and
intellectual pride which might well be named a "Ballad of
Humility":

> Go humbly. . . . It has hailed and snowed . . .
>   With voices low and lanterns lit;
> So very simple is the road,
>   That we may stray from it.

"The Song of the Children," reminiscent of Blake in its artless-
ness, its mood, and the exquisite understatement of its tragedy, is
a plea to men to become as these little ones that they may regain
the seeing eye and the understanding heart:

> The world is ours till sunset,
>   Holly and fire and snow;
> And the name of our dead brother
>   Who loved us long ago. . . .
>
> He taught [men] laws and watchwords
>   To preach and struggle and pray;
> But he taught us deep in the hayfield
>   The games that the angels play.
>
> Had he stayed here forever,
>   Their world would be wise as ours—
> And the king be cutting capers,
>   And the priest be picking flowers.
>
> But the dark day came: they gathered:
>   On their faces we could see
> They had taken and slain our brother,
>   And hanged him on a tree.

One of the best known and arresting of Chesterton's poems is
"The Donkey," wherein simplicity mingles with the grotesque
only to rise in the last stanza to a kind of defiant rapture. Memory

stirs within the derided beast and the secret at which he hints invests him with a dignity unperceived before but inalienable now. A mighty virtue is visioned under a form at which the world scoffs—naturally enough, hints the poet, since that virtue is the object of all fools' scorn. "Humility in the guise of an ass!" Yes, but even Humility has its vision, senses the Divine at hand, and shares Its triumph!

> Fools! For I also had my hour;
>   One far fierce hour and sweet:
> There was a shout about my ears,
>   And palms before my feet.

Love is the most abused emotion in the world, derided by the cynic, debased by the carnal-minded, made the occasion of emotional debauches by the sentimentalist. With the greater Browning and the lesser Henley love is a passion, possessive with Henley, curiously complacent with Browning, but with Chesterton it is a sentiment before whose beauty and wonder he prays that his soul may be worthy, his heart clean. Love exalts him to brotherhood with the stars; under its spell the world is endowed with a new glory until he cries: "Who am I that this marvel is wrought unto me?"

The most unique of Chesterton's love poems is "A Certain Evening," the finest, "The Praise of Dust," wherein his "Non sum dignus" is deepened by his sense of the loveliness triumphant in one dear face and of the miracle that shaped it from the clay. Thus, he implies, is the last made first, the lowly exalted, the finite mingled with the infinite, Humility lifted to beatitude.

> "What of vile dust?" the preacher said.
>   Methought the whole world woke,
> The dead stone lived beneath my foot
>   And my whole body spoke . . .
>
> "Come down out of your dusty shrine
>   The living dust to see,
> The flowers that at your sermon's end
>   Stand blazing silently. . . .

"Pass them all by: till, as you come
　　Where, at a city's edge,
Under a tree—I know it well—
　　Under a lattice ledge,

"The sunshine falls on one brown head.
　　You, too, O cold of clay,
Eater of stones, may haply hear
　　The trumpets of that day

"When God to all his paladins
　　By His own splendour swore
To make a fairer face than heaven,
　　Of dust and nothing more."

It is significant that Chesterton's three most ambitious poems, "Saint Barbara," "The White Horse," and "Lepanto" are ballads, that they celebrate historic conflicts in which civilization was at stake, and that civilization triumphed to the glory of what he deemed the cardinal virtues. There are magnificent lines in "Saint Barbara"; there are parts of "The White Horse" whose beauty and power neither Chesterton nor any other poet of his day surpassed. But "Saint Barbara" has left more than one Chestertonian dazzled by its rhetoric but at a loss for its meaning, and "The White Horse," despite its emotional sweep, is more superb in parts than as a whole.

But "Lepanto" is perfect. Here Chesterton's vision of life is fulfilled and justified; here the mighty virtues of his world are made glorious anew in the immortal heroism of common men. In "Lepanto" Chesterton caught the mood of western Europe after its escape from the menace of Islam. It is a mood in which exultation is sharpened by memories of fear, fear less of death than of the loss of things more precious than life. It was a fear lighted only by the hope that lived in the prayers of an anxious old priest, in the magnetism of a gay and chivalrous boy, and in the courage of men who knew their cause was all the world's. The battle was not to the strong: victory came to the humble old man, the youthful captain, and the untried seamen by whose arms the crescent was eclipsed and barbarism vanquished. Justice, freedom, civilization itself, met one of the great challenges of history and emerged victorious. And the heart of the West sang for joy! It is this mood which Chesterton magically recreated. Even in the lines that hymn the power of the Soldan, the potency of Mahound, and the weakness of Christendom, his ballad pulses with victory.

In "Lepanto" Chesterton reveals all his poetic gifts at their best: rhetoric in the high sense in which De Quincey defined it; music almost as rich as Tennyson's, varied by a chant wherein the tread of marching men lives again; color varied and brilliant with the splendor of the East. Chesterton ran the danger of overdoing his rhetoric, of raising so loud a paean that all softer notes would be lost, of coloring his pictures so sharply that relief would be sacrificed. Though for no modern poet these dangers were likelier, in "Lepanto" he miraculously avoided them. The softer note, the skilfully gained relief, are an achievement emotionally and artistically. You see it in

From evening isles fantastical rings faint the Spanish gun

in the last three lines but one of

Dim drums throbbing, in the hills half heard,
Where only on a nameless throne a crownless prince has stirred,
Where, risen from a doubtful seat and half-attainted stall,
The last knight of Europe takes weapons from the wall,
The last and lingering troubadour to whom the bird has sung,
That once went singing southward when all the world was young.
In that enormous silence, tiny and unafraid,
Comes up along a winding road the noise of the Crusade.

Again in the third and fourth lines of

King Philip's in his closet with the Fleece about his neck
(Don John of Austria is armed upon the deck.)
The walls are hung with velvet that is black and soft as sin,
And little dwarfs creep out of it and little dwarfs creep in.

Still again in the third, fourth, and fifth lines of

The Pope was in his chapel before day or battle broke,
(Don John of Austria is hidden in the smoke.)

The hidden room in a man's house where God sits all the year,
The secret window whence the world looks small and very dear,
He sees as in a mirror on the monstrous twilight sea
The crescent of his cruel ships whose name is mystery.

The crowning instance of Chesterton's artistic repression comes
at the last. Had his inspiration faltered, "Lepanto" would have
ended with the crashing music of the penultimate stanza. But it
soared, and he chose a new and softer note and an accompanying
thought which at first seems curiously remote from the main
theme but actually grows from the very heart of it. Logic is here,
the subtle logic of a poet in a great moment. True it is that the
fight is over, the battle won, Christendom saved, and God glorified,
but when "the tumult and the shouting dies" men will forget the
hero who wrought those marvels. Memories wane and perish; it
is our emotions that never die. On the day of Lepanto Don John's
is a mighty name, but for countless tomorrows a mightier will be
that of the wounded soldier who fought under his command and
when the sun set on victory laid aside his sword for his pen and
reality for a vision. For

> He sees across a weary land a straggling road in Spain
> Up which a lean and foolish knight forever rides in vain.

Don John did more than save western Europe: he made the world
safe for Cervantes. He restored him to peace and the leisure to
bring his dreams to birth and he made it possible for men unborn
to dwell in freedom and to share the kindly and immortal
laughter of *Don Quixote*.

Chesterton had his weaknesses. At times his rhetoric sounds
hollow and one is inclined to think him a belated member of the
Spasmodic School. Again, thought is overwhelmed in words as a
child by the golden robes of an emperor. Sometimes his ideas are
neither clear nor coherent because (to use his own excuse for
Browning) he set them down hurriedly lest, thronging upon his
mind as they did, any should be lost.

But his virtues are essential ones. His detractors called him a
medievalist to imply that his interest was solely in the past. As a
matter of fact, Chesterton's passionate concern was for the present
and it was that which made him a major literary influence of our

time. His interest in the medieval past was that of Arnold's Scholar Gypsy: his ideal was an age when men were robust of mind and spirit, untouched by decadence, unweakened by divided aims, citizens of a great spiritual republic because inheritors of a common faith vitalized by the essential virtues. Unlike Arnold, Chesterton did not stand between "two worlds, one dead, the other powerless to be born." Free of the Victorian's doubts he knew his world lived though narrowed in bounds and encompassed by foes. Life is warfare but the poet, unplagued by fear or uncertainty, proclaimed it good:

> Lo! blessed are our ears for they have heard;
> Yea, blessed are our eyes for they have seen;
> Let thunder break on man and beast and bird
> And the lightning. It is something to have been.

Chesterton did not believe that the present would be transformed into the past but he was confident that the primary virtues by which men lived then, and at their noblest live still, are too sacred to be surrendered. Thus he was always the crusader, fighting to keep the holy places of the spirit from the hands of the destroyers, and singing as he fought.

Some of Our Contemporaries

The Shorter Stories of Joseph Conrad

THE PHRASE "SHORTER STORIES," IN CONRAD'S CASE, REQUIRES A word of explanation for, apart from full length novels, it means for the purposes of this essay stories as short as "The Lagoon" (4,000 words) and as lengthy as "The End of the Tether" (60,000 words). Conrad's finest stories of less than novel length do not fall within the typical short story bounds. What are his finest shorter stories? I think they are, in addition to the two named above, "Youth," "Heart of Darkness," "Falk," "Secret Sharer," "Typhoon," "Smile of Fortune," "Freya of the Seven Isles," and "Amy Foster," with "Karain," "Tomorrow," and "Outpost of Progress" as additional possibilities.

The problems which concern Conrad's chief characters are not even in "Typhoon" primarily physical but moral and ethical. They have little to do with strength of muscle, everything to do with those inner qualities, that spiritual energy, that loyalty (often unconscious) to standards of conduct, which we imply in the phrase "strength of character." The hostile force against which strength of character must be shown may be the fury of fire or storm or, more subtly, temptations presented in guises uniquely seductive, or the threatened loss of a beloved woman, or ignorance coupled with fear, or human cunning and rapacity, or dangers growing out of the defiance (however benevolently intended) of established law.

The persons with whom Conrad's characters are chiefly concerned are not weaklings. If they triumph they deserve to and the reader applauds. If they fail it is because they have been subjected to tests which no man could promise himself to endure. Most of them are in a real sense tragic figures, at bottom good, wishing the right, struggling to maintain it but finally overcome. Kurtz, Captain Whalley, Yanko, Jasper Allen, Arsat—"There but for the grace of God go I."

Conrad once protested against the popular notion that he wrote "sea stories." What he meant was that the challenges his chief characters face have nothing essentially to do with the sea, but in one form or another confront men at all times and in every corner of the world. Conrad wrote about the men he knew best, who "go down to the sea in ships, who do business in great waters," of whom he was one from his sixteenth till his thirty-seventh year. Captain Whalley in "The End of the Tether" might have been a railroad engineer; Marlow, the hero of "Youth," a flier with his first plane; the Captain in "A Smile of Fortune," almost any young man who toyed to his hurt with half evil, half tender sensations. Significantly, Kurtz, the chief character in "Heart of Darkness," the most powerful of all Conrad's shorter stories, is not a seaman at all and the sea plays no direct part in the tale.

Let us see to what moral test (what test of character if you prefer) the leading figures of his shorter stories are subjected.

In his first short story "The Lagoon," Arsat the Malayan, in his flight with the wife of his chief, is aided by his brother. When the three are cornered by their pursuers, Arsat, compelled to make a choice, sacrifices his brother and saves the woman.

In "Karain," written a few months later and thrice as long, the problem is similar: faced with the choice between the beloved woman and his dearest friend, Karain kills him to save her. In each case the decision must be on the instant, and however made is bound to bring remorse in its wake. Life, Conrad intimates, never tires of posing moral challenges. What complexities usually surround them, what undreamed of consequences are in their train!

The centaur-like hero of "Falk" has his own problem. Loving life with the deep-rooted instinct of an animal, he feels a comparable passion for an Olympian girl so generously alive that "she could have stood for an allegoric statue of the Earth." His conscience bids him confess to her a secret known to himself alone:

once on a derelict ship he saved his life by murder and maintained it by cannibalism. To make this confession is almost certainly to horrify the girl and alienate her forever. But for Falk, with whom conscience and the hunger for life are equally exigent, there is no other way.

If we penetrate beneath the surface of "The Secret Sharer" we discover two ethical problems implied but never brought into the light. The youthful captain who knowingly harbors a murderer aboard his ship acts contrary to law (becoming an accessory after the fact), and in providing him an opportunity to escape imperils the safety of ship and crew entrusted to his care. In following this course the captain yields to the claims of compassion rather than to the claims of responsibility and law; he acts as a private individual rather than as the chief officer of a ship and a good British subject. What he faces, Conrad implies, is a conflict between duties defined by law and universally observed and the generous instincts of his youth, which appear heroic when we realize that in yielding to them he runs the risk of disgrace and ruin.

In "The End of the Tether" Captain Whalley, retired, who "never lost a ship nor consented to a shady transaction," returns to the sea to earn money for his impoverished daughter. When his sight begins to fail he keeps the fact secret, continuing in service and risking the safety of his ship. His conscience bids him resign his post but his daughter's need cries out against it. Love and duty clash but duty is not the victor.

The test which in "Amy Foster" confronts Yanko, the Polish castaway on English soil, is, unlike Captain Whalley's, not an ethical one. He survives homesickness and unreasoning suspicions; but when the dull unimaginative peasant girl who has married him out of pity runs from him in terror, taking their child with her, he can endure no more.

In "Freya of the Seven Isles," Jasper Allen has so long associated his girl and his brig together in his thoughts that they become merged in a single all-absorbing passion, beyond which he has no desire, no future, no life. Thus when his rival, Heemskirk, deliberately wrecks the *Bonito* he wrecks the lives of the lovers as well, for Jasper does not seek out Freya and win fresh hope and courage from her who is so rich in both, or attempt to conquer some brave new world with her at his side, but broods over his loss till he goes insane and leaves to the heart-broken girl no release but death. Allen's weakness, cautiously revealed in the course of the story, is a lack of maturity, a certain want of self-discipline, a fatal flaw in an otherwise attractive character.

In "Youth" Jim Marlow at twenty-one as mate of the *Judea* does not escape his test. Conrad does not picture him tormented by fears, but he does not on that account mean to imply that fears —breath-taking fears—would not be justified. Were it otherwise this story could not have been written. It is not that Jim is unaware of their presence or lacks nerves and imagination but that he is so intoxicated by youth, so uplifted by its unreflecting gusto, that peril is a joy and tragedy but an aspect of a thrilling adventure. Thus, says Conrad, men act in the divine hour of youth; later they may also prevail but then they act stolidly or stoically or cynically or by force of habit or from shame or by an effort of will.

In "Typhoon" a similar test confronts the crew of the *Nan-Shan*, attacked not by fire but by the confederate violence of sea and sky, and attention is focussed no longer on one man getting his first initiation in responsibility but on four men, the Captain and his seasoned chief officers. What effects does this "act of God," this most prodigious storm in the whole of literature, have on each of these men and how, besides, do they react to the problem of justice and compassion involved in the presence of a supercargo locked in the hold and maddened by terror?

"An Outpost of Progress" (ironic title) recalls two similar stories of men isolated from civilization, "The Seventh Man" by Quiller-Couch and "In a Far Country" by Jack London. The scene of Conrad's tale is equatorial heat; the scene of the other two, arctic cold. Solitude and frayed nerves play a part in all three but the significant difference is that Conrad's story deals with moral degeneration. The tragedy which overtakes Carlier and Kayerts is traceable beyond a mental upset to a sly and enormous greed which condones and profits by murder.

In a story of much ampler scope, subtlety, and power, "Heart of Darkness," Conrad returns to a similar theme. Kurtz is gifted, magnetic, and idealistic as Carlier and Kayerts never are, and the temptations which assail and finally destroy him are more insidious in their workings and more completely ruinous in their results than the vulgar ones to which they yield. Their spiritual potentialities are meagre, his enormous; at best they might have been commonplace executives in minor positions but Kurtz has it in him to become a world figure, an immortal in the history of social regeneration. The test comes when he discovers that the way to an independent fortune is heart-breakingly slow, and yet without it the door is closed against both his marriage and his vast ambitions for the altruistic development of central Africa. He finds means to quicken it but his course involves him in hateful alliances and tribal feuds, in sinister practices and monstrous relationships culminating in terrorism, lust, and murder.

While writing his first short story, "The Lagoon," Conrad informed a friend that it was "a tricky thing with the usual forests, rivers, stars, wind, sunrise and so on." By this he meant, I think, that it is in miniature a typically Conradean story in the sense that it provides a vital test of the chief personage's character, and it tries to present that character in different situations, in revealing moments, and in actions whose consequences are more widespread and more tragic than anyone has foreseen. Finally, it provides a setting wherein the power and opulence of Nature are revealed in their fulness, and the sense of fear and solitude, beauty, wonder, and mystery is deepened, till her domain and that of human creatures who in the midst of life walk in the shadow of death, seem to mingle in a cosmic pattern more vast and awesome than they can comprehend.

"The romantic feeling of reality," said Conrad, "was in me an inborn faculty." This sense of reality explains why at the core of his stories is an incident of which he had either personal experience as in "Youth" or direct knowledge as in "Heart of Darkness"; or an episode currently known like Heemskirk's villainy in "Freya" or like the murder at sea in "The Secret Sharer." Conrad's romantic feeling explains why his best tales are not merely sailors' yarns but great stories that have been lifted into literature through the power of his emotion and imagination. Thus, to take "The Secret Sharer" again, he broods on what seems to be a vulgar homicide committed by a nameless sailor, until the wrong-doer is transformed from less than a shadow into a living man who, instead of being sent to England, to trial and imprisonment (as in the original episode), falls into the hands of a person responsive to the claims of compassion and poetic justice.

Once the murderer and his deed become actual to Conrad he faces what he called "the problem." "The problem," he wrote, "was to make unfamiliar things credible. To do that I had to create for them, to reproduce for them, to envelop them in, their proper atmosphere of actuality," so that the reader may see what Conrad has come to see and every aspect of the setting: not only, for example, the storm which assails the *Nan-Shan* and makes every sailor's nerves tense, not only the other ship (in "Secret Sharer") on which the murderer Leggatt seeks refuge, but the friendly young captain's compassion, his curious notion that Leggatt is a kind of *alter ego,* the suspicions of the crew that the captain is getting "queer," and finally the scene at night when the captain (to the consternation of the crew) orders his ship to stand in close to shore to give his dangerous guest a chance to escape: "The black southern hill of Koh-ring seemed to hang right over the ship like a towering fragment of the everlasting night. . . . Then stillness again with the great shadow gliding closer, towering higher, without light, without sound. Such a hush had fallen on the ship that she might have been a bark of the dead floating in slowly under the very gate of Erebus." The fugitive noiselessly lowers himself into the sea and as the ship edges away strikes out for the shore and the chance—shrouded in similar darkness and mystery—of a new life.

The facts of this story, as of all Conrad's best tales, might be told in a few words but then it would not be his; the distinguishing features would be gone. The readers must share the captain's sympathy for the murderer; therefore they must know something about him: his background, his upbringing, his courage, his inherent decency; about the murdered sailor: his meanness, insolence, and cowardice; about the captain, who is going to be so impressed by the mitigating circumstances surrounding the crime and to feel such compassion for the murderer, that he will harbor him in defiance of law and risk everything to give him a chance to escape. The incredible must be made credible, and to solve that "problem" by the only medium open to him, words, "the old, old words," as he called them despairingly, "worn thin, defaced by ages of careless usage," Conrad toiled in a very agony of resolve, sometimes in tears. It is the proof of his genius that his successes were striking, his failures few.

To Conrad a character in his stories is immeasurably more than a person to whom something happens. He is a creature of immense importance partly because he is a human soul endowed with fears, longings, hopes, the capacity to foster illusions and to die of heartbreak, and partly because he possesses a conscience which, no matter what name he gives it, plays an inescapable role in his life. As an entity in that human creation which is the sum and crown of things, he commands attention not only for what he does and for what happens to him but for what he thinks and feels, since his thoughts and emotions help to explain the course he pursues and his reactions to the consequences. He is a complex being whose name is mystery, and Conrad, understanding this, leaves to the reader the sense of a secret truth, of a hidden reality in his full length characters that lie beyond the reach of any probe. It is with reverence no less than with despair that he notes "how incomprehensible, wavering, and misty are the beings that share with us the sight of the stars and the warmth of the sun." It is typical of Conrad that he succeeds in probing so deep, revealing so much, and conceding with fine but gratuitous humility his limitations of vision.

In order to make unfamiliar things credible—scenes, events, people—to make us, as he once put it, "hear, feel, before all, *see*" with his own sense of reality, Conrad has recourse to certain devices. Like More in *Utopia* (to take one instance out of many) he employs in all his finest shorter stories, except "Typhoon" and "The End of the Tether," a narrator who is alleged to speak with first hand knowledge. Conrad does not handle this device with unfailing skill and in spite of his best efforts he sometimes wearies or exasperates. Many a reader would gladly proclaim the willing suspension of his unbelief if on such terms this supernumerary might be banished! As another expedient, Conrad adduces reinforcing testimony as to facts and goes to almost grotesque lengths to establish the moral and personal antecedents of his characters and to reveal the varied estimations in which they are held. The three officers of the *Nan-Shan* are one regarding the fury of the typhoon but not regarding Captain MacWhirr's idiosyncrasies; Captain Whalley discloses to the friendly VanWyk the story of his pride and his humiliation and we are permitted to see him through the eyes of VanWyk, Massy, and Sterne. So also with Kurtz: to Europe he is a great name, associated rather vaguely with a kind of humanitarian crusade; to the Company officials, an amazingly successful producer of ivory, a result made possible, it would seem, by some curious influence he wields over the natives; the natives themselves think him a kind of God whose ways are strangely wrought of good and bad; in Marlow's eyes he is evil, in those of the sweetheart who awaits his return to Paris and who cherishes beautiful memories, another Bayard without fear and without reproach.

How are so many points of view possible? How does it come about that Kurtz is known to two continents and why are judgments so divergent? Conrad cannot answer these questions lightly. Being Conrad, having a passion for establishing the reality of his stories, he must answer carefully, meticulously, even at the risk of wearying his readers. We must be informed that it is Marlow who tells this story, that as he does so he is on board a cruising yawl. What is her name? The *Nellie*. Where is she? Anchored in the Thames. What time of day is it? As dusk is falling on the river and London is becoming "a lurid glare under the stars." To whom does Marlow tell the tale? To the Director of Companies and three other men. Who are they? Who is Marlow? How did he happen to go to Africa and specifically up the Congo river? All these questions are answered and countless more as the story slowly gathers itself together and begins to move. As it moves it gains not speed but weight, the weight of endless detail added bit by bit with infinite patience; nothing is overlooked, from the two women "knitting black wool as for a warm pall" in the waiting-room of the Company, to the black helper in the wheelhouse who, spitted through the heart by a spear, "looked at me over his shoulder in an extraordinary, profound, familiar manner, and fell upon my feet." Conrad is in no hurry. If a story seems to him worth telling he insists on telling it in his own way, that is, in the only way which will make you see it—people, setting, and events—full of light and darkness and mysterious emanations, as he sees it himself. A lover of Conrad unendowed with patience and imagination is a contradiction in terms.[1]

The strange seas and remote shores, the lonely rivers whose virgin waters have never been ploughed by a white man's craft, the alluring islands that "lie upon the level of a polished sea, like a handful of emeralds on a buckler of steel," are as unknown to Conrad's readers as the Aegean and the adjacent lands were to Byron's and they are invested with a similar lure. Says Marlow in "Youth": "The mysterious East faced me, perfumed like a flower, silent like death, dark like a grave."

Therein lies a phase of Conrad's problem, of his task of making the incredible credible. He must present this mysterious East to his readers as it appears to him, to Marlow, his other self, for it does things to men, especially to sensitive and imaginative men, the kind whose stories he likes best to tell and the kind through whose eyes he watches those stories unfold. This explains why his descriptions of nature are so interpenetrated, so curiously colored, by human fancies and moods that it becomes impossible to say how much of the scene the senses perceive and how much they create. Instances are countless: "The contorted mangroves seemed to writhe at us in the extremity of an impotent despair." "The woods were unmoved, like a mask—heavy, like the closed door of a prison—they looked with their air of hidden knowledge, of patient expectation, of unapproachable silence." The fury of sky and tropical sea in "Youth" is released upon Marlow's ship: "Whenever the old dismantled craft pitched heavily with her counter high in the air, she seemed to throw up, like an appeal, like a defiance, like a cry to the clouds without mercy, the words written on her stern: *Judea,* London. Do, or die." Who can remain unaware of these seemingly insentient forces that work their mysterious and evil will on everything that dares approach them? We

[1] When Massy decides to fill his pockets with metal in order to wreck the *Sofala* by deflecting the ship's compass, he goes to a small room on board filled with rubbish, scrap iron and eight other listed things. As Conrad is obviously bedeviled by fear lest this vile trick seem incredible he goes to extraordinary lengths to make it credible: among the rubbish is a discarded hat which (a) once belonged to a man now dead, (b) formerly a mate on the *Sofala,* (c) who died of fever, (d) on the coast of Brazil; (e) this hat had remained for years (f) jammed forcibly (g) behind a length of (h) burst (i) copper pipe, (j) flung at some time or other out of the engine room. Was Defoe at his best more painstakingly meticulous than this?

read of the tall, emaciated Kurtz: "The wilderness . . . had caressed him, and—lo!—he had withered; it had taken him, loved him, embraced him, got into his veins, consumed his flesh, and sealed his soul to its own by the inconceivable ceremonies of some devilish initiation."

Read again the description of the *Judea* burning in the night and you cannot fail to notice the transforming power of certain words. A good journalist, a writer devoted to reality stripped of romantic feeling, could write, "At daylight she was only a charred shell, floating still under a cloud of smoke and bearing a glowing mass of coal within." But only Conrad, to whom "the romantic feeling of reality," to repeat, "was an inborn faculty," would write of "the blood-red play of gleams," of "a disc of water glittering and sinister," of "an immense and lonely flame," or speak of the burning craft as "mournful and imposing like a funeral pile" and of her "magnificent death" which came "like a grace, like a gift, like a reward" at "the end of her laborious days. The surrender of her weary ghost to the keeping of stars and sea was stirring like the sight of a glorious triumph."

It is easy to point out in such passages as these the similes, the analogies, the metaphors, the instances of the pathetic fallacy, the "fresh choice and allocation of words and phrases, somewhat in the Gallic order" (to quote Dean Cross), but the important thing is that magic, mystery, and beauty rise from these pages like exhalations, beguiling the fancy till it roam whither "no eye can follow, no hand can grasp," conveying to us some realization of the restless and invincible illusions through which, each in his own degree, his men and women wander.

The word illusion, like the words mystery, fear, evil, and loneliness, are common in Conrad. He uses it to express those conceptions known to most men which approximate reality but are too painful or too joyful, too gloomy or too bright, too full of hope or of despair, to conform with it exactly. Few of us have such complete command of our fears and hopes that we can confront for what it is a world whose naked facts seem so brutal. Some illusions pass only to be replaced by others; some suffer a disenchantment from which there is no recovery; but almost universally illusions of one kind or another remain for they are "invincible." Generally Conrad uses the word to imply a conception that gives more joy, hope, serenity or courage than reality warrants; but he tells us that illusions may imply the opposite as was the case with Falk who was tortured by the illusion that his guilty tale of murder and cannibalism would stir his Juno to revulsion but found with joy that she was moved to pity instead.

Virtually all Conrad's chief characters have their own peculiar illusions: Jasper Allen that he is beyond the reach of Heemskirk's vengeance; old Nelson that Freya does not love Allen and so will stay on to comfort his own old age; Yanko that marriage to an Englishwoman will win him peace of mind and the security of his own hearth; the youthful Marlow that life will always remain thrilling and wonderful; Captain Whalley that his physical powers will never flag; Kurtz that his idealism will survive the forces of evil which lie in wait for him in the tropics, far from the steadying influence of Europe, and so on to the end of the long Conradean gallery. When the cold touch of reality destroys a bright illusion the victim occasionally finds refuge in another, as Kurtz does for a time when he tells himself that he can play with the fires of lust and murder and remain unscathed; or he re-creates it by an effort of memory and for an hour tastes the heady joy of it again, like the middle-aged Marlow when he recounts his early experiences in "Youth." Kurtz, from the very fact that he is intellectual, imaginative, and idealistic, manages to create a succession of fresh illusions as his earlier ones fall from him, but in the end on his way back to the coast, broken in health and will, death overtakes him; in that dark presence, earth's last reality, his final illusion dissolves, and with a cry, "The Horror," he sees himself as the thing he is. Jasper Allen swings from one illusion to its opposite, from the extreme of confidence to the extreme of despair, for after tasting Heemskirk's vengeance he falls victim, not to the reality, harrowing though it is, but to the hope-destroying illusion that the wreck of the *Bonito* is the wreck of his world.

Whether or not Conrad studied the *Apologia* it is hard to say, but he is as sensitively aware as Newman of the isolation of every individual soul. In the hour of crisis each of us must make his own decisions, play his own part, fight his own battle, morally as remote from his fellows as Crusoe on his island. Conrad's Slavic temperament, reinforced by his years at sea, helps to explain his consciousness of this truth, as when he speaks of "the tremendous fact of our isolation, of the loneliness, impenetrable and transparent, elusive and everlasting." By no other writer of English fiction is this note made so pervasive, so insistent; in no other English work but *Everyman* and *The Dream of Gerontius* is it so pronounced. You find it everywhere in Conrad's tales; Kurtz, Leggatt, Il Conde and Gaspar Ruiz *(A Set of Six),* Yanko, Arsat, Jasper Allen, Renouard ("The Planter of Malata"), each is alone in his fateful hour, alone with fear, with despair, with the passion for life, with the mystery of death. So it is with Captain Whalley upon the deck of the sinking *Sofola,* as the shouts of his crew and the sound of their hurrying feet die away; so with Karain, tortured not only by the memory of the friend he has killed but by the desolation that loss has brought him.

The most gripping pages of the "Typhoon" are, as Conrad intended, those which describe Captain MacWhirr on the bridge of the *Nan-Shan,* clawed at by wind and tumultuous waters and in the sudden darkness "feeling stricken by a blind man's helplessness." In the duel between the elements and this man he can expect neither a helping hand nor an encouraging voice; he is alone with his iron courage, alone with his responsibility for the safety of his ship and of every soul aboard. Jukes, the mate, stumbles through storm and darkness to join him, not helping but adding to his burdens. "Our boats are going now, sir." Then "with a penetrating effect of quietness in the enormous discord of noises, as if sent out from some remote spot of peace beyond the black wastes of the gale" he hears the Captain's voice—"the frail and indomitable sound that can be made to carry an infinity of thought, resolution and purpose, that shall be pronouncing confident words on the last day, when heavens fall, and justice is done —again he heard it, and it was crying to him, as from very, very far—'All right.' "

Almost all Conrad's finest shorter stories belong to tragedy or tragi-comedy. Even "Youth," that paean of joy in remembered gusto, has as its refrain regret over precious, irrecoverable things, while "Falk" and "The Secret Sharer" though ending "happily" grow out of tragic episodes.

Why should this be so? Why did tragedy capture Conrad's attention and commend itself to him under a variety of guises, as the stuff from which he could—and did—shape his finest stories?

The answer, I think, is to be found in several things: in his childhood, darkened by the savage repression which followed the insurrection of 1863; memories of an exiled mother treated with ruthless severity and of a cultured and talented father recalled from exile only to follow her to the grave; in a racial strain in which melancholy has always been deeply marked; in an imagination shadowed by apprehensions and fears; in his twenty years of struggle as a writer in the face of poverty and popular indifference; in, finally, a supersensitive nature which Conrad's wife tells us was not a happy one.

Life, Horace Walpole once observed, is a tragedy to him who feels, and Conrad no less than Thomas Hardy is a notable instance. Hardy's rebellion against what he deemed the pitiless injustice of the ultimate force (Chance, Destiny, God, "It," President of the Immortals,) made him so complete a pessimist that he sometimes creates the impression of trying to justify his attitude by loading the dice against his chief characters. It is significant that Conrad entered a spirited denial of the charge that he was either a pessimist or a cynic. It is true that there are passages in his tales which the casual reader may cite in support of one or both charges. But if Conrad said that the history of men might be written in the phrase: "They were born, they suffered, and they died," he was prompt to confess that it was as difficult to be wholly sad as wholly joyous on this earth. If he was acutely aware of the isolation of the individual soul, he cherished nevertheless an invincible belief in the spiritual and emotional solidarity of all human kind, in a communion uniting "the dead to the living and the living to the unborn." If he bears testimony to a universe full of haunting terror, pain, sorrow, toil, uncertainty, and disillusionment, he bears equal testimony to "its wonder and beauty, its infinite passion, its illimitable serenity." He never lets us forget that if men hate, they love; if they despair, they hope; if they are deadened by the ugly and the commonplace, they are uplifted by the sublime.

All writers, he says, give themselves (and their morality) away "in about every third sentence" and he himself is no exception. Let us see. All lands and they that dwell therein "lie under the inscrutable eyes of the Most High" and must run their course and meet the challenges of good and ill. Man, the universe, the ways of

God, are full of mystery; nevertheless there is a supreme law which He established and through which He operates, and the individual conscience to which He speaks. Each of us has an appointed task on this earth; we must endure the vicissitudes of life with a "steeled heart" and see in death the very condition of immortality. Add courage, compassion, love capable of faith and abnegation, a stern sense of duty, the wisdom of discipline, and you have a glimpse of the "morality" (or if you prefer, the philosophy of life) in which Conrad believed and which he reveals "in about every third sentence." In moods when the burthen of the mystery chilled his heart he spoke of life as "a futile tale," but in a loftier and truer mood he could look upon the face of a man dead and say: "His soul, delivered from the trammels of his earthly folly, stood now in the presence of Infinite Wisdom."

These things explain why Conrad denied that he was either cynic or pessimist and why he declared, "I have never sinned against the basic feelings and elementary convictions which make life possible to the mass of mankind."

Lytton Strachey, Biographer

WHEN LYTTON STRACHEY DIED IN JANUARY 1932 HE WAS ACCLAIMED on all sides the father of the "new biography." A fortnight before that event, when advertised to lecture on the new biography in a great Eastern city, I was amazed to be questioned as to what the *new* biography was. Everybody seemed to know the meaning of biography, uncharacterized, and would probably have described it as the life of a distinguished person. If that were the case, why *new* or *old* either for that matter?

As a plain fact the new biography is different, not because it has ceased to be the life of a distinguished person but for three important reasons. First, its chief interest is not in what its subject did but in what he was; next, it regards him not as an essentially superior type but as marked by faults and virtues; and finally, in place of the Plutarchian aim (which was to win the reader to imitate virtue and avoid vice) it holds itself aloof from all moral purposes. The biographer of the new school is convinced that the biographer of the old school went to extremes; that he set hero-worship above truth and contrived by hook or by crook to paint an agreeable portrait of his subject. Follies and indiscretions were not to be mentioned; scandals were taboo. The great man was always on dress parade and on good behavior. He was never revealed either morally or socially off his guard. Moore's *Byron* is a classic instance of the biographer's refusal to lift the veil, and Tennyson's comment is a classic revelation of the Victorian attitude of mind toward such reticence: "What business has the public to know about Byron's wildnesses? He has given them fine work and they ought to be satisfied." If a biographer told too much and stripped the heroic toga from the great man's shoulders he was promptly damned: witness Froude whose revelations of Carlyle have not even yet been forgiven. The case of Ruskin provides an instance of the other extreme. In 1893 W. G. Collingwood published a two volume life of the author of *Modern Painters* and never once mentioned the name of Euphemia Gray! Such reticence was a two-fold evil: it called attention to the very thing it so studiously ignored and it awakened uneasy doubts as to the number of other "discreet silences" biographers of the prevalent tradition had observed. Such false delicacy offended even Newman, most prudent of men, who wrote of it impatiently and that too in the case not of laymen but of saints.

It was the first World War which brought the dissatisfaction with Mid-Victorian biography to a head. Tried as by fire in those devastating years many a high reputation perished. Men accounted great in peace played traitor in politics or dunce in battle, and disenchanted millions knew them at last for the Lilliputians they were. Disillusionment became the order of the day. About those that sat in high places brutal truths were entertained and sometimes whispered but, thanks to the censorship, seldom committed to print. But no censorship protects the dead, and the statute of limitations has run against Horace's merciful *De mortuis, nil nisi bonum.* Thus, in the last year of the war, embodying this mood with its ironic challenge to accepted appraisals, came Lytton Strachey with *Eminent Victorians.*

What exactly did Strachey do? He selected four outstanding characters, a nurse, a churchman, a soldier, and a teacher, all of whom had won and held the veneration of England for a generation, and he subjected them to keen scrutiny. The first thing notable was his method of approach. He professed a perfect detachment, a complete freedom from prepossessions, a coldly scientific impersonality. He did not aim to heighten his subject's virtues or his weaknesses. He merely desired to paint a true portrait of the outer and especially of the inner man and that within about one-twentieth of the space required for the typical old-fashioned biography. To achieve this Strachey had first to study his man from every point of view, to consider his career in its failures no less than in its achievements, to decide upon his inner nature, and to discover the secret of his character, that key which unlocks the countless hidden chambers of his heart and mind and brings to light the passions that lurked there and were the mainsprings of conduct.

Strachey's method required him to select and to reject, to select the material which supported his conception and to reject that which might raise a doubt of its accuracy. If he had before him a score of letters, he must select therefrom the paragraph, the sentence, the phrase, which conveyed the desired impression; all else must be swept aside. Clearly the responsibility of such a biographer is enormous. Everything depends on the accuracy of his interpretation of his subject's character, and that accuracy depends in turn—at least negatively—on his own freedom from prejudice and prepossessions.

Eminent Victorians made Lytton Strachey famous overnight. Its four studies were admittedly so brilliant, so vivid, so psychologically keen, so attuned in their irony to the prevailing mood of disillusionment, that they caught the popular eye at once. In 1921 Strachey's next venture, *Queen Victoria,* appeared. Here was a more sustained work which required, for obvious reasons, highly judicious handling. Strachey was conscious of the obligation and equal to it. He slowed down his *tempo,* added to his gravity a touch of conscious dignity which at times approached the "grand manner," and sustained in striking fashion the characteristics which had marked *Eminent Victorians.* In 1928 he again challenged success with a major work and again he won. *Elizabeth and Essex* was acclaimed on all sides. Strachey was pronounced "the most eminent biographer of our day," his latest volume "an exquisite work of art," and its medium "imperishable prose." Two men whose reputations flashed through Europe, the German Ludwig and the French Maurois, were accounted Strachey's disciples (Maurois so proclaimed himself), a host of imitators followed at his heels, and thus we beheld an amazing phenomenon: the English Strachey, virtually unknown before 1918, achieved a world-wide reputation in a dozen years, established virtually a new *genre,* and became the father of a literary school.

His career raises some interesting questions: If he was not

entirely *sui generis,* who were his literary creditors? Granted his brilliancy, was his mind open, entirely free from prejudice, eager only for the truth? Finally, where does he "belong" as a biographer?

Picking up one of Strachey's three major works blindfolded and opening it almost at random one encounters this: "The public schools of those days were a system of anarchy tempered by despotism. Hundreds of boys, herded together in miscellaneous boarding-houses, or in that grim 'Long Chamber' at whose name in after years aged statesmen and warriors would turn pale, lived, badgered and over-awed by the furious incursions of an irascible little old man carrying a bundle of birch-twigs, a life in which licensed barbarism was mingled with the daily and hourly study of the niceties of Ovidian verse. It was a life of freedom and terror, of prosody and rebellion, of interminable floggings and appalling practical jokes. Keate (the Head Master) ruled unaided by sheer force of character. But there were times when even that indomitable will was overwhelmed by the flood of lawlessness. Every Sunday afternoon the whole school assembled shouted him down. The scenes in Chapel were far from edifying: while some antique Fellow doddered in the pulpit, rats would be let loose to scurry among the legs of the exploding boys. But next morning the hand of discipline would re-assert itself; and the savage ritual of the whipping-block would remind a batch of whimpering children that, though sins against man and God might be forgiven them, a false quantity could only be expiated in tears and blood."

There is no mistaking that: *aut Caesar aut nullus.* It is Macaulay to the life, from the topic sentence at the beginning to the overstatement at the end. The Long Chamber "at whose name in after years aged statesmen and warriors would turn pale," the "furious incursions of an irascible old man carrying a bundle of birch-twigs," "licensed barbarism mingled with the daily and hourly study of the niceties of Ovidian verse"—the tone, the method of development, the diction, all bear the impress of Strachey's chief creditor, the greatest Victorian master of non-fictional narrative—Macaulay. From him Strachey learned the value of the concrete word, the casual allusion, the specific instance, the picturesque detail, and the infinite and effective possibilities of contrast. He mastered the art of painting vivid scenes (the mustering of the Mahdi's army in *Eminent Victorians* is one of the finest descriptive passages in twentieth century prose) and speaking likenesses of his chief actors.

Strachey proved himself an apt and skilful pupil and with him as with Macaulay contrast is the core of his art. In *Queen Victoria,* the Queen's almost middle-class complacency sharpens the tragedy of the Prince Consort's eagerness for a life of action in the arena of politics, and the frustration of his great ambition becomes the more poignant in the face of his minor successes. Again, Disraeli's attitude to the aging Queen is darkened to duplicity while Gladstone's bluntness is lightened to candor. Finally, as the grand *motif,* is implied on every page the contrast between the majesty of the British empire and the commonplaceness of the plump, domestic little woman who symbolized it.

Elizabeth and Essex is fundamentally a study in contrasts. On the one hand a queen, on the other a subject; she selfish, old, and ugly, he generous, young, and handsome; she with brain dominating heart, he with heart dominating brain; she coldly unspiritual, he knowing moments of spiritual exaltation; in the event, she the powerful sovereign determined to wreak vengeance, he the impotent subject beaten in the game of cat and mouse.

In *Eminent Victorians* Strachey's flare for contrasts is no less evident. Florence Nightingale's overmastering efficiency has a foil in Dr. Hall, her restless energy in the willing but physically feeble Sidney Herbert; impulsive Gordon is set against his coldly restrained superior, Sir Evelyn Baring; Manning is contrasted with Newman, one the "eagle," the other the "dove." Only in the study of Thomas Arnold does contrast play no part and it is significant that it is the briefest and least effective of the four.

Macaulay loved those scenes on which he could lavish his pictorial powers, the impeachment of Warren Hastings, the execution of Monmouth, the death of William III. The limitations Strachey set himself kept him from Macaulay's opulent detail but he caught the Victorian's trick, employed it often in distinguished miniatures, and once let himself go and matched his hand against the master's. Read his elaborate description of the execution of Essex who, in his "scarlet waistcoat, with long scarlet sleeves . . . tall, splendid, bareheaded, with his fair hair about his shoulders, stood before the world for the last time." Then read Macaulay's

description of Monmouth on the scaffold in the fifth chapter of
the *History of England*. Each is marked by animation, a perfect
mastery of detail, vividness, dignity, and by the painter's scarcely
concealed joy in a subject nicely suited to his talents.

Strachey, disillusioned, in revolt against the smugness of Victorian biography, found a weapon in irony. For this he owes
nothing to Macaulay; the slashing invective and naked sarcasm
of the Victorian leave him cold. He sought what he desired in
French literature and found it in Voltaire. Strachey knows his
Voltaire. In his volume called *Books and Characters* (1922) he
published for the first time an original dialogue of the French
ironist and devoted to him three of the essays in the book.

It is in *Eminent Victorians* that the Stracheyan irony is most
obvious and most brilliant. Four "personages" are to be subjected
to pitiless scrutiny from a new angle. Letters and diaries are
ransacked, speeches studied, conduct at critical moments analysed,
and such instances noted as reveal devastating contradictions between appearance and reality, between the pose and the attitude
offguard, between profession and practice. This selective process
(let me repeat) is highly artificial, its aim (professedly) is to lay
bare the truth, and its most efficient instrument is irony. If
Strachey were bent on mastering it he went to the right source,
for among the modern lords of irony Voltaire stands alone.
Strachey proved an apt pupil. His irony, like his master's, is never
blatant, a fact which explains why it escapes the dull-eyed; he
handles it with an ease so studied that it appears to be unconscious, and an impersonality of tone so skilfully preserved that it
seems no longer an acquirement. And most important of all, again
like his master's, it never by a hairbreadth swerves from its aim.
About Strachey's irony as about Voltaire's there is something
unmistakably feline. The Frenchman never forgot how to purr
but he often bared teeth and claws, drawing blood. Strachey's
manners are sometimes better but his intentions are always the
same. His claws emerge less often from their velvet sheaths but
the thin crimson lines unfailingly follow them. We read: Dr.
Arnold in his Sunday evening sermon, the culminating moment of
the week, "propounded the general principles of his own conduct
and that of the Almighty." [1] How Voltaire would have chuckled

[1] In this and the two following instances the italics are mine.

over the deadliness of that! Here is another, a fitting mate: "While the Prince Consort had lived, the Queen had worked, indeed, with regularity and conscientiousness; but it was work made easy, made delicious, by his care, his foresight, his advice, *and his infallibility.*"

Sometimes the Stracheyan, like the Voltairean, claws rip their way deep below the skin. A typical instance occurs in his sketch of General Gordon. Strachey dilates upon the calculating ambition of Sir Evelyn Baring, Consul-General at Cairo (who, rather than risk a temporary setback to his own fortunes, permits Gordon to be trapped in Khartoum) and the ministry's aversion from despoiling the Arabs and shedding blood. What preventive measures are taken by Baring and the ministry? None. What happens? The inevitable; Khartoum falls and Gordon perishes. What then? For the moment nothing, but England bides her time and finally at Omdurman wreaks bloody vengeance. Thus Strachey: "It had all ended very happily—in a glorious slaughter of twenty thousand Arabs, a vast addition to the British Empire, *and a step in the Peerage for Sir Evelyn Baring.*" Strachey the ironist, like Voltaire, knows how to flesh his claws, all the while with narrowed eyes and (to use a phrase of his own) "a subacid smile."

Although Strachey learned important lessons from Macaulay and Voltaire he sought for something more which neither of them could give him. He was not content to describe men from the outside or to explain them, like Macaulay, as if all the pulses of the machine were stopped. Quite the contrary. Minds and the complex round of human passions as he desired to present them are dynamic, not static, never halted but always functioning. Obviously the psychological method of approach was the thing but just where would one turn to see it in action? Certainly not to biography, for biography had usually held psychology at arm's length and never admitted her as an intimate. In the novel perhaps? The thought must have come upon Strachey with the joy of an inspiration. There were George Eliot and the long line of her heirs and assigns who sought to reveal the hidden springs of human action, to pursue complexities, to calculate the imponderables in human motive. They presented the mind and heart objectively and we listen, like students at a lecture, trying with more or less success to grasp by an effort of intellect what is most often comprehensible only by an effort of emotional sympathy. Strachey did not have far to go to find this general method skilfully followed out and in a fashion more suited to twentieth century tastes and contemporary psychology than George Eliot's. It was then that he discovered his third chief creditor who may be symbolized by John Galsworthy.

Galsworthy sought to improve on the George Eliot technique by giving us the sense of sharing the inner thoughts of his characters, not indirectly by description but directly by revelation. To achieve this, he employed a deceptively simple but highly effective device which he used at first tentatively but more often and more convincingly as time passed, until by 1916 he showed his mastery of it in *A Stoic*. This device, which came into wide use as "the stream of consciousness" technique, consists of admitting us directly into the thought-current of the characters and recording their self-communion in words. Here is an instance from *A Stoic*: Old Heythorp has just foiled an attack by his business associates. "The old man who could not get up without assistance stayed musing in his chair. He didled 'em for the moment into giving him another month and when that month was up—he would didle 'em again. A month ought to make the Pillin business safe, with all that hung on it. That poor funkey chap Joe Pillin! A gurgling chuckle escaped his red lips. What a shadow the fellow had looked, trotting in that evening just a month ago, behind his valet's announcement 'Mr. Pillin, Sir.' What a parchmenty, precise, threadpaper of a chap, with his bird's claw of a hand and his muffled-up throat."

This device, which effects so obvious an enlargement in the reader's sense of reality, was not lost on Strachey who saw its possibilities in the new and more subtle kind of biography which he meditated. Once having taken it over he soon was adept in its use. Here is a typical instance. The aged Manning would often delve into his scrap-books filled with newspaper cuttings concerning himself over a period of thirty years. Animosity toward his detractors would stir within him. "And then he would suddenly begin to doubt. After all, where was he? What had he accomplished? Had any of it been worth while? Had he not been out of the world all his life? Out of the world!"

Other biographers of the new school have tried their hand at this device, Shane Leslie slightly in *The Skull of Swift,* Harold Nicolson in a few clever pages of his *Byron,* and Strachey's brilliant French disciple, André Maurois, in *Disraeli,* but none with such confident mastery as Strachey himself. In the concluding page of *Queen Victoria,* Strachey has made daring and skilful use of it. The Queen's last hour has come; Strachey is eager to let us peer in upon the current of her dying thoughts, but in default of diary or document to lend color to conjecture, he must confessedly fall back upon his imagination. What he gives us is a companion piece to the final pages of Galsworthy's *Indian Summer of a Forsyte,* and here if ever, by creating the illusion of reality in what purports to be serious biography, the biographer justifies his debt to the novelist. The Queen "herself, as she lay blind and silent, seemed to those who watched her to be divested of all thinking—to have glided already, unaware, into oblivion. Yet, perhaps, in the secret chambers of consciousness, she had her thoughts, too. Perhaps her fading mind called up once more the shadows of the past to float before it, and retraced, for the last time, the vanished visions of that long history—passing back and back, through the cloud of years, to older and older memories— to the spring woods at Osborne, so full of primroses for Lord Beaconsfield, to Lord Palmerston's queer clothes and high demeanour, and Albert's face under the green lamp, and Albert's first stay at Balmoral, and Albert in his blue and silver uniform, and the Baron coming in through a doorway, and Lord M. dreaming at Windsor with the rooks cawing in the elm-trees, and the Archbishop of Canterbury on his knees in the dawn, and the old King's turkey-cock ejaculations, and Uncle Leopold's soft voice at Claremont, and Lebzen with the globes, and her mother's features sweeping down toward her, and a great old repeater-watch of her father's in its tortoise-shell case, and a yellow rug, and some friendly flounces of sprigged muslin, and the trees and the grass at Kensington."

So much for Strachey's methods as he developed them from a study of his chief literary creditors. It is time to remind you that his avowed purpose was to discover and present the truth about the persons he treated, to draw a psychological portrait of them not as their adorers or defenders conceived them but as they appeared to his penetrating scrutiny as an impartial student. As an ideal that was beyond criticism; as a practical matter it takes too much for granted. Are we quite certain of Strachey's impartiality and his penetration?

Strachey's saturation with Voltaire colored his mind. His flair for irony became an obsession, and one suspects that he selected the subjects of his biographical studies less because of their eminence than because of their apparent susceptibility to ironic treatment. Like the inveterate punster who sees a possible play on words even before their valid significance, Strachey instinctively noted obvious or possible contrarieties on whose adroit positing irony might be made to turn. Nothing escaped his ferret glance, from a cabinet reversing its policy to an adoring widow emerging from her weeds. He became so adept that, like Voltaire with the same instrument and like Macaulay with his infinite contrasts, he obeyed second nature in beholding men, their virtues, views, and actions, not under the guise of truth but under the guise of irony. Thus his boasted interest in the facts as they are became a cynical quest of weaknesses, self-contradictions, ignoble compromises between good and evil, and his skill in selecting and organizing material was made to minister to what even his admiring disciple Maurois called his iconoclasm. Let us see how Strachey's obsession with irony makes a mockery of his alleged detachment.

Was it an accident that Strachey selected for treatment in *Eminent Victorians* four persons whose spiritual sensibilities were unusually responsive? That three of them went through a period of *Sturm und Drang?* That of these, two, Manning and Arnold, were clergymen? It is a striking fact that against the great convert and the Head Master of Rugby his irony is given fullest play, mockingly in Arnold's case, mercilessly in Manning's, and that with both it is their preoccupation with religion which draws his sharpest fire. When he states that Arnold introduced a religious principle into the educational system of Rugby, his tongue is in his cheek. When he turns to Arnold's personal religious problem he announces with mock gravity that, thanks to Keble's advice, Arnold's doubts on the Blessed Trinity soon vanished, adding: "One other difficulty, and only one, we hear of at this period of his life. His dislike of early rising amounted, we are told, 'almost to a constitutional infirmity.' This too, he overcame, *yet not quite so successfully as his doubts upon the doctrine of the Trinity.*" [2]

It was when Strachey attempted to portray Manning that he most completely betrayed the limitations of his boasted detachment. To this study he gave lavishly of his skill for it was designed to herald the "new biography" and to display the Stracheyan gifts at their fullest. Let us see. Manning, after bitter doubts like Newman's, followed him from the Church of England to that of Rome. Says Strachey sagely: "The Church of England is a commodious institution; she is very anxious to please; but, somehow or other, she has never managed to supply a happy home to *superstitious egotists.*" That shaft is skilfully aimed: it is intended for Manning and the Catholic Church. Later Mr. Strachey has his doubts; perhaps Manning's egotism (or was it his superstition?) needed an extraneous lure to make Romanism attractive. At once he is on the scent. He recalls that three years before Manning had a "mysterious interview" with the Pope. "What," queries Mr. Strachey, finger to lips, "what did Pio Nono say? It is easy to imagine the persuasive innocence of his Italian voice. 'Ah, dear Signor Manning, why don't you come over to us? Do you suppose that we should not look after you?' " When we succeed in controlling our laughter we ask if the man who could write that is capable of "cool detachment"? Is he the master of a science or the victim of romantic illusions? Is he following the tradition of Plutarch or that of Exeter Hall?

Later we come to Canon Kingsley. Strachey says solemnly: "Kingsley's hatred of Popery was, at bottom, simply ethical—an honest, instinctive horror of the practices of priestcraft and the habits of superstition." The voice is the voice of Strachey, but the words are the words of the anti-Catholic tradition. Listen further: When Catholic sees were reëstablished in England in 1850, Lord John Russell stirred the unthinking to frenzy by raising the cry of "Papal aggression" and unleashing a storm of hysterical resentment. Does the coolly aloof Mr. Strachey deplore this shameful outburst? "The instinct of Lord John," he declares gravely, "and of the English people was in reality sound enough." Why? Because Wiseman's installation was a "quickening in England of the long dormant energies of the Roman Church"— a consummation bitter

[2] In this and the following instance the italics are mine.

as wormwood to the inheritors of the anti-Catholic tradition in 1918 no less than in 1850.

When Strachey looked back upon the Vatican Council of 1870 he was cruelly plagued. He clung to the delusion that its bearing was political; he was embittered by the thought that the English Manning had taken a leading part in its deliberations. But what goaded him beyond endurance was Acton's failure to follow Döllinger out of the Church. In the face of that his last pretence of detachment vanishes; even his polished irony and his good manners are forgotten. "Lord Acton," he snarls, "while straining at the gnat of Infallibility, swallowed the camel of the Roman Catholic Church." At last we have it; the mask is off: detachment, so vital a part of the Stracheyan concept of biography, fails, in the master's own hands, to remain either unwarped by irony or unpoisoned by prejudice. Fate played a cruel trick on Strachey. She decreed that this despiser of mid-Victorianism should be the prey of the most childish of mid-Victorian bugbears, hatred of the Catholic Church!

Strachey's psychological insight deserves consideration next. As a psychologist he never got to the bottom of a complex mind and when it was complicated by spiritual elements it allured but always baffled him. His *Elizabeth and Essex* has the air of having been written to catch the tide of popular favor. Despite its glitter it is thin, the character of Essex is imperfectly realized, and that of Elizabeth is so simplified as to be unconvincing. The distinction of the book does not lie in its psychology but in its Macaulayan portraits and passages of vivid description. For his *Queen Victoria* he selected a major figure solid, four-square, and entirely innocent of complexities, and in his portrayal of her foil, the Prince Consort, he revealed the shrewdest psychology he knew. This of all Strachey's biographical studies has the best chance to be remembered. The task of picturing a British Sovereign imposed certain wholesome restraints on him from which his art profited, and he approached his task with more seriousness, perhaps with more intellectual honesty, and certainly with irony more astutely controlled than in the case of *Elizabeth and Essex* and *Eminent Victorians*.

It was *Eminent Victorians,* Strachey's most brilliant work, that offered the severest test of his psychological insight. None of the four persons presented there was simple or free from spiritual complexities, Gordon and Manning least of all. To Gordon from young manhood religion grew so important that " it became a fixed and dominating factor in his life." Florence Nightingale was beset with doubts as to her proper state in life and cried in agony: "My God! What is to become of me?" Of Arnold and Manning I have already spoken. With how real a penetration does Strachey ascertain their secrets? So far as the figures treated are dynamic, ego-centric personalities prone to consider themselves instruments of the Divine Will, Strachey presented them with unusual power, but when we seek to know what part spiritual cravings played in those complex, eager, restless souls, we get no satisfying answer. In Gordon's attitude toward the Soudan was he a conqueror or a religious crusader? Did he regard himself as an active or as a passive agent of the Divine Will? Did Florence Nightingale's doubts about her vocation and her revolt against her shallow social environment indicate an authentic yearning for satisfaction of soul or simply an efficient woman's sense of frustration? If she had a genuinely spiritual nature, to what degree was it satisfied by her activities in the Crimea and by her post-war efforts to effect permanent reforms? What qualities did Arnold possess which made it possible for him to revolutionize education in the great English public schools? Were they largely a moral endowment? How did they affect his personality? These questions are left unanswered.

The case of Manning deserves special consideration. For sheer brilliancy it is the most effective study Strachey ever wrote; for convincingness it can impress only the uncritical or the innocently unaware. For the fact is that Strachey failed to understand Manning, he failed to understand the Church for which Manning forsook his ease in Anglicanism and to whose service he devoted the last forty-one of his energetic years and, as if to prove these things no accident, he failed to understand Newman whom he set up as the "angelic" foil to the "diabolical" Manning. His sharp Voltairean glance could not discern the crusader in a great spiritual cause, spending and being spent with a divine prodigality, the passionate lover of a social justice that should bring the kingdom of God closer to earth, the priest with body bowed in humbleness, with heart lifted high in adoration. What he presents

is a play-actor's Manning, a tall gaunt creature in ecclesiastical
robes who "struts and frets his hour upon the stage" and utters
words he has learned by rote, a selfish, cruel churchman, warped
of conscience, petty of soul, the prey of "exorbitant ambitions," a
Victorian Machiavelli in soutane and biretta, a merely theatrical
figure reminiscent of the melodramatic stage and the anti-Catholic
tradition.

Another—and vital—weakness of Strachey remains for mention.
Carlyle, writing of the author of the greatest biography ever
written, insisted that Boswell possessed the first and most necessary
gift for such a task: he hero-worshiped Johnson. That was the
Carlylean way of saying that sympathy is essential to understanding, that without it a true psychological portrait is impossible,
that with it even a second-rate writer may sometimes work a
literary miracle. Carlyle was right. Unwittingly he pointed out,
two generations before Strachey, an elemental quality in which
the "father" of the "new biography" was wanting. For Strachey
found in men the weaknesses he sought. Whatever good they
possessed, especially of the nobler kind, he failed to see or he
looked upon with cold suspicion. He never wrote a page which
showed that his heart was stirred by heroism, self-sacrifice, or the
spiritual yearning of sensitive souls. The quality which made
Macaulay stand hushed and reverent beside Monmouth's grave,
which silenced Carlyle in the death chamber of the ignoble Louis
XV, which stirred Hilaire Belloc as he pictured Danton standing
at the foot of the guillotine, straight and unafraid in the glow of a
summer sunset, was unknown to Lytton Strachey. The magnanimity which no genuinely great writer has ever lacked passed
him by.

Strachey's was a conception of biography which, as Macaulay
confessed of his own ideal of history, it is virtually impossible to
attain. The penetration and detachment of Sainte-Beuve com-
manding a narrative gift equal to Macaulay's (expressed in a
lighter, swifter style) would approach it. When, if ever, will that
come?

Meanwhile Strachey's influence has been twofold: it has been in
the direction of a fearless presentation of facts and a candid
appraisal of eminent persons, women no less than men. Biography
returns from the business of gazing in hushed wonder at distant

luminaries to the business of dealing with human beings whose talents and achievements did not remove them from the necessity (as Carlyle puts it) of maintaining their bodies and saving their souls. That is good. On the other hand it has encouraged a flock of imitators (mostly pedestrian) in the belief that invention is more important than research, that it is necessary to insinuate scandals if none can be found, and that the function of a biographer is to "debunk."

"No man is a hero to his valet." To which Carlyle dryly rejoined that that is the fault of the valet.

John Galsworthy—An Appraisal

THE UNTIMELY AND UNEXPECTED DEATH OF THE ENGLISH NOVELIST John Galsworthy, January 31, 1933, evoked universal regret for a distinguished man of letters, who was also a winner of the Nobel prize and a fine gentleman. It did something else. It moved a large section of the reading public here and abroad to refresh their memories regarding his career, and the discriminating minority to turn afresh to his books and, with their excellences and short-comings in mind, attempt to decide upon their author's place among the masters of British fiction.

Everybody knows that Galsworthy was born in 1867, that he was educated at Harrow and at Oxford, that he studied law and was admitted to the Bar in 1890, that he made a journey around the world, and that he gave up law for literature.

For the first years of his career as novelist (1898-1901) Galsworthy wrote under a pseudonym. In 1904 he published *The Island Pharisees* with his own name and followed it two years later with what is probably his masterpiece, his first Forsyte novel, *The Man of Property*. During the next fourteen years he wrote seven novels and in 1920, after a lapse of fourteen years, he returned to the Forsytes and produced a sequel, *In Chancery*. This move opened the way for further chronicles of the family, and the very next year Galsworthy produced *To Let,* a third volume in the Forsyte series. In 1922 these three novels, with two connecting Interludes, appeared in one volume with the title *The Forsyte Saga*.

Having gone so far and made a new generation of Forsytes his concern—with generous applause from critics and public—Galsworthy was tempted to continue, and for the next six years (1922-1928) his interest in fiction was centered on the further doings of that long-tailed family. *The White Monkey, The Silver Spoon,* and *Swan Song* were published biennially in succession, and, with two connecting Interludes, appeared in 1929 as *A Modern Comedy*. It is with these two trilogies that Mr. Galsworthy's name has been most intimately associated and on them that his reputation as a novelist seems likely to rest.

With the evidence before us of such industry and skill as they unquestionably present, precisely what are we to think of Galsworthy?

Of the success he achieved there can be no question. His books have sold widely, they won him recognition at home and abroad, they so impressed us in America that during the last fifteen years of his life we considered him the foremost living English novelist and probably the superior of any contemporary American. The ablest and best-balanced of American critics goes so far as to declare that only *The Forsyte Saga* among recent novels in our tongue will last a century.

Galsworthy's celebrity was not secured by long fiction alone. It was paralleled by short stories, essays, sketches, often published in popular magazines, and by dramas which won him a place with Barrie and Shaw. All these productions bore the impress of a single shaping hand and of a unique personality. They appeared at frequent intervals, kept Galsworthy's name constantly in the public eye and were, to a striking and (for Galsworthy) fortunate degree, mutually reinforcing.

Above all things else Galsworthy was a conscientious workman. He could no more indulge in the Arnold Bennett type of pot-boiler than he could make a balloon ascension in order to advertise his books. His work was never hastily done, in fact it was planned with the same forethought and executed with the same care as would have characterized the briefs of John Galsworthy, solicitor, charged with important litigation. It was not merely an accident that the court episodes in *One More River* and *The Silver Spoon* were done with gusto as well as brilliancy, and that his chief and most completely realized male character, Soames

Forsyte, "the man of property," is a lawyer, meticulously attentive to every detail of his life; that he has, in a word, the Galsworthian conscience. Soames' daughter Fleur has a similar sense of orderliness and efficiency despite the post-war environment in which she moves, and it serves her equally in selecting the right sort of people to give atmosphere to her drawing room and in operating a soup kitchen during the great strike. So too Michael, Soames' son-in-law, who must give business details his honest consideration and on entering Parliament must, in lieu of convictions, at least find and espouse definite principles.

Galsworthy's orderliness, his sense of conscience in all his work, are evident in his style no less than in the fashioning of his novels. It is an unusual style, smooth, graceful, supple, and in the competent hands of its master, it became a skilful instrument. It lacks the point and precision of Shaw's and the virility of Bennett's. It is the mirror of a different type of mind, a more impressionable, a more sensitive, a less masculine type than theirs.

A mind like Galsworthy's, with its feminine side, was not necessarily lacking in vital interests or in the tenacity to cleave to them. His particular concern was with social conditions as affected by the injustice, selfishness, and lack of vision of the wealthy and aristocratic classes, and even his love episodes were colored by that concern and projected against that background. With a quicker sensitiveness than his contemporaries and a deeper pity, he saw poverty and its attendant evils not primarily as super-scientific questions like Wells, not as merely personal conditions like Bennett, not as things to be triumphed over by an imagination, a fairy godmother, or a happy turn of fortune like Barrie, but first of all as objects of human sympathy and after that as intolerable effects of a social and economic situation for which well-to-do Britons must be answerable.

In *The Forsyte Saga*, Galsworthy turned his attention to the well-to-do middle class in England whose roots were already struck deep at the beginning of the nineteenth century. The industrial revolution had brought them property and wealth, and from one generation to another they clung to both tenaciously, watching them increase by natural growth, by fortunate investments, and by far-sighted inter-marriages with wealthy families of their own caste. They were narrow, self-satisfied, grasping, and unconscious of social obligations in any broad sense. Soames, a man of property, who adds to an inheritance already great, whose possessive passion extends from lands to houses, to pictures, and even to his wife, exemplifies the instinct of his class, and his defeat at the hands of his wife Irene prefigures the downfall of the social order of which he is a part.

To the generation of Soames' daughter Fleur, the generation that lived through the First World War and felt old ties loosed and social conventions flouted, Galsworthy turned to study further the evolution of the middle class. An unforeseen situation greeted him. The process had not ceased to be arresting in its economic aspects but had become both arresting and frightening on its moral side. He beheld in Fleur the undying possessive passion of Soames and his forbears but diverted from the acquisition of property toward the gratification of merely social ambition, personal vanity, and even lust. The Decalogue had gone overboard and with it restraint, reverence, and pity itself.

What was Galsworthy's attitude toward the two aspects of the phenomenon in which he felt so compelling an interest—the evolution of the upper middle class? In *The Forsyte Saga* he implied with skilful irony and keen satire that the rifts in the structure of society were growing steadily wider and more menacing; in *A Modern Comedy* with irony no less skilful and satire no less keen he implied that things were drifting toward moral chaos. For the former situation he seemed to have a nostrum. He speaks of art and says: "Art is the one form of human energy which really works for vision and destroys the barrier between man and man." About seventy years ago Matthew Arnold expressed similarly high hopes in the case of culture. It was going to assimilate what was "best in religion," provide yearning souls with an approach to God, turn the minds of the masses from a belief in "machinery," in coal mines and population, in railroads and exports, and transform them from Philistines to seekers of "all things that are lovely and of good report," eager to make reason and the will of God prevail. There is a startling similarity between the nostrum suggested by Arnold and that advocated by Galsworthy, and it is as impossible to be sanguine of the one as it is of the other.

In *A Modern Comedy,* where the moral situation edges its way into the limelight, it is through the lips of his most attractive character, Michael Mont, Fleur's husband, that Galsworthy speaks. Michael notes the self-consciousness of his generation, its poses, its affectation of cleverness, its lack of joy, its restlessness, "the effort to escape from something that couldn't be got away from." Michael asks himself what his generation has put in the place of the things they discarded and finds no answer except, "We must be after something." When a son is born to Fleur and Michael, they wonder in what creed they will bring him up. "Without faith," Michael asks himself, "was one fit to be a parent? Well, people were looking for faith again," but, warped as they were, would, he feared, fail to recover it. Fleur puts the key into the lock but leaves it unturned when she remarks: "The Catholics really do get something out of their religion." In the end Fleur and Michael arrive nowhere.

And where does Galsworthy arrive? As a matter of fact he has no way out. To him life is a muddle and it is in an observation of one of his characters, Young Jolyon, that his philosophy is revealed: "To be kind, and keep your end up—there's nothing else in it." At the conclusion of *Swan Song* when Michael, aware that Fleur has played him false, seeks a brief refuge from his bitterness of soul out under the summer stars, he finds no thought to comfort him or to lighten his bewilderment in the face of the enigma of life. In the three Charwell novels (published with the inclusive title, *End of the Chapter*) Galsworthy went no deeper. He remained an excellent workman, a meticulous recorder of the contemporary English scene with its tattered moral patterns, and a spectator of the widening breach between the new generation and the old, but one became aware of a lessening preoccupation with solutions as if, though neither acquiescent nor apathetic, he tacitly resolved, like Michael Mont, to plague himself no more with distressing (and seemingly unanswerable) questions.

Let us now turn to a consideration of Galsworthy as the artist in fiction. Without question we grant him the merits of a keen observer, a scrupulously careful craftsman, an accomplished and resourceful stylist, an ironist of the Addisonian tradition grown more obviously conscious, and finally the merit of a deep and sincere human sympathy. These assets carried him far. It remains to ask: Have they carried him so far that *The Forsyte Saga* is the finest work of fiction produced by any British novelist of his generation? Does his masterpiece seem to assure to Galsworthy a distinguished claim on the attention of our great-grandchildren?

On March 27, 1931, Galsworthy lost his only serious rival among his English contemporaries. Arnold Bennett did more than his share of ephemeral work and was too often deaf to the protests of his artistic conscience. Occasionally, however, he gave ear to it and turned his undoubted talents to good purpose. Once inspiration came to his aid, he drew upon every resource of experience and art at his command, and "with an impressiveness unmatched since Thackeray" (to borrow a judgment from Dean Cross) achieved his only undoubted masterpiece, *Old Wives' Tale*. Here is a novel entirely unconcerned with those social problems which Galsworthy always found absorbing and which occupy so large a place in the world's thought today. It boldly turns its back on our generation, and its historical high point is not the nineteen-twenties but 1870. Its concerns are limited, personal, almost petty. It is (you remember) merely the chronicle of the childhood, youth, marriage, subsequent fortunes, and death of two sisters, and it is about the same length as the three novels that make up *The Forsyte Saga*. The personages of *Old Wives' Tale* are no whit less selfish, narrow, and self-centered than the figures in Galsworthy's *Saga*. And yet there is a difference emphatic enough in treatment, but even more emphatic in the result accomplished. Neither by conscience nor inclination was Bennett bedeviled into attempting two roles; he was completely the novelist dedicated to an all-absorbing task, and not even by a stroke of the pen or a flicker of the eye did he aim to be a conscious critic of society. Not even in his mind did he have a divided aim, but the abundance of his vitality flowed into his story and he achieved that mysterious blood transfusion, so to speak, by which a novelist who pretends to greatness must fill the veins of his creatures and transform them into independent entities who think, will, and act for themselves.

Galsworthy's men and women lack this vitality. Annette, Soames' second wife, is only a name; Bosinney and Irene are scarcely more vital than the fog into which Bosinney walks to his death. Others—most of the older Forsytes in fact—are brought as near to a three dimensional existence as they ever get by the device of a pet interest or a pet phrase in the Dickens manner. It was on Soames and Fleur that Galsworthy lavished his skill as a creator of character and the result is significant. Only in *The Man of Property* does Soames emerge from the shaping hands of the novelist and appear upon the retina of the mind's eye, a breathing human creature, capable of thought and action. Throughout the five subsequent novels he becomes constantly less corporeal and it is only at occasional moments, as in *Swan Song*, when he rescues his pictures from the burning gallery, that he steps out of the shadows into reality or when (ironic fact!) dying, alone with Fleur, who peers into his dull eyes, he declines her offer to bring in the others; he wants *her*. As for Fleur, the most successfully drawn of all Galsworthy's characters, she achieves a life of her own thanks to the device of presenting her through Soames' and Michael's eyes; and her eager, selfish heart, with its passion to possess, awakens her pulses to a living response. She overshadows Michael whose veins are warm only in her presence, and neither of them experiences any essential development, but each, in the manner of Dickens, remains static.

I have implied that Galsworthy's failure to endow his characters with complete reality is due to his preoccupation with the contemporary English scene, with his interests as a student and critic of society. That is a part but only a part of the explanation. The rest is to be found in two other directions. It is a singular and highly significant fact that Galsworthy's women more nearly approach reality than his men. A certain feminine strain in him, noticed before, an unvirility, from which Wells, Bennett, and Barrie (for all his fancifulness) are free, revealed in his style and in his eye for decorative non-essentials of deportment, appearance, or *milieu,* got in the way, and prevented the elements that went to the making of his men from cohering and taking form. (You are aware of this also in his best short stories, "The Apple Tree," "The First and the Last," and even in "A Stoic".) Finally, as a result of his preoccupation with social phenomena and of the inherently feminine strain in him, he achieved neither as man nor as artist the needed fusion of opposing elements. There grew up a certain self-consciousness, an inability to surrender himself completely, passionately, to his task as a novelist. The creative fires glowed but never—except briefly and at rare moments—burst into flame.

Of course the Forsytes are commonplace people, but common-

place people may be as real as one's own brothers and as fascinating to read about as queens or adventurers. Except for Becky
Sharp the people in *Vanity Fair,* the greatest of English novels, are
commonplace; they are Forsytes of an earlier generation. The characters are commonplace in *David Copperfield,* in *The Mill on the
Floss,* in Hardy's *Tess,* in *Old Wives' Tale.* It is not the quality of
the people but life that is important and everlastingly fascinating,
and even commonplace men and women can command our interest once the creative genius of the novelist endows them with life.

Saintsbury says finely of Thackeray: "He could not introduce a
personage, no matter how subordinate, without making him a
living creature. He may be introduced to say a couple of lines,
and never appear again, but Thackeray has no sooner touched him
than there is a human thing—an entity. He could not introduce
a footman, saying some half-dozen words, 'My Lady is going to
Brighting' or something of that sort, without presenting the fellow for his trouble with life and immortality."

Fundamentally Galsworthy's weakness, despite (to say it once
more) his undeniable virtues, is vital. It is to be found in a phrase
used by Henry James when he said that the supreme virtue of a
novel was to "produce the illusion of life." That is the secret, "the
illusion of life," and it sanctions any method (Bennett's, Galsworthy's, Hardy's, or any other) which can perform the miracle of
producing it. How the novelist shall achieve this, whether by the
use of description, dialogue, or incident, in addition to the
reality of character, no one can say. That is a secret, as James
pointed out, between the novelist and his good angel. In what
proportions his elements are mixed is no man's concern provided
only the novelist "catch the very note and trick, the strange irregular rhythm of life." To demand this is to demand much. It is
to demand what only the masters can give and what, when given,
proves their genius. The greatest of British critics, paying tribute
to the greatest of British romancers, wrote: "All that portion of the
history of his country that he has touched upon, the manners, the
personages, the events, the scenery, lives over again in his volumes.
Nothing is wanting—the illusion is complete. There is a hurtling
in the air, a trampling of feet upon the ground, as these perfect
representations of human character or fanciful belief come thronging back upon our imaginations. . . . His works, taken together,

are almost like a new edition of human nature." And he adds, half between applause and envy: "This is indeed to be an author!"

Herein lies the reason for Galsworthy's failure to be a great novelist. The "illusion of life" in his fiction—to use again the phrase of Hazlitt and of Henry James—is faint and when it occurs is neither compelling nor long sustained. At times we catch it, as in that fine scene at Mrs. Magussie's rout in which the social duel between Fleur and Marjorie Ferrar reaches its climax and society takes its revenge on Fleur. Again we catch it in *Swan Song* when Fleur, denied an assignation by Jon, drinks the bitterness of humiliation to the dregs. But instances such as these are rare in Galsworthy. Not in his as in genuinely great novels does the reader feel the tide of life flowing all about him, eddying at his feet, ebbing and returning, in never-ending motion, like the sea. It is such a sense of life that Galsworthy attributes to Michael Mont; it is such an illusion of life that his novels seem so often *on the verge of providing* but so seldom do. It is as if we got sight of people—but through opaque glass; as if we heard the sound of their voices and laughter—but through closed doors.

The critics, deeply impressed by the many-sided talents of John Galsworthy, gentleman, have been highly generous to John Galsworthy, novelist. But in treating his works, they have closed their eyes to the real function of fiction, and by emphasizing the wrong things have declared in effect that that function is to provide posterity with pictures of contemporary society rather than to create the illusion of life. Thus, supported by this interesting but disastrous doctrine, typical of our socially conscious age, they have created the myth that Galsworthy, painstaking, conscientious, observant, with the temper of a critic and a propagandist rather than an artist, is a great novelist.

But time will settle all that. We cannot, by a kind of *mortmain*, impose our idols on our grandchildren. And besides, our grandchildren may be too busy setting up idols of their own.

The Short Stories of Thomas Hardy

WHATEVER MAY BE THOUGHT OF HARDY'S POETRY OR WHATEVER preference one may personally have felt for it over his fiction, there can be little doubt that his fame will end only when the finest of his novels are forgotten—*The Return of the Native, Tess of the D'Urbervilles, The Woodlanders, The Mayor of Casterbridge,* and *Far from the Madding Crowd.* The stir of life is in their pulses as it is in *Copperfield, Vanity Fair,* and *The Mill on the Floss,* and Hardy's creative vigor and abundant vitality during the period from 1872 to 1891 prove him a direct—and the last—inheritor of the great traditions of the Victorian novel.

The widespread recognition given Hardy in the heyday of his power and the revelation of that power through a quarter of a century were equally striking. He came into his own with little delay, moved on from one masterpiece to another, reached his zenith in *Tess* in 1891, blundered badly in 1896 with *Jude the Obscure,* and, following the storm which that ill-starred performance evoked, observed in fiction an unbroken silence during the thirty-odd years that remained to him of life.

To that statement one exception must be made. Between *Jude* and the year 1900 Hardy wrote three short tales, and in 1913 he published them with nine others written between 1881 and 1895, with the title *A Changed Man and Other Stories.* This volume was notable for three reasons: first, because it was by Thomas Hardy; secondly, because it appeared after seventeen years of

117

silence; thirdly, because it reminded a world to which Hardy as novelist was rapidly lapsing into a memory that he had already published three other volumes of brief tales and that, were it not for the fame of his longer masterpieces, he would have achieved celebrity as one of the greatest of modern short story writers.

Of the twelve tales included in *A Changed Man* four were typical and powerful, "The Waiting Supper," "A Mere Interlude," "A Committee-Man of 'The Terror,' " and the introductory tale from which the volume received its title. In spite of this notable group *A Changed Man* was inferior to the three volumes of short stories which had preceded it: *Wessex Tales* (1888), *A Group of Noble Dames* (1891), and finest of all and unquestionably a classic of its type, *Life's Little Ironies* (1894). A few of the tales in these volumes are brief; some are of ordinary length; others are almost long enough to be considered short novels. But no matter what their length all of them bear the indubitable marks of Hardy's genius, his constructive skill, his vitality, his power of characterization, his vigor, his vividness. Besides, they are colored by his philosophy, a philosophy strange, ironic, and depressing. But in justice to Hardy it must be conceded that life is usually strange, often ironic, and sometimes depressing even to those of us who do not share his philosophy.

His themes were not epic. He did not attempt anything so sweeping as Kipling did in *The Man Who Would Be King* nor did he turn for a setting to some remote country around which clung the glamour of romance, as Kipling did in India, Bret Harte in California, and Jack London in the Klondike. Even the great cities where men foregather—O. Henry knew that lure—failed to attract him. On the contrary he accepted as a fitting stage for his short stories, no less than for his novels, what he called a "nook of civilization" and named "Wessex." The heaths, the farm-lands, the hills, the dales, the streams of Wessex, he knew as he knew the reflection of his own face in a mirror, and he knew the common folk of Wessex with their oddities of speech and manner, their peculiar points of view and, most important of all, their altogether human yearnings, weaknesses, and passions as he knew his own soul.

Coleridge once said of Schiller that, to be tragic, he had to destroy armies and burn cities, while Shakespeare could achieve equally moving results simply by dropping a handkerchief. This is not merely one of the innumerable ways in which Shakespeare shows his genius but one of the proofs he offers that he is a modern of the moderns. From an inn he infers a city, from a town or a camp, the world. There are no bounds to his horizons.

More than a little of a similar genius belonged to Hardy. In his chosen corner of England he beheld the great world in miniature, recognizing no essential difference between the tragedies and tragi-comedies enacted there and (the words are his) "those which, enacted on more central arenas, fix the attention of the world." For the most part he was content to weave his stories about the lives of rural people; and though his heroines in *A Group of Noble Dames* possess rank and fortune they dwell far from the madding crowd and are as essentially unsophisticated as their own dairymaids.

Hardy's choice of country-folk was not an accident. In an essay published in *The Forum* for March, 1888, he declared that the conduct of the upper classes was screened by conventions and thus their real characters were not easily seen; whereas, in the lower walks, conduct was a direct expression of the inner life, and thus a character could be directly revealed through action. Accordingly, conventionalized expressions of hidden emotions failed to interest him, and his art was saved from the tenuosity which results when a dozen pages are devoted to some subtle reaction that finds ultimate expression in a gesture. This does not mean that Hardy considered his rural folk, the small farmer and his family, "simple." Christine Everard in "The Waiting Supper," daughter of a squire, warns against that error even in the case of the peasants. "You little think what they see and meditate! Their reasonings and emotions are as complicated as ours."

A generation and a half ago New England was "discovered" by short story writers, among them Mary Wilkins and Alice Brown. But the New England story as such petered out. The reading public grew weary of church-fairs, mince pies, and quilting-parties, not primarily because these things seemed trivial but because the emotions and the actions of the people for whom they provided the setting were devoid of universal appeal. Maurice Francis Egan once remarked that the writer who pictures dull or commonplace people must never do it in a dull or commonplace way. Hardy learned that lesson early. At the very outset of his career he grasped a fact which it is a sign of genius never to forget—that trivial doings are not interesting merely because they are recounted with meticulous fidelity but only when they give us revealing glimpses into a human soul. And when they do that they are no longer trivial.

Hardy was endowed with the seeing eye. When he turned his glance on the citizens of Wessex it was to penetrate their stolid demeanor, and to lift the veil that concealed an elemental world of passions and desires. He looked upon a village vicar and saw him struggling against his love for the promised wife of another man; upon a humble schoolmaster and perceived in him an ambition so eager that he would be guilty of murder sooner than allow it to be thwarted; upon the mother of children and beheld such a passion awaken in her for a poet she had never seen as neither marriage nor motherhood had ever evoked before; upon a peddler hawking his wares and knew that he was cherishing at fifty an affection for a middle-aged widow he had loved in boyhood; upon a matter-of-fact merchant and watched him cheat death to save the wife who had been making his home an inferno.

They are not cheerful themes, these of Hardy, and tragedy seldom fails to cast its shadow over them. And yet, strangely enough, Hardy was capable of comedy too. But his comedy was typical of his genius; there was something massive and almost serious about it. In fact it belongs rather to the ironic than to the merry; its laughter is of the head rather than of the heart; its forbear was the sardonic mirth of the grave-digger in *Hamlet*.

Hardy's short stories were written for the most part after he was forty-five, when the lightness of youth had long since passed and he had become a convert to a philosophy of life which beheld only its devastating irony. And that irony as he saw it was not the result of chance but of a malevolent Fate that played tragic pranks on helpless mortals. In Hardy's eyes indeed irony was the most striking thing about life. To him Tantalus was not an arch-malefactor punished by inexorable justice, but a symbol of humanity innocent of evil intention yet the victim of an endless diabolic jest. Thus man seeks a supposed blessedness only to find it the ashes of roses; he challenges chance twice and wins, doubles the stakes and loses, loses everything and irrevocably. He falls in love, marries, and learns too late that it is not the woman he has won who has actually engaged his heart but the wife of another man. He risks his good name to repair an ancient wrong only to see his act of reparation rendered starkly futile. Perhaps he has waited long years for a woman, bravely repressing his feelings until the day when he is free to express them. That day comes but the letter in which he declares his love goes astray, while the woman waits, first in hope and then in bitter disappointment. He waits in his turn for a reply to his declaration and, receiving none, interprets silence as a refusal and with no further sign drops forever out of her life. And so by the most casual of accidents—and most bitter of ironies—two people that love each other are denied happiness.

It is thus that Hardy's men and women go on, the unsuspecting sports of a diabolical Fate. Most of them, hesitating like blind men at a crossing, miss the high road to comedy by a hairbreadth and plunge along that of tragedy. And therein lies a poignant element of Hardy's irony: it is usually by the merest chance that tragedy is wrought: a vagrant breeze whisks a letter away; a word only half-meant is taken in earnest; a bit of evil gossip overheard by chance poisons a soul all confidence before.

With these things in mind let us consider a few of Hardy's short stories. In "The Duchess of Hamptonshire" the youthful vicar is the beloved but unsuccessful suitor for the hand of the pretty Emmaline. Her unwilling marriage to the harsh Duke of Hamptonshire is more than the vicar can bear and he determines to emigrate to America. Emmaline, bitterly unhappy in her marriage, begs to accompany him but he declines because "it is wrong." The next day he sets sail on the *Western Glory* and on arriving in Boston buries himself in unremitting clerical labors for nine years. One day by chance he reads in a discarded English newspaper of the death of the Duke of Hamptonshire. His old passion for Emmaline, now (he supposes) free at last, reawakens, and he sets sail for England to claim her, only to find on arriving that the widow is an utter stranger. Amazed at the discovery he makes inquiries about Emmaline in the village. Gossip, now become a kind of tradition, says that she had loved the vicar too well to remain with the Duke and had fled with him to America on board the *Western Glory* nine years before. Dumbfounded at

such news the vicar pursues his inquiries further. A young unknown woman, he discovers, actually took passage on the ship at
the last moment and mingled among the passengers in the steer-
age. The second day out she was stricken with a swift and fatal
illness; and when death claimed her, poor child, a stranger among
strangers, it was he, the vicar, who was called upon to solemnize,
all unwitting, the last rites of her he loved.

Could Fate play a more cruel trick than this? The vicar was
upright, not evil and he made his renunciation like a true man.
The young bride, whose heart and motives recall Pompilia's
in *The Ring and the Book,* sought escape from a marriage which
had become unbearable. Of what wrong were they guilty? Of
none, answers Hardy who, while sharing George Eliot's belief
in an inescapable retributive justice, holds with equal conviction
that Fate imposes on the well-intentioned and the guiltless even
greater sufferings which are neither retributive nor just but are
equally inescapable.

In "A Tragedy of Two Ambitions," the brothers Joshua and
Cornelius drudge for years in the class room in order to send their
sister to a continental boarding-school and open the way for her
to a good marriage and a "lady's life." They are not without their
own ambitions: they seek ordination and advancement in the
church. The sole obstacle to their desires is their drunken father
whose follies have kept the family impoverished and whose dissipa-
tions have made away with the pittance his dead wife had saved
for her sons' education. For years Joshua and Cornelius have seen
nothing of their sire, and their steady toil has brought them near
their goal. One day, utterly without warning, the father appears,
intoxicated and belligerent, with some strange woman clinging
to his arm whom he calls his wife. Fearing disgrace and sick at
heart they manage to get rid of him but at the cost of all their
meagre savings. Once again they resume the drudgery they had
thought past, the scrimping and self-denial, until at long last the
efforts of years seem on the point of yielding their reward: Joshua
and Cornelius are safely ordained and their sister is about to be
betrothed to a young gentleman of excellent family. Then the
blow falls.

Their father turns up again, one autumn evening, intoxicated and vainglorious over the news that his daughter is "mak-

ing a fine match," and to crown the ill-starred encounter he is
at that very moment trudging along the country road which
leads to his prospective son-in-law's home, the "big house," bound
on declaring himself and "borrowing a small sum." The sons
remonstrate, foreseeing the downfall of all their hopes. At first
the father is obdurate, then abusive, and finally in a rage he flings
in their teeth a gross insult against their mother's memory. Then
with a grunt of satisfaction at the success of this shot he lurches
on toward the "big house." Cutting across his path runs a narrow
stream. He mounts the bridge which spans it, sways, makes a mis-
step, loses his footing, and plunges headlong into the brook. The
brothers, watching, for a fatal moment stand stock still, their wills
as if paralyzed. Another instant and the spell is broken, their
lethargy passes, and they run forward to the bank of the stream.
But already the body has disappeared, wedged solidly within the
culvert below. . . . The brothers are saved from disgrace. Soon
afterward their sister, never guessing the truth, is married.

Months pass. Spring comes. The brothers meet again and,
moved by a common impulse, turn their footsteps toward the
scene of the tragedy. There they halt and each reads in the other's
eyes the confession which is already mounting to his lips. They
are tortured by remorse; the image of their father haunts their
sleep. They have achieved their ambitions only to find them bitter
as death. This would seem tragedy enough but the inexorable
Hardy does not stop here. Some day soon, he hints, the remorse of
the brothers will take a new and awful turn. They will divulge
the secret to their sister, thus poisoning the happiness they sought
to insure, and they will crown their errors by taking their own
lives.

This story is so typical of Hardy's method that, gruesome
though it is, it deserves further consideration. In the first place he
has turned our sympathies away from the worthless father at the
very outset and directed them to the sons, who, however narrow,
are energetic, persistent, and devoted to an honorable ambition.
The father was always a drain on the family and neglectful of
his children and his wife. It is to her self-sacrifice that the boys
owe their start; her memory is sacred to them, but not to the
brutal old man in his drunken passion. Hardy has made the sons'
momentary hesitation, their paralysis of will, appear almost par-

donable. With what result? The magnitude of their remorse and intended expiation is made to seem overwhelmingly ironic and Fate grotesquely unfair in wreaking vengeance on her victims because, when tantalized to madness, they could endure no more.

In the next place we notice that the shadow of the tragedy lengthens not only to envelop the guilty brothers but eventually the innocent sister as well. Fate, as Hardy sees it, takes a monstrous satisfaction in making the guiltless suffer here just as it does Mrs. Twycott in "A Son's Veto," Barnet in "Fellow-Townsmen," and Gertrude Lodge in "The Withered Arm."

Finally, we notice the part that Nature plays in the story. When the Spring comes and all the world is astir with new life, the drowned man's body rises to the surface and the beauty of stream and sky mocks the ghastly thing. Then, as if to add a final effect, there comes a typical Hardian touch, worthy of Hawthorne in such a masterpiece as "Roger Malvin's Burial": the dead man's rough walking-stick has taken root among the sedge and become a tiny sapling with gay silvery leaves. Thus Fate laughs as, with infinite mockery, she marks the place of death with a symbol of life.

Read "Fellow-Townsmen" and see the reverse of the situation presented in "A Tragedy of Two Ambitions." The amiable Barnet has married the wrong woman who revenges herself by making his home life wretched. Her horse runs away and she is flung into the sea and almost drowned. A physician who tries to resuscitate her gives up the task as hopeless. But Barnet, to whom her death will be a relief, tries in his turn and with infinite patience succeeds at last. Surely the breach between them will now be healed and all will be well. No; Barnet's reward is not appreciation but an even more bitter disdain than before. Hardy's point is clear: whether one resist temptation like Barnet or yield to it like Cornelius, Fate denies the longed-for happiness; life's "little ironies" will be played out to the end.

Hardy almost never employs the happy-ending formula; to do so, as he sees it, would be to risk violating the facts of life. In "The Distracted Preacher" as it first appeared (in the *New Quarterly Magazine* April, 1879) and was published in *Wessex Tales* (1888), the Rev. Mr. Stockdale marries Lizzie who has given up her association with a band of smugglers. "He took her away from her old haunts to the home that he had made for himself in his native county, where she studied her duties as a minister's wife with praiseworthy assiduity." That ending however did not sit easily on Hardy's conscience. Thirty-three years later he appended a note in which he declared he had followed a "convention almost *de rigueur* in an English magazine at the time of writing," and added that the ending more in accordance with the facts *and his own preferences* [1] would have been entirely different.

Hardy, like Meredith and Conrad, is extraordinarily sensitive to Nature. The knowledge he ascribes to Angel Clare of "the seasons in their moods, morning and evening, night and noon, in their temperaments; winds in their several dispositions; trees, waters, and clouds, shades and silences, *ignes fatui;* constellations, and the voices of inanimate things," is his own. In "A Tryst at an Ancient Earthwork" he surrounds an old Roman bastion with an air of wonder and awe as it lies beneath the blanket of night, while the atmosphere heaves "like the sigh of a weary strong man" and the thunder and lightning create the illusion of the ancient dead returning to renew their battles. In "The Three Strangers" it is not mere chance but the wild March rain that brings the three ill-assorted men under Fennel's roof and reinforces the air of mystery that surrounds their advent. Sometimes Nature directly reflects the mood of a character and even appears to assume a personality of its own. Christine and Nicholas, chilled by jealousy, "sat apart . . . each looking afar off at vague objects and not in each other's eyes. Thus the sad autumn afternoon waned, while the waterfall hissed sarcastically of the inevitableness of the unpleasant."

Hardy's characters were all too often the sport of chance but never his employment of Nature or any other aspect of his story telling. At seventeen he had chosen architecture as a profession and later he won prizes for his designs. Thus early he learned the value of form, and his short stories no less than his novels are devised with unfailing skill. Every word spoken, everything done, every emotion hinted at or disclosed, plays a distinctive part in advancing the action. He thought out each detail with the minute care of Poe himself, and with as definite a conception of his aim. There is no wastage but a supreme and artistic economy as infal-

1 The italics are mine.

lible in the Englishman as in the American. Behind the seemingly inevitable art of each man's tales are the perfectly contrived plot and the concealed but ever-present hand of the contriver. An analysis of "Fellow Townsmen," "On the Western Circuit," or "The Marchioness of Stonehenge" will reveal at once how interdependent are the parts, how nicely articulated, how completely of a piece they are, and heighten your respect for Hardy the master of form, the architect turned story-teller. And if you are moved to reread one of his novels try that supreme piece of characterization and construction, *The Return of the Native.*

Hardy's men are drawn with less success than his women, or perhaps it would be more accurate to say that his heroes are seldom as attractive or interesting as his heroines. In *A Group of Noble Dames* he naturally keeps the spot-light trained on women, but even in his novels it is his women rather than his men who absorb us and refuse to be forgotten. At heart all Hardy's people are pagans, and while he can draw men as fine-grained as Stephen Reynard in "The First Countess of Wessex" and Barnet in "Fellow Townsmen," he gives us for the most part in his short stories men with more than a drop of satyr in their blood, like Lord Uplandtowers in "Barbara of the House of Grebe," prigs like Sir William in "The Lady Penelope" and Captain Northbrook in "The Honorable Laura"; cads like Raye in "On the Western Circuit" and Randolph Twycott in "The Son's Veto." Most of the men in *A Group of Noble Dames* are bullies or boors despite their blue blood, and to their innermost thought a woman is scarcely more than an object of primitive desire. If it be objected that they belong to the bluff old days of roast beef and ale, it may be answered, as Henley hinted some years ago, that sex was never absent from the undercurrent of Hardy's consciousness. Only a man of whom this was true could have given us the ending of "Lady Icenway," where for a moment we seem to look into the knowing eyes of another Sterne rather than the grave features of the Wessex sage. This intense interest in sex explains why Hardy's genius was taxed to lend his women freshness and charm, to endow them with that subtle appeal which his men experience in their company and that touch of mystery which is a part of their enchantment. His success is striking; even those women whose heads are empty, like Betty Dornell in "The First Countess of Wessex," or whose affections lack a balancing will-power, like Mrs. Harnham's Anna in "On the Western Circuit," are fragrantly feminine. Almost all Hardy's women win the reader just as they win lovers; and the first and most devoted of those lovers is Hardy himself.

Hardy, like Conrad, treated his short stories as no mere by-product of his novels but as works of literary art worthy of his talents. Hence no selection of either man's finest fiction can be limited to his novels; in Hardy's case that would exclude at the very least "The Waiting Supper," "The Three Strangers," "Fellow Townsmen," "The Withered Arm," "A Tragedy of Two Ambitions," and "On the Western Circuit." In short as in long fiction Hardy is distinctly superior in mastery of form to Conrad, the seaman turned writer. Both often exceeded the typical short story length, but Hardy can tell as good a tale as "A Committee-Man of 'The Terror' " in a little over 5000 words and Conrad "The Lagoon" in a thousand words less.

Conrad takes us to far-away places, to coasts on the under side of the world, while Hardy centers on the "nook of civilization" he knows best. Both reveal an abiding compassion for their fellows, the result of the spectacle of human suffering on meditative and sensitive minds. Both present characters who must pay expiatory debts to Justice and both are prone at times (Hardy more often than Conrad) to imply that the payment exacted is much heavier than the payment due. Again, they have a marked interest in characters who follow their more generous instincts to their own undoing.

Hardy would not have written "Heart of Darkness." The many-sided and overwhelming irony of the tale would have commended itself to him, but what he would call its "arena" is too vast for his taste. Besides, he would have considered Kurtz's descent to Avernus too steep and sure and the revelation of that erstwhile idealist too indirect and too long postponed. Hardy might have written Hawthorne's immortal "Roger Malvin's Burial" but he would never have permitted Reuben to know the relief of expiation: his philosophy found no balm in Gilead. To Hawthorne, Fate was an instrument of Divine Justice; to Hardy, a perverse and malevolent thing to which he gives a variety of names and which he considered either God or the executor of His designs. Conrad was often bewildered (as who is not?) by what seem the cruel injustices of life, by the evil consequences of well-intentioned acts, by the inexplicable sufferings visited on the innocent. But his spiritual heritage was different from that of the others and, while it did not permit him to find complete satisfaction in Hawthorne's philosophy, it saved him from one as bitter and hopeless as Hardy's.

These problems on which Hardy centered his thought so long ended by almost completely absorbing him. Hence nearly all of his stories are essentially tragic, and it is seemingly casual events, life's "little" ironies, that make them so. "Strange conjunctions of circumstances," he wrote, "particularly those of a trivial everyday kind, are so frequent in ordinary life that we grow used to their unaccountableness, and forget the question whether the very long odds against such juxtaposition is not almost a disproof of its being a matter of chance at all." Which means that if chance is eliminated, a malevolent intention (whose, I have already indicated) takes its place.

Quite apart from this philosophy Hardy's employment of what appears to be chance is managed so adroitly that the casual reader never questions it. But the diligent reader of the eleven hundred pages of his short stories does. The paper "accidentally swept to the floor" in "The Grave by the Handpost," the letter which arrives just too late in "Fellow Townsmen," the drowned man wedged in the culvert in "A Tragedy of Two Ambitions" and the other who meets a similar fate in "The Waiting Supper," bring back to mind a lengthening series of comparable mischances and lead to the suspicion that, after all, it may be Hardy who pulls the strings and lays the blame on the wanton malevolence of Fate.

It is surprising that Hardy, holding to such a conception of life, retained his desire either to live it or portray it. Did he find compensation in recording that occasionally Fate relented before the tragedy had run its course, as in "A Mere Interlude," or in studying humankind in its infinite variety and noting how curiously we react to the evils that assail us? What surprises await the surest predictions! To what heights the weak ascend, to what depths the strongest sink! How indomitable are the yielding, how compliant are the firm!

Hardy as already indicated felt infinite pity for his fellows, but his chronicles of their fateful hours reflect his pity less than the fascination which the unfolding drama of their lives held for him.

It is part of his genius that he infects his readers with this same fascination. As we read we are absorbed. The *advocatus diaboli* whispers to us in vain. "His plots are artificial"; we have forgotten it. "His philosophy of life is false"; we decline to think of it. "He has pre-determined to wreck his characters"; we find the suspicion unwelcome. "He is going to imply that Fate not Hardy is the destroyer"; we resent the warning. We are lifted above his theories and his philosophy. We are under the Master's spell; we are the willing victims of an illusion. We seem close to life, peering into her face, feeling the warmth of her breath and the thrill of her pulses, shuddering at her agony, pitying her tears.

Something About Kate Chopin

LITERARY HISTORY PLAYS CURIOUS PRANKS. IT PERMITS CERTAIN writers of high talent to fall into neglect, exalts others temporarily into a cult, and rescues others from seeming oblivion. Optimists like to believe that, in the long run, justice is accomplished, the unworthy dislodged, the truly great seated among their peers and the neglected recalled to their place in the sun. Among these last must be remembered that writer of mixed French and Irish stock, Kate Chopin, whose work included two striking volumes of short stories, *Bayou Folk* (1894) and *A Night in Acadie* (1897). What Hamlin Garland did for the middle west, Mary Wilkins Freeman for New England, Thomas Nelson Page for the middle south, and Miss Murfree for the Tennessee mountain country, Mrs. Chopin did for the dwellers along the sluggish marshy streams that meander among the sugar plantations of upstate Louisiana. Louisiana was not her undivided domain for Grace King and G. W. Cable made it the scene of such classic tales as *Balcony Stories* and *Old Creole Days;* but Mrs. Chopin left New Orleans to Miss King and the pre-war years to Cable, while she sought her material without distinction of class and among people whose knowledge of ante-bellum opulence was largely a tradition.

Both *Bayou Folk* and *A Night in Acadie* were treated kindly by the critics but not so generously as they deserved, and though both contain masterpieces, they have long been caviar to the general. You look in vain for them even in our largest book shops or in any but a handful of our greatest public and university libraries.

Mrs. Chopin, like H. C. Bunner, was a student of Maupassant. Her Celtic warmth of blood and romantic spirit rejected his icy cynicism, and her human sympathy kept her point of view from the rigorous impersonality of his. But she enriched her innate talent for story telling by studying his virtues and making them her own: economy of words, beginnings which start the reader off like a shot from a pistol, and infallibly "right" endings.

Mrs. Chopin knew before setting pen to paper exactly whither she was bound and her conclusions bear proof of it. They are never flat, trite, weak, or forced. They seem to be there not as the result of a clever device or for a calculated effect or—as with O. Henry—to startle the reader, but as if they were inherent in the situation or in the psychology of the chief character. In "Tante Cat'rinette" and "Ozème's Holiday" situations which might become romantically unreal are saved and perfected by right endings, and "A Wizard from Gettysburg," the tale of a demented tramp who returns accidentally to his own plantation three decades after Appomattox and digs up long buried gold, is lifted from banality to art by its final sentence. The old man's wife recognizing her husband greets him, and he, looking long into her imploring face, makes a courtly bow. " 'Madame,' he said, 'an old soldier, wounded on the field of Gettysburg, craves for himself and his two children your kind hospitality.' " The conclusion of "In and out of Old Natchtoches" foreshadows O. Henry; so too does that of "In Sabine" which, though without the passion of Bret Harte's "Brown of Calaveras" and Hamlin Garland's "Love Among the Corn Rows," is superior to Garland's tale and only a shade less fine than Harte's. The conclusion of "After the Winter" has beauty, of "At the 'Cadian Ball" drama, of "Nég Créol" irony, of "Azélie" a sense of the inevitable, of "Athénaïse" tenderness and pathos as real as the maternal instinct it reveals.

Mrs. Chopin's people are not mere names. She endows them with three dimensions in a sentence or two. "Mamzelle Aurélie possessed a good strong figure, ruddy cheeks, hair that was changing from brown to gray, and a determined eye. She wore a man's hat about the farm, and an old blue army overcoat when it was cold, and sometimes top-boots." Here is Lacodie, locksmith and radical: "He was small, frail, and hollow-chested, but his head was magnificent with its generous adornment of waving black hair, its sunken eyes that glowed darkly and steadily and sometimes flamed, and its moustaches which were formidable."

The important thing with Kate Chopin as with Maupassant is character rather than situation, the response of men—and even more of women—to the passion of love. Maupassant's interest is in the blasé, the sophisticated, when confronted by the ingenuous and unspoiled (or the reverse), while Mrs. Chopin's is chiefly in young men and women in the first blush of romantic passion. There are no elopements as in Garland, no roués suddenly moved to a change of heart by innocence or a sense of pity as in Harte, no parade of bleak lives as in Mrs. Freeman, or of worn out elderly ones, pathetic or gracious but remote from the verve and joyousness of the young, as in Grace King. The elderly appear, like Monsieur Jean Bo, who for thirty years has awaited the return of his dead brother Alcibiade from the war, but youth is almost always at their side, softening their decline with tenderness, profiting by their experience, or implying the onward flow of life and its unquenchable hopes.

Kate Chopin's youths and maidens are unspoiled. They have not toyed with their emotions until they become their victims nor are they afraid of the promptings of their hearts. They are not unduly introspective or tormented by indecision. They have no need to be for their instincts, like homing birds, fly straight and true, though the young women, true daughters of Eve, sometimes make pretence of fluttering away. Thus Clarisse, after playing the coquette with Alcée Laballière, follows him to the 'Cadian ball and rescues him from the vampish Calixta. "I thought, Alcée, maybe you were going to—to Assumption. I got wild. An' then I knew if you didn't come back, *now,* tonight, I couldn't stan' it,—again."

These boys and girls are not selfish; they seem to have no concern for what they deem the mere accessories of life. Hence the girls are capable of simple—and magnificent—loyalties which triumph over everything but contempt and abuse. For them love is the great, the crucial and transfiguring experience, the door swinging open to whatever earthly paradise there be, glorified by nothing but the abiding satisfactions of the heart. Euphrasie, having promised to marry Placide Santien whom in the ignorance of her youth she thinks she loves, cleaves to him even when she knows her heart is elsewhere. Madame Célestin, left in the lurch by her husband for six months, is ready to seek a divorce in defiance of confessor and bishop, but melts when her errant spouse comes home "an' promise me on his word an' honor he's going to turn ova a new leaf." Mentine, slender and lovely, marries Jules Trodon only to become, in seven years, what with children and poverty, a faded, bedraggled old woman. But when Doudouce, well-to-do and still her adorer, goes to thrust Jules aside and rescue her and her children, he finds himself little more than a stranger. Departing, he "looked back at Mentine, standing at the gate with her baby. But her face was turned away from him. She was gazing after her husband, who went in the direction of the field." Azélie Pauché, poor as a church mouse, lovely as a flower, answers without a thought or a regret 'Polyte's plea to marry him: "Ah, b'en, no. I ain't goin' to stay yere wid you, Mr. 'Polyte; I'm goin' yonda on Li'le river wid my popa."

Mrs. Chopin touches passion with a deft hand. In the case of young women she is sensitively aware of its revelations, its hesitancies, its fears, while she senses how deeply young men are troubled by its bitter sweet torment and bewildered by its divine illogic, and always she treats them with a certainty and convincingness which owe as much to reverence as to art. Thus 'Polyte, young plantation store-keeper, half in love with Azélie with the red curved lips, the "dark wide innocent questioning eyes, and black hair plastered smooth back from the forehead and temples," discovers her one night stealing from his supplies. Shocked, he lets her go. "He sat for a long time motionless. Then overcome by some powerful feeling that was at work within him, he buried his face in his hands and wept, his whole body shaken by the violence of his sobs."

"After that 'Polyte loved Azélie desperately. The very action which should have revolted him had seemed, on the contrary, to inflame him with love."

Of course Mrs. Chopin does not confine herself to this sole *motif* nor, when treating it, does she limit herself to a single formula. Love dawns and its loyalties find expression in infinite ways; in recounting them she sometimes hints at twists of thought whose subtleties she, like Maupassant, leaves the reader to divine. Thus it is with 'Polyte, instanced above; thus it is with Madame Delile who, on the brink of eloping with the charming M. Sepincourt, learns of her husband's death in battle and at a stroke dismisses Sepincourt from her life and dedicates her youth and beauty to hallowing the memory of the dead.

These subtleties sometimes take another direction as with the middle-aged Mamzelle Fleurette, a sentimental soul who feels attracted to Lacodie, the perky little locksmith, and experiences a secret thrill when he comes to her shop each evening to buy a paper. She checks the feeling rigorously but, when Lacodie dies and his widow remarries, she feels that he has been forfeited to her and exultingly takes charge of his grave and hangs a picture of him in her room. Chicot, a half starved, dull witted old negro, is faithful as a dog to an impoverished, worn out old woman because she bears the adored family name of Boisduré. She dies: his loyalty experiences a curious recoil, abandoning her and centering itself in the large, vague glory of the name she bore. The withered form "was doubtless that of some Boisduré of *les Attakapas;* it was none of his." Tony Bocage, a giant boatman with primitive instincts, smitten by Claire Duvigne, a city belle, is hired to take her for a pleasure row and on returning "is stirred by a terrible, an overmastering regret that he had not clasped her in his arms when they were out there alone, and sprung with her into the sea." He resolves not to miss a second chance. So Maupassant might have written, without elaborating on Tony's thought or curiously delving into his mind but with a statement at once laconic and authoritative. But Tony's story in Mrs. Chopin's hands takes another turn into a new—and convincing—subtlety, fashioned to her own pattern for she was a student of Maupassant's art not of his psychology. On learning months later that Mlle. Claire has died, Tony first is stunned, then filled with despair, but next morning feels mysteriously content. The thought, he explains to his mother, that another man might one day possess Claire drove him mad. "But now she is where she belongs; there is no difference up there; the curé has often told us there is no difference between men. It is with the soul that we approach each other there. Then she will know who has loved her best. That is why I am so contented. Who knows what may happen up there?" Recalling Browning's "Evelyn Hope," in which death does not quench but kindles the lover's faith, one divines subtleties here of a kind that intrigued the great Victorian.

The emotions which for the most part concern Mrs. Chopin are elementary even when their roots are struck in hidden places, and it is not surprising that the maternal instinct should provide the theme for some of her finest stories. We have it in the tale of Mme. Carambeau, long at feud with her son for marrying an American girl but reconciled at the sight of her granddaughter; of Mamzelle Aurélie, self-centered and middle-aged, who, on sending back home four children she has mothered for a fortnight, "let her head fall down upon her bended arm and began to cry. Not softly, as women often do. She cried like a man, with sobs that seemed to tear her very soul." Most notably this theme appears in the tale of Athénaïse who, scarcely out of school and married to the widower Cazeau, resents his having married her and hides away from him in a kindly city *pension*. A month later, troubled and half ill, she seeks out her motherly landlady. "She stayed a long, long time, quite still, quite stunned, after her interview with Sylvia, except for the short, uneven breathing that ruffled her bosom. Her whole being was steeped in a wave of ecstasy. When she finally arose from the chair in which she had been seated, and looked at herself in the mirror, a face met hers which she seemed to see for the first time, so transfigured was it with wonder and rapture. . . . Cazeau must know. As she thought of him, the first purely sensuous tremor of her life swept over her. She half whispered his name, and the sound of it brought red blotches into her cheeks. She spoke it over and over, as if it were some new, sweet sound born out of darkness and confusion, and reaching her for the first time. She was impatient to be with him. Her whole passionate nature was aroused as if by a miracle."

None of Kate Chopin's short stories is told with greater beauty or more exquisite understanding than this, and only one, "Désirée's Baby," outranks it. Here is a tragedy, miniature in proportions, overwhelming in effect, told in a bare 2000 words, every one significant, from the incisive opening sentence to the final startling one, which matches O. Henry's "Furnished Room" in the suddenness of its surprise and in the irony and pathos of its revelation. All Mrs. Chopin's gifts are here in their perfection: directness of approach, sureness of touch, and delicate shading, and the swift strokes which provide the setting create the atmosphere and introduce and realize the characters. With unerring instinct and an amazing economy of words which even she never equalled and Maupassant never surpassed, she probes the psychology of Désirée and her husband to the quick, after first opening the way by what seem to the unwary scarcely more than casual phrases. The sense of impending tragedy comes early, as it should in so brief a thing, with perfect naturalness and in the turn given a sentence by two words, and is deepened by the disclosure that Désirée's foster-mother, visiting her and her baby, "shudders at the sight of the Aubigny house as she always did. The roof came down steep and black like a cowl, reaching out beyond the wide galleries that encircled the yellow stuccoed house. Big, solemn oaks grew close to it, and their thick-leaved, far-reaching branches shadowed it like a pall."

As one reads recollections of other short story masters arise with whose revelations of power and skill in evoking the spirit of tragedy this perfect tale takes its place, Poe, Hawthorne, and Thomas Hardy.

From Kate Chopin's two volumes of short stories a modest book could be made containing half a dozen tales which her only American superiors in that field would not disdain to own, a volume which those most proud of American literature would gladly proclaim an addition to its masterpieces.

The Case for Louise Imogen Guiney

"SHE HAS DONE," SAYS ALICE BROWN, "THE MOST AUTHENTIC AND exquisite verse America has yet produced." "Much of her work," says Louis Untermeyer, "is poeticizing rather than poetry." These judgments, so sharply at variance, are reflected in half a dozen anthologies published within the last decade and a half. The *Oxford Book of American Verse* (1927) edited by Bliss Carman (a poet in his own right) finds room for ten of Miss Guiney's poems; *American Poets* (1932) edited by Mark Van Doren excludes her entirely. With due allowance made for the subjective element in all such appraisals we are, none the less, confronted here with opinions too conflicting to be reconciled and we are by that very fact led to weigh, consider, and pass judgment for ourselves.

To begin with it is admitted that Louise Guiney's output was not large and that her artistic scruples led her to ban all but the poems included in the small definitive volume named *Happy Ending*. This must not tell against her for bulk of itself is no asset, and a dozen stanzas, a dozen lines, yea, a quatrain or a couplet of authentic poetry, outweighs tons of the other thing. "He must carry a slender baggage," said Anatole France, "who would fly to immortality."

With this point made we are prepared to ask: how does the case stand for Louise Guiney? What qualities do Alice Brown and other lovers of her poetry find in it to support their enthusiastic praise?

I.

To understand Louise Guiney it is important to remember four things: her race, her faith, her feeling for her father, and the absence from her life of one of the most vital and universal of emotional experiences.

She was of mixed blood, Scotch, French, English, and Irish, but the Irish predominated and stood revealed in her enthusiasms, her loyalties, her impracticalities, her romantic hero-worship, and her devotion to lost causes and dead yesterdays. She had courage and verve like those of the charging Irish at Fontenoy, sympathy and the insight which springs from it, a disregard of the present, an unconcern for the future, a vitalizing sense of the past.

Her religious faith was ardent. To her eyes it lay at the very heart of life, illumining its darkness, lightening the burden of its mystery, transfiguring it from the winnowing place of death to the flowering field of immortality. Without it she would have found life not only devoid of chivalrous impulses to action and of joyous idolatry of the great dead but utterly without meaning. Louise Guiney's was a demanding faith: it gave much, it exacted much in return. If she deemed it the most precious thing in the world and accepted it with infinite gratitude, it required in return the cultivation of an unflinching will, disciplined emotions, and the courage to accept life as a ceaseless challenge.

Louise Guiney's one passion was her worship of her father, General Guiney, a hero of the Civil War, cruelly wounded at the Wilderness, who lived on for twelve years within the daily shadow of death. To his friends and above all to Louise, he was a Bayard *sans peur et sans reproche* who doffed his uniform in peace but never the shining armor of his spirit. Even in childhood Louise regarded his arms as relics rather than playthings, mementoes of an authentic figure of chivalry. General Guiney had entered the war as a high duty, unblinded by passion, and his ardor as a soldier sprang from his conviction that he was answering no casual call to the colors but a direct and imperative summons from a more than earthly Voice. His death was in perfect accord with the faith and gallantry of his life. One day, said Louise, while "crossing the square toward his house, he had sudden warning, by a slight spurt of blood to the lips. He took off his hat and knelt down by a tree; his loyal and instinctive way of meeting his Lord. A child playing near, who knew him, was the first to reach his side; but already he was no more."

Louise never forgot she was a soldier's daughter nor did the final vision of that romantic figure ever fade from her memory. When she thought of men striving with life it was under the guise and color of a chivalry ennobled by tradition and heroically exemplified in her sire. She idolized certain dead poets and men of letters, beholding them as knightly figures, soldiers at heart and usually by profession, in whom she recognized a kinship with her father and who on that account were doubly dear. Thus romantically conjoined, the two vocations she knew best proved mutually glorifying.

A tradition, too nebulous to trace, says that Louise Guiney in her late teens had a love affair, that it met with no encouragement at home, and that, having feeble roots, it perished. What would have happened had it been otherwise is an idle question now. Perhaps she would have given us love lyrics charged with such beauty as Alice Meynell's, such intensity as Emily Dickinson's, or such passionate renunciation as Christina Rossetti's. The fact remains that she has not done so and that emotions whose full powers only a great love might have awakened went to enrich her friendships, her hero-worship, and, with advancing years, her almost maternal affection for younger adventurers in letters who sought her aid.

Once, it is true, and in a lyric of beauty, Louise Guiney's heart seems to speak but the emotion has no fire, only a kind of timid adoration as of one worshiping at a distance, and, significantly, the dedicated hour is the passionless hour of twilight. Judge for yourself:

> When on the marge of evening the last blue light is broken,
> And winds of dreamy odour are loosened from afar,
> Or when my lattice opens, before the lark hath spoken,
> On dim laburnum blossoms, and morning's dying star,
>
> I think of thee (O mine the more if other eyes be sleeping!),
> Whose greater noonday splendours the many share and see,
> While sacred and for ever, some perfect law is keeping
> The late, the early twilight, alone and sweet for me.

The energizing elements then in Louise Guiney's life and—since she was essentially a lyrist—in her poetry, sprang from her race, her faith, and her adoration of her father, all as affected by a pervasive sentiment which under other circumstances might have been a confined but intense passion. These elements rarely if ever remained completely distinct: mysticism blended with the clatter of arms and gallop of horses, the iron nerve of soldierly stock resisted the ravishes of spiritual desolation, Celtic *élan* and faith mingled with her optimism, as faith and affection sweetened her human sympathies.

II.

The impulse to withdraw from the pursuit of ambition and pleasure, in answer to a higher call that will not be denied, is not uncommon and has been celebrated in verse under a variety of guises. Louise Guiney's thought played about this mystical theme of self-surrender and the result is unique. She is not concerned with renunciation, there are no tears, no rendings of the heart; her hero hears the summons and heeds it as a soldier, weary of the inactive life of the barracks, welcomes the call to arms. He is a Knight of the Grail, another Galahad whose quest ends only "beyond the sunset and the stars," but no Galahad ever swung into the saddle with so ringing a cheer or followed his Leader with more impetuous speed than he. Where but in "The Wild Ride" with the galloping beats of its anapestic meter, its stirring notes that move the heart "more than with a trumpet," will we find mysticism sustained by such gusto!

I hear in my heart, I hear in its ominous pulses,
All day, on the road, the hoofs of invisible horses,
All night, from their stalls, the importunate pawing and neighing.

Let cowards and laggards fall back! But alert to the saddle
Weatherworn and abreast, go men of our galloping legion,
With a stirrup-cup each to the lily of women that loves him.

The trail is through dolor and dread, over crags and morasses;
There are shapes by the way, there are things that appal or entice us;
What odds? We are Knights of the Grail, we are vowed to the riding.

Thought's self is a vanishing wing, and joy is a cobweb,
And friendship a flower in the dust, and glory a sunbeam:
Not here is our prize, nor alas! after these our pursuing.

A dipping of plumes, a tear, a shake of the bridle,
A passing salute to this world and her pitiful beauty;
We hurry with never a word in the track of our fathers.

(I hear in my heart, I hear in its ominous pulses,
All day, on the road, the hoofs of invisible horses,
All night, from their stalls, the importunate pawing and neighing.)

We spur to a land of no name, outracing the storm-wind;
We leap to the infinite dark like sparks from the anvil.
Thou leadest, O God! All's well with Thy troopers that follow.

If faith has its exultations as in the splendor of charging horse-
men it has its desolating fears as well. The coward no less than
the hero leaves a heritage behind, and defeated fathers may seal
the doom of sons wavering in the press of battle.

> The terrible Kings are on me
> With spears that are deadly bright;
> Against me so from the cradle
> Do fate and my fathers fight.

To that cry of fear and anguish is given an answer that belongs
with Browning's "Childe Roland," Tennyson's "Light Brigade,"
Arnold's "Last Word," and Henley's "Invictus":

> While Kings of eternal evil
> Yet darken the hills about,
> Thy part is with broken sabre
> To rise on the last redoubt;
>
> To fear not sensible failure,
> Nor covet the game at all,
> But fighting, fighting, fighting,
> Die, driven against the wall.

In "The Colour-Bearer" Louise Guiney sounds the battle note
again; it is no longer an exhortation that we hear but a grave
acquiescence in commanded duty; the meter is so adroitly handled

that the martial note is transformed to the beat of muffled drums: here is warfare stern and joyless, doomed to end in "the nakedness of defeat" but not in dishonor.

Victory arising from defeat, defeat which *is* victory, came to have a peculiarly personal significance for Louise Guiney. She had begun her literary career young, had been praised by distinguished poets, and had found a ready market for her verse. But as the years wore on it became clear that in America she had missed not only popularity but wide recognition, while in England, despite the enthusiasm of certain discriminating critics, her work met with general indifference. There were moments when the bitterness of that discovery was especially hard to bear and when only loyalty to traditions of pluck and abnegation made endurance with an air seem possible.

In being faced by virtual failure she was not unique for among her intimates were men and women whose merits had been as cruelly ignored as her own. They too, else sinning greatly, held fast to ideals and loyalties and for reward saw their work ignored by the lords of literary opinion. The history of art was full of such tragic cases: at the stony feet of Apathy lay unnumbered pearls scattered by talented souls whom the world called failures. At the thought an age-old question arose to plague her: Who *are* the failures? she asked, and her answer took form in a lyric gravely tender, mystical, perfect in form.

The Vigil-at-Arms

Keep holy watch with silence, prayer, and fasting
Till morning break, and every bugle play;
Unto the One aware from everlasting
Dear are the winners: thou art more than they.

Forth from this peace on manhood's way thou goest,
Flushed with resolve, and radiant in mail;
Blessing supreme for men unborn thou sowest,
O knight elect! O soul ordained to fail!

III.

It was natural that Louise Guiney's thoughts should turn to chivalry for she was not only a soldier's daughter but a

Dreamer of dreams born out of her due time

homesick for that colorful epoch when knighthood was still an ideal and the age of "sophisters, economists, and calculators" was yet to dawn. Her especial love was seventeenth century England whose firmament glittered with "starrie gentlemen," and the griefs of whose martyred King she found less endurable than her own. The objects of her warmest worship were "the sworded poets of the Civil Wars," Montrose, Lovelace, and, cherished only this side idolatry, Henry Vaughan ("my Vaughan" she called him) whose thoughts dwelt far from war's alarms in the world of light.

The arc of her worship swung wide, from Hazlitt and Stevenson to the poet Surrey and the recusant poets whose songs were stilled only by rack and rope. To Surrey she dedicated a sonnet whose sestet reveals as nothing else could the reality of her heroes and the ardor of her devotion.

> At Framlingham tonight if there should be
> No guest beyond a sea-born wind that sighs,
> No guard save moonlight's crossed and trailing spears,
> And I, your pilgrim, call you, Oh, let me
> In at the gate! and smile into the eyes
> That sought you, Surrey, down three hundred years.

When Louise Guiney set out for England it was to begin a passionate pilgrimage. She wandered delightedly about London, visiting York Stairs, the British Museum, and the Church of St. Peter-ad-Vincula, in whose shadow many a noble head had fallen, and she stood breathless with adoration in Westminster Abbey glorying in its Catholic traditions. Even the docks, the lights, the Sunday chimes in the city, and—most beautiful of all—the doves of St. Paul's, inspired her to poetry. She sought out the Brecon valley for Vaughan's sake and the river Usk from which her beloved poet drew

> A play of thought more mystic than the dawn
> And death at home; and centuried sylvan sleep.

But the Mecca of her spirit was Oxford whose "dreaming spires" and enchanted past haunted her thoughts as they haunted Newman's and Matthew Arnold's, luring her less as an intellectual than as a poet. To her the contemporary significance of the University was remote; she gave scant heed to the challenges it was called upon to face in a day of new doubts and disintegrating beliefs, but she yielded her imagination to the beauty of its colleges slumbering "in old pleasaunces of peace," with birds a-flutter among their ivy and clocks that were "wardens of hours and ages." Her emotions were stirred by the memory of pre-Reformation traditions, by the magic names of Erasmus, Aubrey, Keble, and Newman, and by the presage of the return of

> The long-arrested, the believing years,

and when at last she takes her leave it is with reluctant step and backward glance:

> Sweet on those dim long-dedicated walls
> Silver as rain the frugal sunshine falls;
> Slowly sad eyes resign them, bound afar.
> Dear Beauty, dear Tradition, fare you well.[1]

As a devotee of Arnold's "Scholar-Gipsy" and "Thyrsis" and as an unconquerable romantic who confessed to a gypsy strain in her blood, Louise Guiney missed none of the natural beauty with which England delights the seeing eye. Wherever she might be, in old England as in new, hills and trees, meadows gay with flowers, the sky with stars, rivers seeking the sea, the wonder of dawn, the magic of twilight, all performed for her their endless miracles. Sometimes they made her conscious of a strange lassitude (as in "The Still of the Year"); sometimes she revealed how they could pull upon the heart and evoke wild tears (as in "In Leinster"); sometimes they awakened a kind of wistful questioning (as in "Temperaments"); again (as in "Sanctuary"), true to the Wordsworthian tradition, they lifted her spirit into a felicity from which the agonies of life seemed

> . . . winnowed into silence on that wind
> Which takes wars like a dust, and leaves but love behind.

[1] Her farewell to Winchester (dear for Lionel Johnson's sake as well as for its own) evoked lines equally beautiful and nostalgic.

But sometimes when her spirit wandered in the desert, disconsolate and alone, they failed, despite their beauty, to bring her solace. It was in such an hour that the loveliness of sea and shore and trees, the dancing midges, the sportive singing of the blackbird, the herds going "hillward in the honeyed rain," tortured her with their gladness until, unable to endure more, her own inner desolation, finding voice, cried out to The Infinite Giver

> Whose heart
> Remembers each of these: Thou art
> My God who hast forgotten me!

Here and in that poignant lyric "An October Litany," one seems to hear another soul, another poet, Christina Rossetti, similarly eager for the consoling sense of the nearness of God.

If at times Louise Guiney knew the anguish of spiritual desolation she shared the experience of all other sensitive and aspiring souls from David to Newman, and her cry did not go unheard. Consolations were granted which flooded her being with light and fragrance and a sense of ineffable grace. Once her compensation came as a delight so sudden, so imminent, so intense, that it reveals a mystical strain already foreshadowed in "The Wild Ride" and "The Vigil-at-Arms." It comes upon her in no tangible form but as an exhalation of the scented April twilight, a glimmer from among the trees, a shadow from out the dusk, bearing in upon her soul intimations of a Mystical Presence she dares not name that leaves her faint with love and awe.

> Through all the evening,
> All the virginal long evening,
> Down the blossomed aisle of April it is dread to walk alone;
> For there the intangible is nigh, the lost is ever-during;
> And who would suffer again beneath a too divine alluring,
> Keen as the ancient drift of sleep on dying faces blown?
>
> Yet in the valley,
> At a turn of the orchard alley,
> When a wild aroma touched me in the moist and moveless air,
> Like breath indeed from out Thee, or as airy vesture round Thee,
> Then was it I went faintly, for fear I had nearly found Thee.
> O Hidden, O Perfect, O Desired! O first and final Fair!

In that last cry of awe and spiritual love, this New England girl transcends Wordsworth with his awareness of Nature's mystery and Shelley in ecstasy beneath the spell of Intellectual Beauty, and for a divine moment she shares the passionate rapture of St. Augustine.

IV.

As a romanticist and a Celt, Louise Guiney could never become insensitive to the tears of things even though she met the tragic issues of her own life with a more than Roman fortitude. Her note is never false; it is always felt at the heart no matter how restrained. Here is "A Last Word on Shelley" which, by the way, deserves to be compared with Tabb and Watson both for form and insight:

> Each vast inrolling wave, a league of sound,
> All night, all day, the hostile crags confound
> To merest snow and smoke. The crags remain.
> Smile at the storm for our safe poet's sake!
> Nor ever this ordainèd world shall break
> That mounting, foolish, foam-bright heart again.

At times, as in "Astraea" and "A Dog's Memory," one is aware of unshed tears, and again in the sudden pathos at the close of the first—and finest—of her "Five Carols for Christmastide":

> The Ox is host in Judah stall
> And Host of more than onelie one,
> For close she gathereth withal
> Our Lorde her littel Sonne.
> Glad Hinde and King
> Their Gyfte may bring,
> But wo'd to-night my Teares were there,
> > *Amen, Amen:*
> Between her Bosom and His Hayre!

In "Fifteen Epitaphs"—imitations from the Greek Anthology—Miss Guiney caught the note of resigned sadness so perfectly that she deceived many even of the elect who accepted them as translations. The first, fourth, seventh, eleventh, and fourteenth are very lovely; the fifteenth is perfect:

Praise thou the Mighty Mother for what is wrought, not me,
A nameless nothing-caring head asleep against her knee.

Mingled sadness and resignation (as to "the one inexorable
thing") pervade the beautiful longer lyric, "A Friend's Song for
Simoisius": diction, tempo, and mood are at one; no voice is
raised in protest against Fate; all is subdued as befits a lament
uttered at twilight when "the honey-bees unrifled sleep" and the
"early moon" rises above Mount Ida:

> Upon the widowed wind recede
> No echoes of the shepherd's reed;
> And children without laughter lead
> The war-horse to the watering. . . .
>
> Thou stranger Ajax Telamon!
> What to the lovely hast thou done,
> That nevermore a maid may run
> With him across the flowery Spring? . . .

Marked by pathos of an utterly different kind is the first sonnet
of "Friendship Broken." There are tears here but neither eye nor
voice betrays them; the eyes are cold, the voice has the ring of
steel and the lines are sharp with challenge. Turn now to Watson's
"Estrangement" and beside its grave composure you will sense
the depth of Louise Guiney's grief over such sundering of an
ancient sacred bond "as never truth again can mend."

Sunt lacrimae rerum et mentem mortalia tangunt.

For many years Louise Guiney's life was a "petty round of
irritating concerns and duties." Uncongenial tasks required for a
livelihood, researches well-loved but cramped by mounting dis-
couragements, the bitter pinch of poverty—these neither quenched
her optimism nor the gay gallantry of her spirit.

At times, it is true, when weariness weighed upon her she sighed
for the ultimate peace, as in "Beati Mortui," "To T. W. P.,"
"To One Who would not Spare Himself," but even those betrayed
neither self-pity nor a hint of frayed nerves:

> Be mine to ride in joy, ere thou art gone,
> The flame, the torrent, which is one with thee!
> Saint, from this pool of dying sweep us on
> Where Life must long to be.

Once, in London, before St. Paul's, vexed by an ancient question, she asks herself if "man's advance be vain,"

> If each inheritor must sink again
> Under his sires, as falleth where it clomb
> Back on the gone wave the disheartened foam?

The voices of her heritage answer: optimism, courage, and faith are exquisitely at one:

> What folly lies in forecasts and in fears!
> Like a wide laughter sweet and opportune
> Wet from the fount three hundred doves of Paul's
> Shook their warm wings, drizzling the golden noon,
> And in their rain-cloud vanished up the walls.
> "God keeps," I said, "our little flock of years."

V.

In many ways Louise Guiney invites comparison with her English friend Alice Meynell. In demeanor Mrs. Meynell suggested the gravity of a Sibyl, Louise Guiney the spriteliness of Puck. Both were spiritually ardent, high-souled, sensitive of mind, shrewd observers of men and things. Not in personality, but in innermost spirit each was austere, cleaving to an ideal of deportment before God and man, and, like Wordsworth's nuns who "fret not at their convent's narrow room," finding heaven in surrendered liberty. Both were in the world but not of it, their thoughts busy with those tantalizing matters

> On Man, on Nature, and on Human Life,

which have always been the concern of poets. Both were adept in prose and verse, meticulous artists whose divine dissatisfaction rested only in perfection of thought, phrase, and music. Both gave a swift response to Beauty in all her forms and to Nature in her

infinite variety. Both were under obligation to Keats, to Wordsworth, and to their especial loves, the "metaphysical" poets of the
seventeenth century. Each had her peculiar problems, those mundane exigencies which even souls the most withdrawn do not
escape, but each faced them with quiet courage. Both had infinite
reserves of strength, tenderness, and sympathy, counted brilliant
men of letters among their friends and admirers, and gave glad
encouragement to younger followers of the Muses.

Mrs. Meynell found in the domestic circle inevitable distrac-
tions but compensating stimulation; Louise Guiney ran her course
alone, with what depths of feeling unplumbed, what high desires
unawakened, we can only surmise. Beneath Mrs. Meynell's austerity and restraint lived a passion that, burning like a flame, intense
and clear, found arresting utterance in more than one lyric, and
was the ultimate secret of all her poetry.

Mrs. Meynell was typically at home in her huge living-room
at Palace Court, attentive but slightly aloof in the circle of Sunday
afternoon visitors; the typical Louise Guiney tramped the English
countryside on literary pilgrimages, a staff in her hand, a pheas-
ant's feather in her hat.

When Alice Meynell wrote letters to the *Times,* it was to break
a lance for woman's suffrage; when Louise Guiney sought publicity, it was to complain that the grave of the poet Vaughan, dead
two hundred years, had fallen into neglect. Mrs. Meynell never
lost touch with the practical issues of her day; Louise Guiney,
yielding more and more to the lure of the past, echoed Lamb's
decision to write for antiquity. To Alice Meynell the complexities
of the present revealed the simplicity of some great moral truth;
to Louise Guiney they brought depression and bewilderment.
Thus in "The Motor," like a latter-day Ruskin, she execrates the
"hell-smoke" discharged into the "patient eyes" of the cattle, the
"bawling ruin" caused by the car as it speeds by "in wrecking
fury," declares that "Nature dispossessed" looks on in "helpless
hate," and concludes:

> False God of pastime Thou, vampire of rest,
> Augur of what pollution, what despair?

Mrs. Meynell in "The Threshing Machine" marks the rhythmic
rods, the "unbreathing" engine, "inhuman, perfect, saving time,"

and, answering Ruskin (and, unwittingly, Louise Guiney) concludes:

> "No noble strength on earth" he sees
> "Save Hercules' arm"; his grave decrees
>   Curse wheel and steam. As the wheels ran
>   I saw the other strength of man,
>   I knew the brain of Hercules.

When the war came Louise Guiney was overwhelmed by its
horror:

> Lost on the wind is Belgia's holy cry,
>   And Poland's hope shrinks underground again,
>   And France is singing to her wounds, where lie
>   The golden English heads like harvest grain.

Alice Meynell, amid the serene beauty of England, also thinks of
the agony of war and of "man's unpardonable race" that supplants
Love by Hate. But—

> Who said "No man hath greater love than this,
>   To die to serve his friend"?
> So these have loved us all unto the end.
>   Chide thou no more, O thou unsacrificed!
> The soldier dying dies upon a kiss,
>   The very kiss of Christ.

These two poems deserve careful camparison for they point the
way to conclusions which are supported by a re-reading of all the
verse of the two poets.

What are those conclusions? Primarily, that the more certain
touch, the ampler vision, the greater restraint and penetration are
Mrs. Meynell's.[2]

Other conclusions must be added. Mrs. Meynell's is not the
finer but the more pervasive intellect, Miss Guiney's are not the
richer but the more warmly responsive emotions. Mrs. Meynell
was more intense, more subtle, and her thoughts were more in-
genious as became a poet who rejoiced in paradox. Miss Guiney
let her imagination play about a thought: her artistry was re-

[2] Cf. Miss Guiney's "Nocturne," "Winter Boughs," "The Recruit," "Nam Semen
est Verbum Dei" with, respectively, Mrs. Meynell's "To O——, of her Dark Eyes,"
"Winter Trees," "Free Will," "The Unknown God."

vealed less in the formal perfection of a lyric than in the beauty of single lines. Mrs. Meynell conceived of a poem as so severely a unit that it became (to use an exquisite phrase of Miss Guiney's in another connection) "rich in forborne felicities." In three lines Mrs. Meynell sought to present three aspects of a thought, Miss Guiney a single aspect in three striking ways. Miss Guiney's verse is intellectually less pointed, emotionally more diffuse. To read a poem of Mrs. Meynell's is to discover that a new idea vitalized by fancy or an old one radiant with a fresh flame has pierced your mind like an arrow. To read Miss Guiney's poems is to hear great names reinvoked and glorified, to behold them enriched by long treasured memories and adorations, and in the domain of the spirit to feel your coldness reproved, your courage rekindled, your faith reborn.

Louise Guiney will never be popular. Her optimism demands too much faith, her courage too much will, her joy too much austerity; the passion that inspired her was too much the vestal flame, and from such things mundane tastes turn away. But when all is said she has her place for she has left, in Keats' fine phrase, "great verse unto a little clan."

To those who shrink from dubious compromise, or hail Duty as the voice of God, or scorn to allege a sorry inheritance against a deed of shame, or who decline none of the moral challenges of life, Louise Guiney's finest poetry—and that of few is finer—will always be as the sound of bugles calling in the dawn.

The Dramas of J. M. Barrie

MY FIRST INTRODUCTION TO BARRIE WAS IN THE AUTUMN OF 1898 when Miss Maude Adams appeared for one night in *The Little Minister* at Springfield, Massachusetts. The box-office was besieged but, by a stroke of fortune and my idol's determination to give his young high school brother a treat, we secured the last—and loftiest —pair of seats in the house. As we toiled up the final flight of stairs we murmured like Charles and Mary Lamb, "Thank God we're safe."

That night three memorable things happened: I experienced a romantic delight such as few plays have ever given me since, I fell desperately in love with Maude Adams, and I became at once and for ever a Barrie fan.

In the novel from which the play was made and in the earlier volume of sketches *A Window in Thrums* (1889), Stevenson in his far-away Samoan paradise sensed the high talents of his younger brother-Scot and the greater achievement they promised. "I am a capable artist," he wrote, "but it begins to look to me as if you were a man of genius." Barrie's best answer was to write *Sentimental Tommy*, the portrait of a genius growing up, whose publication the glamorous exile did not live to see, and whose hero was Barrie's most unique contribution to English fiction. The sequel, *Tommy and Grizel* (1900), with its gratuitously grim conclusion, was a disappointment; obviously it was not written for his own delight but as a duty to his public.

All this work was interesting and distinguished but a mere

prelude to what came after the turn of the century, for it was then that Barrie, virtually abandoning fiction, gave his matured genius to drama and came into his own. Up to 1900 he had scored three stage successes: *Walker, London* (1892), a farcical comedy, *The Professor's Love Story* (1894), a sentimental comedy played by E. S. Willard (who can forget the magic of his voice?), and *The Little Minister.*

The twelve-month that began with September 1902 was Barrie's *annus mirabilis.* For in that period he had three plays running simultaneously in London to packed houses, *Quality Street, The Admirable Crichton,* and *Little Mary,* an hilarious farce-comedy. The first two are among his best and one of them, *The Admirable Crichton,* has been called the finest English comedy since Sheridan. Maude Adams was a memorable Phoebe in *Quality Street,* a delicious play of the period of the Napoleonic wars. The *Cranford*-like tempo, setting, and costumes provide satisfactions of their own, but what gives the play its grip is that the imp in Phoebe comes to light, insists on having its fling, and finds her—to our surprise and delight—only too willing to respond. Of course it may be a strain on the incurably unromantic to suppose that a woman of thirty who looks forty can cast off twenty years in as many minutes, but it can be done (read Barrie's *Rosalind* and see) and thanks to Barrie's genius the audience *wants* to believe that Phoebe at least can do it.

One of the great roles of the late William Gillette was that of the inspired butler in *The Admirable Crichton.* (You may have forgotten that "the admirable Crichton" was an historical character, a sixteenth century Scotchman and prodigious scholar but "vain, heedless, a babbler"—as the Scotch Carlyle said of the Scotch Boswell—who was killed in a drunken brawl in Paris at the age of twenty-three.) Crichton in the play is admirable for things even rarer than scholarship, for insight into character, courage and resourcefulness, love of truth, and a common sense which amounts to genius. For sheer greatness he stands alone among Barrie's men and his only match among Barrie's women is Maggie Shand. What a pair they would have made!

Crichton is so perfect a butler that neither upstairs nor down does he express disapproval of anything done by his master Lord Loam—except at his lordship's invitation. Then he objects to the monthly teas at which his lordship, "a peer of advanced ideas," is present and his daughters (not "advanced" but under paternal duress) entertain the servants. Lord Loam, stung by Crichton's disapproval, calls him a "pitiful creature."

> CRICHTON (*shuddering under his lord's displeasure*). I can't help being a conservative, my lord.
> LORD LOAM. Be a man, Crichton. You are the same flesh and blood as myself.
> CRICHTON (*in pain*). Oh, my lord!
> LORD LOAM (*sharply*). Show them in; and, by the way, they were not all here last time.
> CRICHTON. All, my lord, except the merest trifles.
> LORD LOAM. It must be every one. (*Lowering.*) And remember this, Crichton, for the time being you are my equal. (*Testily.*) I shall soon show you whether you are not my equal. Do as you are told.

Did Shaw ever set such a smile upon the face of Irony?

What the dull Lord Loam fails to suspect but what Crichton senses is not only that these monthly democratic gestures are an empty farce (because merely a disquieting suspension of the established social order) but that when and if "Nature takes matters into her own hands," artificial ranks will disappear and he will rule who proves himself best fitted. Barrie decides to put this theory to the test; hence the shipwreck of his lordship's yacht on an uninhabited island with four men and four women survivors, and the astonishing revelations that follow.

In the new social order Lord Loam is last and Crichton first; indeed his lordship is the least efficient member of the company. His two younger daughters show their mettle: Catherine and Agatha are almost as valuable as Tweeney their erstwhile maid; the eldest, Lady Mary, rises close to Crichton's level. Crichton is a miracle of resourcefulness; he is "admirable" in the eyes of all the others and not undeservedly so in his own. (After all, genius is never unaware of itself, and all males, says Barrie, are vain.) After eighteen months on the island everybody is efficient, fit, and contented. Crichton is called "governor" (Gov. for short) and relishes the title; the highest female privilege is to wait on him at meals. He looks with favor on Lady Mary ("Polly" now) and says:

> I am lord over all. They are but hewers of wood and drawers of water for me. These shores are mine. Why should I hesitate; I have no longer any doubt. I do believe I am doing the right thing. Dear Polly, I have grown to love you; are you afraid to mate with me? . . .
>
> LADY MARY (bewitched). You are the most wonderful man I have ever known, and I am not afraid.

The rest of that great third act is beyond praise: here are irony, humor, and pathos intermingled, revelations of human vanity and affection as old as the world, an enchanted moment when joy soars high and all the hostile forces of life seem suspended, that other desperate moment when "duty and inclination come nobly to the grapple," and finally the vision of a tiny Utopia, where individuals and their traditional social order have conformed for a golden hour to the designs of Nature, sinking forever below the horizon.

The play is provocative as great plays are. What should Crichton have done when the rescuing boat turned back? Why? What would *you* have done? Do you remember these lines:

> LADY MARY. Gov., let the ship go. (She clings to him, but though it is his death sentence he loosens her hold.)

For my part that scene is one of the most challenging in modern drama. My heart echoes Lady Mary; my conscience applauds Crichton.

How will Barrie bring this play to a close? Must we choke upon an anti-climax? For answer Barrie provides us with an act which is never over till Crichton, "an enigma to the last," answers Lady Mary's final question and dutifully turns out the lights in Lord Loam's London drawing-room.

Is this play a comedy or a tragedy? Comedy yes, you say. But it has its tragic side. Why? Because back in England these people abandon the normal for the abnormal, the natural for the artificial, sinking into physical and spiritual flabbiness, playing the endless game of marrying and giving in marriage, not where love is but wealth and the flesh-pots of Egypt. The chief tragedies are Lady Mary's and Crichton's, hers because she becomes the willing victim of such an unlovely sacrifice, Crichton's because his genius is doomed to be frittered away. Barrie of course does not accent the tragedy but he leaves it there interwoven with the comedy like threads of black and gold, and it is for the individual eye to decide which is the more compelling. *The Admirable Crichton* is not only full of dramatic surprises but of challenges and questions. Beneath the humor and irony of its brilliant surface it is one of the most provocative dramas ever written, and if you want to awaken a psychologist or a sociologist from a dream of peace get him to discuss it. (How Carlyle, whose bent but still Jovian figure Barrie often saw as a boy, would have applauded this revelation of "The Hero as Butler"!)

One day in London Barrie confided to Charles Frohman, producer and friend, that he had written two new plays, the first so close to his heart that it *must* be produced even though a commercial failure, the second so certain to succeed that it would more than finance the other. On both counts Barrie erred. The sure hit was *Alice-sit-by-the-Fire,* a clever but unconvincing drama of situations, faintly reminiscent of Sheridan's *School for Scandal,* which proved to be a comparative failure; the doubtful play was *Peter Pan.*

Peter Pan has taken its place with the child-classics of the language and has been translated into nearly every civilized tongue and produced in almost every civilized country. It probably holds the world's record for performances. Here Barrie wrought the miracle of recapturing the dreams of childhood, of making them visible, of giving them a local habitation and a name, and of evoking for grown-ups whose souls still live the delights of the vanished but unforgettable land-of-make-believe. *Peter Pan* was written for the immediate joy of two people, a little boy named George Llewellyn Davies and the undying boy that dwelt in the heart and the memory of Barrie.

After a lapse of three years Barrie emerged in 1907 with one of his finest plays, *What Every Woman Knows,* the memory of which with Maude Adams as Maggie Shand is still a joy. The irony, as brilliant as that of *The Admirable Crichton,* is not directed against the English social system but against the vanity, stupidity, humorlessness, or whatever it may be that keeps the male of the species from knowing what every woman knows, that for subtlety, resourcefulness, and a realistic sense he is as a child in her hands.

Of the great modern English dramatists Barrie is the most daring. He dared to write *Peter Pan* where a single false touch would have meant ruin; he dared to write *The Admirable Crichton* whose great second act seemed to defy him to match it with a third; in *What Every Woman Knows* he challenged fate in the very first act by the long silence which followed the rise of the curtain, by the explanation of the burglarious Shand's presence in the Wylie home, and by the discussion (so serious to the participants, so hilarious to us) in which Maggie is bargained off to the trespasser. That last is masterly even for Barrie and scarcely less so is the final half of Act III where Maggie, seemingly stripped of trumps, plays her hand with a skill which leaves Lady Sybil, John, the three stalwarts of the Wylie clan, and the entire audience dumb with admiration.

At the end of the play Maggie performs two final feats: while telling John *half* of what every woman knows (what woman ever tells more?) she affects a humility which saves his face, and she opens the somber chamber of his vanity to its first beam of humor. Does that seem like a feat? It is more: it is a near miracle and the beginning of another; for some day John will laugh at himself and the miracle will be complete.

MAGGIE. Look at me, John, for the first time. What do you see?

JOHN. I see a woman who has brought her husband low.

MAGGIE. Only that?

JOHN. I see the tragedy of a man who has found himself out. Eh, I can't live with you again, Maggie. *(He shivers.)*

MAGGIE. Why did you shiver, John?

JOHN. It was at myself for saying that I couldn't live with you again, when I should have been wondering how for so long you have lived with me. And I suppose you have forgiven me all the time. *(She nods.)* And forgive me still? *(She nods again.)* Dear God!

MAGGIE. John, am I to go? or are you to keep me on? *(She is now a little bundle near his feet.)* I'm willing to stay because I'm useful to you, if it can't be for a better reason. *(His hand feels for her, and the bundle wriggles nearer.)* It's nothing unusual I've done, John.

Every man who is high up loves to think that he has done it all himself; and the wife smiles and lets it go at that. It's our only joke. Every woman knows that. *(He stares at her in hopeless perplexity.)* Oh, John, if only you could laugh at me!

JOHN. I can't laugh, Maggie.

(But as he continues to stare at her a stronger disorder appears in his face. Maggie feels that it is to be now or never.)

MAGGIE. Laugh, John, laugh. Watch me; see how easy it is.

(A terrible struggle is taking place within him. He creaks. Something that may be mirth forces a passage, at first painfully, no more joy in it than in the discoloured water from a spring that has long been dry. Soon, however, he laughs loud and long. The spring water is becoming clearer. Maggie claps her hands. He is saved.)

Is this a provocative play? Of its kind as provocative as Barrie's two other masterpieces, *The Admirable Crichton* and *Dear Brutus*. If you doubt it drop any of these questions in a mixed gathering; one will do: Is Maggie "every woman" or a uniquely clever one? Is her humility (pretended, of course) typically feminine? Are her efforts to save John inspired by love, by the maternal (or protective) instinct, or by vanity? Which of these three impulses has the chief part in a woman's relations with her husband?

In 1916 *A Kiss for Cinderella* [1] was produced and proved to be uniquely Barrie's in its conception, its whimsical humor, its pathos, and its skilful skirting of the pit of sentimentalism. Dickens would have rejoiced in Cinderella, the London child who does a charwoman's work and is so curiously wise and naively imaginative. Only Barrie in all the world would have pictured Cinderella as counsellor-at-large, good angel-in-general, mistress-of-all-trades for the empty-pursed and soul-troubled folk in her neighborhood; only Barrie would (only Barrie *could*) have created and sustained a play in that middle land where fact and fancy, reality and dreams, are fused and vitalized.

A Kiss for Cinderella was so clearly in the boy-Barrie tradition of *Sentimental Tommy* and *Peter Pan* that many unsuspecting souls, oblivious of the serious Barrie of *The Admirable Crichton* and *What Every Woman Knows*, were confirmed in the belief that

[1] It is now (April 1942) enjoying a successful revival on Broadway.

he had never grown up. But they were soon undeceived for in 1917 *Dear Brutus* appeared and in 1920 *Mary Rose*.

In that London aerie where Barrie had his home high above the teeming streets, he dwelt not only with thought and imagination but with memories inestimably sweet (as we know) and others desolatingly bitter (as we may guess) and finally with those reflections on the burthen of the mystery of life which with most of us grow more exigent with the years. If you read *Margaret Ogilvy,* Barrie's exquisite biography of his mother—and you can never know Barrie till you do—you will realize how his dearest memories clung to that part of his life which preceded her death in 1894. Had he made a vital mistake since then, taken a wrong turn at a moral cross-road? Did he, do we, act blindly, are we mere pawns of Fate as Hardy held, or are we what our own characters make us, as Barrie's friend Henley had sung so roundly in "Invictus"? Shakespeare, posing the same question, put an answer into the mouth of Cassius:

> The fault, dear Brutus, is not in our stars,
> But in ourselves, that we are underlings.

Suppose the clock-hands were turned back and we, young once more, were given another chance: would we make the wise choice this time? It was around that theme that Barrie wrote *Dear Brutus*.[2]

The same and yet a different Barrie are in this play. It has Barrie's daring, extraordinarily justified in the result, his whimsy, his fantasy, his power to create the atmosphere essential for his needs and to make the unreal real and the impossible probable. He even persuades the moonlight outside Lob's windows to do magic things for him and a distant wood to creep up so near that when the guests peer out they find it standing where the garden was, moonlit, thrilling with a nightingale's song, and offering in its enchanted depths the coveted "second chance." But there is another Barrie here, foreshadowed four years earlier in that miniature tragedy *The Will,* the Barrie who then presented a picture of moral deterioration too grim for a smile and who now returns to another aspect of the same problem, to probe deeper into its

[2] Did O. Henry also have Shakespeare's lines in mind when he wrote his short story "The Roads We Take" (1904)? And Shaw in the Epilogue to *St. Joan* (1923)?

dark mystery than he was ever to do again. The combination of these two roles in one play suggests the possibility that Barrie, the dramatist, had been studying Hawthorne, the novelist, and had mastered certain of that wizard's secrets.

Lob, who has adroitly gathered together a group of week-end guests and is the magician of this second chance, is a Puckish little wonder-worker of comedy and tragedy. To the guests he is at first comic, then mysterious, then frightening, for he does more than invest the wood with enchantment, more than evoke the past and let his guests repair their early error; he awakens their consciences for an hour of such utter candor as they have never experienced before and will never reveal again. They have their new chance in the wood, seize it, and find it as disastrous as the old; dazed and shaken they return to Lob's house and, to their unutterable relief, to their former state. As they recognize one another and blurt out secret things they comment on Dearth, the bibulous artist, and his wife Alice, the last couple to emerge.

> COADE. Did you see that his hand is shaking again?
> PURDIE. The watery eye has come back.
> JOANNA. And yet they are both quite nice people.
> PURDIE (*finding the tragedy of it*). We are all quite nice people.
> MABEL. If she were not such a savage!
> PURDIE. I dare say there is nothing the matter with her except that she would always choose the wrong man, good man or bad man, but the wrong man for her.
> COADE. We can't change.
> MABEL. Jack says the brave ones can.
> JOANNA. "The ones with the thin bright faces."
> MABEL. Then there is hope for you and me, Jack.
> PURDIE (*ignobly*). I don't expect so.

Purdie's confession is ignoble but honest. The trouble with him and with all these others is that they are not brave, that their faces, however "thin and bright," reveal neither spiritual powers nor nobility of soul. The divine spark, rekindled by the revelations in Lob's wood, is already dying within them and Purdie knows it.

But there are two people in that typical company for whom there is hope. Joanna asks Matey, Lob's servant, whether the strange experience they have undergone (tried annually in mid-summer week by Lob on other selected guests) ever has any permanent effect.

MATEY *(on whom it has had none)*. So far as I know, not often, Miss; but, I believe, once in a while.

(There is hope in this for the brave ones. If we could wait long enough we might see the Dearths breasting their way into the light.)

Why is there hope for the Dearths? Barrie describes Alice Dearth as a woman "of smouldering eye and fierce desires" in "the labyrinth of whose mind murky beasts lie in ambush," but he answers our question when he adds later that though "the darkest spirit" she is "the bravest." She has some humor, blunt honesty, a passionate nature which can sweep all selfishness away, the stuff from which great penitents are made. And Dearth? In his better days he was an artist, a lover and creator of beauty, who wanted to give something ennobling to life, a man of infinite tenderness, to whom the children, yearned for but denied, would have made all the difference. In the enchanted wood it is he alone whose might-have-been proves worthy, whose unfulfilled dream is a lovely thing. That dream is a daughter, Margaret, and the scene of joy and banter between her and Dearth (the impending sword of reality poised to fall) is almost too poignant to be borne. Suddenly, you remember, as they talk, he catches sight among the trees of a blurred light; it is from a window of Lob's house, in the world from which for a little space he is dissevered.

MARGARET *(in a frenzy)*. Don't go into that house, Daddy! I don't know why it is, but I am afraid of that house!

(He waggles a reproving finger at her.)

DEARTH. There is a kiss for each moment until I come back.

(She wipes them from her face.)

Oh, naughty, go and stand in the corner.

(She stands against a tree but she stamps her foot.)

Who has got a nasty temper!

(She tries hard not to smile, but she smiles and he smiles, and they make comic faces at each other, as they have done in similar circumstances since she first opened her eyes.)

I shall be back before you can count a hundred.

(He goes off humming his song so that she may still hear him when he is lost to sight; all just as so often before. She tries dutifully to count her hundred, but the wood grows dark and soon she is afraid again. She runs from tree to tree calling to her Daddy. We begin to lose her among the shadows.)

MARGARET *(out of the impalpable that is carrying her away).* Daddy, come back; I don't want to be a might-have-been.

Barrie's is a very human world in which laughter is a blessed thing as it is with Chesterton, and courage, as he said in his famous rectorial address at St. Andrews, the crowning virtue. In all his great plays there is not only humor, but courage carrying redemption in her hands. He portrayed life as he saw it and as the thing it is, a tragi-comedy.

Mary Rose troubled both critics and public and raises the question how seriously we are to take it. Are we to believe that a little girl of six picnicking with her parents on a lonely island of the outer Hebrides, mysteriously disappears for several days and on mysteriously returning remembers nothing of the incident? And that long after, as a young mother vacationing with her husband, she visits the same island and is rapt away again, this time for twenty-five years? The theme—not uncommon in folklore—presents little difficulty to a man of Barrie's imagination, Celtic blood, and announced belief in fairies, and the problem of making it so credible that it chills the audience provides another of the challenges he loved to meet. It is when at long last Mary Rose reappears among her kind, and the distant household where she once lived as child, bride, and mother awaits her coming, that we grip the arms of our chairs. How will these elderly people, long reconciled to their tragedy, greet their daughter? What will this grizzled sea-captain, schooled to an iron self-command, find to say to his wife? What common ground can there be between the living and this revenant? Miraculously Barrie discovers the way in a memorably strange and poignant scene and thus, up to the last half of the last act, holds us captive. Then comes the final test: how to bring this eery drama to a close? Barrie presents a scene supposedly enacted years later in the same house (now dank and half-ruined) where Mary Rose appears as a ghost, talks to her son whom she does not recognize, and sits on his knee. Suddenly a call is heard such as Mary Rose had answered among the forlorn and empty seas of the north; now once more she answers and finds peace at last. . . . That is a valiant attempt but, as Maurice Baring wrote on seeing it on the London stage, it is not enough.

Audiences have always asked what *Mary Rose* means. I am not sure. But Barrie had lived through the first World War when men's minds were busy with death and the mysteries that lie "beyond the veil," and in this mood he had written the one-act play *A Well-Remembered Voice* (1917). At longer range and in a softer mood he returned to a new aspect of the mystery in *Mary Rose,* but the final curtain leaves us questions. Is there a middle ground between life and death similar to the middle ground between fact and fantasy presented in so many of his plays? Does consciousness lapse there? What calls the dwellers in this twilight land back to earth? Mother-love, to Barrie the most noble and compelling of feminine instincts? Should they return, what would greet them? Love? Bewilderment? Fear? Is it not best that life should be only for the living? And lastly, *beyond* the twilight country, are there those blessed and abiding things we mean when we say "peace"?

In Barrie's life were two influences which never waned: his joy in his boyhood and his adoration of his mother. She was his "one woman" and the greatest influence he ever knew. Whatever of mind, heart, and charm his women possess were hers—he says as much in *Margaret Ogilvy*—from their maternal instinct to their seductive little vanities. His boyhood was a golden day of haunting delights whose very tears were sweet. Thus in nearly all his plays he reveals a certain nostalgia, a wistful turning back to memories of his childhood and of his mother's, recounted to him so often and brooded over so long that they became merged and glorified with his own. *Peter Pan* dramatizes his boyish play-world. In *What Every Woman Knows* the Wylies, father and sons, are Kirriemuir products; Maggie Shand is Margaret Ogilvy even to her genius for self-education. In *Quality Street* he returns to a house rich in heirlooms and "lavendered delights"; the period was his mother's childhood; characters, incidents, even the color-scheme of the Throssel parlor (blue and white) are borrowed from *Sentimental Tommy* and *A Window in Thrums*. The island in *The Admirable Crichton* was once Robinson Crusoe's which the boy

Barrie dreamed of as his own. Cinderella is the feminine counterpart of Barrie himself, the little sister he should have had to play with growing up. In a certain sense *Dear Brutus* betrays Barrie's nostalgia most poignantly of all, for the man whose love of children led him to adopt Pauline Chase and the four little sons of the dead Llewellyn Davies, still at fifty-seven could share Dearth's dream of the daughter that might have been (Margaret, for his mother) and awake, I suspect, to bleak reality with a similar cry of despair. The great moment in *Mary Rose* comes when the poor soul, returning home from her long and mysterious absence, forgets the years between and tiptoes to the door of the empty nursery. Barrie did grow up; what joyous memories, what unrealized hopes, what poignant might-have-beens, he carried with him!

Our final record of his work is *The Boy David* written for Elisabeth Bergner, heralded around the world, produced only a few months before his death, and doomed to failure. Barrie lovers could wish the play to have been an overwhelming success, the crowning event of their seventy-seven-year-old idol's career. With that denied they are consoled to remember that posterity will be concerned only with his triumphs.

Barrie as dramatist challenges comparison with his two great contemporary rivals, Galsworthy and Shaw. Galsworthy was an honest mind, a careful workman, and a sincere humanitarian whose admirers believe that his novels and plays are important social documents to which a later generation will turn for a picture of post-war England. Shaw's gifts are more brilliant than Galsworthy's, and though he can be more dull his great moments like his great characters cling to the memory as Galsworthy's fail to do. As a craftsman Shaw ranks last, largely because he is so victimized by his own volubility and wit that he constantly indulges them at the expense of the action. Primarily, Galsworthy is a preacher exposing the social abuses of his day and place; Shaw a propagandist harboring opinions on social, economic, and moral questions and feeling the zealot's urge to proclaim them at all costs; Barrie is the born artist, the stuff of whose greatest plays is ideas and whose abiding concern is to express them with power, convincingness, and beauty. The earmark of Galsworthy's plays is high seriousness; of Shaw's, wit (laughter of the mind); of Barrie's, humor (laughter of the heart) and imagination, both full of whimsy and surprises. There is some beauty in Galsworthy's plays, much beauty in Barrie's; as to Shaw, Professor Weygandt laments, "There is so damnably much of Shaw and no beauty at all." [3] Galsworthy had everything a carefully cultivated talent could give him; Shaw reveals flashes of genius but like his moments of dramatic power they are rare. It is Barrie alone who proves his right to be accounted in the great tradition.

Professor Phelps summarizes him eloquently: "Barrie's plays are the shows of this world. He gives us pictures of all humanity— our follies, our impossible and futile dreams, our sordidness, our nobility, our vanity; and he accomplishes this without a trace of venom or of scorn, without a flavor of superiority; he loves men, women, and children. But in him love is never blind."

[3] *St. Joan* should be excepted, thanks to its heroine, who quite on her own account is one of the most vivid and fascinating personalities in history. She got out of Shaw's hands and stole the show. Even Candida's charm is Katherine Cornell's. Shaw's Candida does not inspire love in anybody, even in her young admirer, and what he deems love he will, being young and a poet, soon get over.

In Praise of Mary Coleridge

A CONTEMPORARY WOMAN CRITIC IS ON RECORD AS LAMENTING THE paucity of women poets in literary history and asserting that those who have achieved fame are inferior to their brother lyrists even in the writing of cradle songs. My concern is not with the fact alleged or with possible explanations of it, but with the danger of overlooking real poetry because its author was a woman who, being dead, can depend on no clique to press her claims. Specifically I am interested in an Englishwoman who died in 1907 at the age of 46 after writing some two hundred poems, mostly lyrics, all brief, amazingly free from inequalities, and at their finest worthy of inclusion in any anthology of English lyrical verse which pretends to adequacy.

In blood no less than in certain aspects of her poetic talent Mary Coleridge was related to the author of "Kubla Khan" and "The Ancient Mariner." Born in 1861, the year of Mrs. Browning's death, she was thirty-one years younger than Christina Rossetti and Emily Dickinson. Her poems, published in various periodicals, were either anonymous or signed with the pseudonym Ἄνοδος ("Wanderer"), and against the urging of her friends that she abandon this concealment she urged her "fear of tarnishing the name which an ancestor had made illustrious in English poetry." A limited edition containing forty-eight lyrics published in 1896 is now a collector's prize; a complete collection numbering two hundred and thirty-seven lyrics appeared with her name in December, 1907, a few months after her death, and three more editions were issued in rapid succession. Mary Coleridge's admirers numbered such discriminating critics as the poets Henry Newbolt, Robert Bridges, and Maurice Baring; in the ordinary sense her work was not popular, as Mrs. Browning's was but as Emily Dickinson's and Christina Rossetti's was not.

What Mary Coleridge's friends knew was a keen-minded woman, widely read, a wise and sincere thinker who had the tender sympathies of a woman, the self-dependence of a man, and a humor all her own. They saw her devotion to a great cause, for she devoted much time to teaching working-women in her own home and gave lessons in English literature at the Working Women's College. What the public knew was that her novel, *The Seven Sleepers of Ephesus*, won praise from Stevenson and that another, *The King With Two Faces*, brought her fame. What her intimates sensed and the careful readers of her poems cannot miss is that she looked on life with the eyes of a sensitive, tender, passionate, and profoundly spiritual soul and recorded in intimate and spontaneous poetry the thoughts it evoked.

True to her heritage she loved nature not as something merely decorative but as something endowed with power to transform gloom to light long afterward; or to give joy to the dreams of grieving men; or, in its darker aspects, to presage some unguessed fatality, or to commemorate in some withered tree an evil secret thing like that which lay in wait for Childe Roland beyond the blasted heath. Flowers, even in their loveliness, the iris blooming, the cyclamen opening its buds, give her delight but evoke thoughts that lie too deep for tears and awaken a memory too conscious of the world's sadness and ironies to forget for long. Wind, sea, and stars intrigue her most: to dwellers in another planet, our earth, though flaming to destruction, would seem but like a shooting star taking a swift and casual flight into darkness; the winds are things of mystery, driven on by some relentless force, symbols perhaps of those miracles which Carlyle pointed to as all about us and scourged us for ignoring:

> O voice that ever wanderest o'er the earth
>   Lamenting, roaring, sighing,
> Where was thy place of birth,
>   And where shall be thy dying?

In the sea touched by the wind she saw the symbol of eternal
sameness, eternal change, and in the most perfect of her sonnets
she prays for a final resting place, not on Earth's breast but

> Far from thy living, farther from thy dead,
> From every fetter of remembrance free,
> Deep in some ocean cave, and overhead
> The ceaseless sounding of thy waves, O Sea!

Her thoughts turn most often to love, not love as a sentimental
episode but love as a transforming experience. She sings of its
intuitions, its delights, its bitterness, its disillusionment, its fears,
its memories that turn winter into spring and those others that are
as deathless as beauty's self. To her as to Christina Rossetti, love is
a mighty thing, dawn after darkness, a garden in the desert, a voice
out of the silence, swift as light, sharp as a sword, whose memories
for weal or woe outlast heartbreak and the empty years.

A Moment

> The clouds had made a crimson crown
>   Above the mountain high.
> The stormy sun was going down
>   In a stormy sky.
>
> Why did you let your eyes so rest on me,
>   And hold your breath between?
> In all the ages this can never be
>   As if it had not been.

Christina Rossetti's love lyrics are mournful; she renounced and
laughter left her eyes forever. Mary Coleridge was made of sterner
stuff; she wrote nothing so radiant as "A Birthday" (though her
"News" is lovely in its simplicity and eager joy), nothing so desolating as "When I am dead, my dearest" (read her "Hail and Farewell" and compare them for yourself); her spirit has the bravery
of Emily Brontë's defiance. Read "Whether I live," "We were not
made for refuges of lies" and this, entitled "Knowledge":

> Let weaker souls at His decrees repine!
> To us eternity in time was given.

Whene'er we parted, 'twas your death and mine.
    Whene'er we met again, why then 'twas Heaven.

Now let the tempest rise, the fierce winds blow,
    And shake the house of life from floor to rafter!
Whichever goes, whichever stays, we know
    Both death and what comes after.

In conjunction with this read "A Moment" and ask yourself if
Mrs. Browning ever soared higher. Read this, called "Invocation,"
and see if the gorgeously vestured passion of Dante Gabriel
Rossetti's "House of Life" says more than this Englishwoman's
veiled ecstasy:

Come, long-awaited dawn of wondrous Night,
        Come, heart's delight!
The Moon hath risen, the Sun of lovers' eyes;
The stars are fainting now, the pale moth flies;
The air is still, the bird of darkness cries.

Spirits of Sleep, beware, and come not near!
        Tremble and fear!
When with excess of life the senses numb
Call to the lips of Love, and they be dumb,
Then, to restore defeated nature, come!

What Mrs. Browning and Gabriel Rossetti know and feel she
shares; what they in their abundance pour out as from an over-
flowing cup she distils into a single golden drop. They exhaust
language in an effort to make it convey every aspect of their
thought; she presents her thought in a hint, an implication, a
swiftly suggested parallel, a figure of speech.

A primary secret of her art is understatement; like a true Greek
she knows that in real art the part is greater than the whole. To
the unimaginative she is often enigmatic; to those ignorant of life
and the world of the spirit, always so. Her longest poems are short,
her shortest a quatrain. None is finished before the last word of
the last line; it is only then that the key clicks open on the unguessed treasure of her thought. And that treasure is always surprising, sometimes breath-taking:

> I saw a stable, low and very bare,
>   A little child in a manger.
> The oxen knew Him, had Him in their care,
>   To men He was a stranger.
> The safety of the world was lying there,
>   And the world's danger.

Can you match that among modern Christmas poems? In six lines you have the substance of every Christmas sermon ever uttered; the final line, climaxed by the final word, comes like the discharge of a masked battery. Simplicity? Yes, the simplicity that Wordsworth praised and attained only at his best; the simplicity for which Mary Coleridge never seemed to strive, but always attained, and which accounts in part at least for her abiding power and freshness. What weighty thoughts her frail monosyllables and dissyllables carry, not haltingly but as lightly as thistle-down!

> Is this wide world not large enough to fill thee,
>   Nor Nature, nor that deep man's Nature, Art?
> Are they too thin, too weak and poor to still thee,
>   Thou little heart?

> Dust art thou, and to dust again returnest,
>   A spark of fire within a beating clod.
> Should that be infinite for which thou burnest?
>   Must it be God?

In Mary Coleridge's lyrics one finds the occasional influence of other poets, of Coleridge in poems where things of evil and mystery are abroad as "At Dead of Night" and "Wilderspin"; of Shelley in "Invocation"; of Dante Gabriel Rossetti in "Whither Away"; of Blake (whom she greatly admired) in "High Wind," "Gifts," "The Witch," and "Master and Guest"; of the ballad in such poems as "At Dead of Night," "Over the Hills," and that triumph of simplicity, "Our Lady"; and of the profoundly spiritual Crashaw and George Herbert. Christina Rossetti too was deeply spiritual; she too felt the influence of George Herbert. Most often Herbert prayed against his coldness of heart, Christina Rossetti for patience to endure; Mary Coleridge, like so many of us, confesses her failures—and her love. Read Christina Rossetti's "The Resurrection" and then this to which it must give place:

> Good Friday in my heart! Fear and affright!
> My thoughts are the Disciples when they fled,
> My words the words that priest and soldier said,
> My deed the spear to desecrate the dead.
> And day, Thy death therein, is changed to night.
>
> Then Easter in my heart sends up the sun.
> My thoughts are Mary, when she turned to see.
> My words are Peter, answering, "Lov'st thou Me?"
> My deeds are all Thine own drawn close to Thee,
> And night and day, since Thou dost rise, are one.

The sincerity of that is Mary Coleridge's; the form and development are in the tradition of Crashaw and Herbert purified of all self-consciousness. Sometimes doubts shadow her soul, sometimes she bows in abasement, sometimes, like Christina Rossetti, like Newman, like every troubled soul that seeks God, she is caught in the torment of Yea and Nay, and the conflict of moods is reflected in hurrying antitheses that are reminiscent of Christina Rossetti's "The Three Enemies" and of Herbert's "The Collar":

> Depart from me. I know Thee not!
>   Within the Temple have I sought Thee,
>   And many a time have sold and bought Thee
> In that unhallowed, holy spot.
> Depart from me, I know Thee not!
>
> Depart from me. I know Thee not!
>   Full oft among the poor I found Thee.
>   There did I grieve, neglect, and wound Thee.
> I never strove to share Thy lot.
> Depart from me. I know Thee not!
>
> I know Thee not. Abide with me!
>   More than aught else do I admire Thee,
>   Above all earthly things desire Thee.
> I am Thy prisoner. Make me free!
> I know Thee not. Abide with me!

A two-fold miracle permits true poets to utter their hearts in words and music, while a subtler cadence runs its course far below the surface of the meter carrying, perhaps, the low laughter of lovers or giving the sense of unshed tears. Perhaps it is this latter that Virgil meant by "lacrimae rerum" and Wordsworth by "the still sad music of humanity." In Christina Rossetti's poems it often deepens the sense of sadness to the point where Walter Raleigh confessed he felt more like crying than discussing them. To an often striking degree Mary Coleridge revealed this power. Here is a lyric which in theme, poignancy, brevity, sense of intimate relation, as if One Alone were meant to hear this voice and see these unshed tears, should be compared with Christina Rossetti's "The Lowest Place." In it are Herbertian echoes and haunting repetitions which Christina Rossetti managed so adroitly that they seem the perfection of naturalness. It is Mary Coleridge's and no one else's and in form and feeling it is beyond praise. (Note the effect of the slowly descending second half of the final line.) No English poet who ever heeded the admonition *Sursum Corda* but might envy Mary Coleridge this response:

> Lord of the winds, I cry to Thee,
>   I that am dust,
> And blown about by every gust,
>   I fly to Thee.
>
> Lord of the waters, unto Thee I call.
>   I that am weed upon the waters borne,
>   And by the waters torn,
> Tossed by the waters, at Thy feet I fall.

One secret of Mary Coleridge's power is to say much in little, as becomes one whose verse is the result of "concentrated meditation and desire." Read Browning's "Any Wife to Any Husband" (in 126 lines) and then turn to Mary Coleridge's "Contradictions" (in ten) and her sonnet "Alcestis to Admetus," and you will discover that genius, like victory, is not always on the side of the big guns. When, like Watson and Tabb, she turns her skill to the quatrain, she makes it a thing of beauty, not yielding a gem-like flame like theirs but a softer glow as befitted a deeper emotion. Mrs. Browning in a celebrated sonnet offered an answer to the

question, "How do I love thee?" In the following quatrain Mary
Coleridge answers the question, "How *did* I love thee?" and if it
be with simplicity and passion that heart speaks to heart most
directly Mary Coleridge has nothing to fear by the comparison:

> The sum of loss I have not reckoned yet
>   I cannot tell.
> For ever it was morning when we met,
>   Night when we bade farewell.

The imprint of Mary Coleridge is there: everything is implied in
the two final lines, passion, with all its ecstasy, with all its pain,
equally defying appraisal and oblivion. Here is a song which like-
wise bears her imprint, the imprint this time of that side of Mary
Coleridge which her great namesake, master of the ballad and
lover of the remote and mysterious, would have recognized at
once:

UNWELCOME

> We were young, we were merry, we were very very wise,
>   And the door stood open at our feast,
> When there passed us a woman with the West in her eyes,
>   And a man with his back to the East.
>
> O, still grew the hearts that were beating so fast,
>   The loudest voice was still.
> The jest died away on our lips as they passed,
>   And the rays of July struck chill.
>
> The cups of red wine turned pale on the board,
>   The white bread black as soot.
> The hound forgot the hand of her lord,
>   She fell down at his foot.
>
> Low let me lie, where the dead dog lies,
>   Ere I set me down again at a feast,
> When there passes a woman with the West in her eyes,
>   And a man with his back to the East.

Like Emily Dickinson, Mary Coleridge had an acute sense of
the mystery of life, the soul's secrets, the hidden forces which lie

below all plummets' reach, the seemingly minor things that are charged with high and sometimes frightening significance:

> There with two lives before me did I choose,
> There did I lose to win, and win to lose,
> Not till the day all secrets are displayed
> Shall that Great Angel show the choice I made.

It is this side of Mary Coleridge's gift which, when all is said, is most essentially and characteristically her own. To most of us, bereft of the seeing eye and understanding heart, life is "a petty round of irritating concerns and duties," but to Mary Coleridge it was a curious and infinitely varied journey made through sun and rain, under clouds and stars, whose joys turn to bitterness, whose woes may find a strange beatitude, whose loves breed their own torment, where Fear may follow Love as "lord of one's house and hospitality," where Death, long resisted, is welcomed at the last, where deeds are done too dark for human eye to witness and words spoken that, all unknown, slay a living soul, where a glance thrills a heart beyond all forgetting, and a thought is born, too secret, perhaps too shameful, to be uttered. What casual thing reveals to the lover the duplicity of his mistress so that the "daisies fair" at their trysting place wither away? What unwitting word betrays to the prescient eye of a dying wife her mourning husband in another's arms? Why do men give to those who love them best not their adoration but their tears? Why do we shrink from seeing to its depths another soul or revealing to that other the hidden places of our own? Why will we confess to all the world a secret kept from one? Why does our blessing upon our friend turn to his bane, our curse upon our foe to his advantage? Why must a shadow follow every light? What sudden fears chill the heart at the thought of the soundless hurrying hours that rob us of the happy present, that bring ever nearer the future dark with destiny? What divine alchemy changes the joys of the lowly to the sorrows of the great? How cruelly we punish those who have destroyed our illusions, with what folly we cast aside some priceless irrecoverable thing! Mary Coleridge does not attempt an answer. What she does is to offer us a series of brief lyrics, each "the essence of an experience," sometimes poignantly, often arrestingly, always beautifully done, and it is not her fault as a woman or as a poet if we fail to become aware of new things in earth and heaven that fill us with humility, joy, and unending wonder.

MORTAL COMBAT

It is because you were my friend,
  I fought you as the devil fights.
Whatever fortune God may send,
  For once I set the world to rights.

And that was when I thrust you down,
  And stabbed you twice and twice again,
Because you dared take off your crown,
  And be a man like other men.

Henry Newbolt remarks that at times "she entered very deep shadows filled with strange shapes" but adds truly and revealingly: "Her thought, though clothed in so slender a form, has the courage of the strong, and holds its way through the night like Milton's dreadless angel; but, like him, it is always unsullied, always unscathed, always returning towards the gates of Light."

Some Hardy Perennials

Charles Lamb Falls in Love

CHARLES LAMB, THE SPINDLE-LEGGED LITTLE BOY WITH THE LONG face and the unusual eyes, donned the blue and yellow uniform of Christ's Hospital School in 1782 at the age of seven, left when nearly fifteen, and on the first of September, 1791, began work at a guinea a week at the South Sea House probably at the elbow of his older brother John. The job was shortlived and he laid his pen down for the last time on the eighth of February. Three months later Dame Destiny took a hand, sentencing him to another clerkship, this time at the East India House, where he was to be "chained" to a desk until its "wood had entered his soul" and emancipation came at long last when he was fifty.

It was in the brief idleness between his two clerkships that Charles paid a visit to his grandmother Field near Blakesware in Hertfordshire and first fell in love. The object of his devotion was a fair-haired girl named Ann Simmons and his ardor gave Grandmother Field serious concern. Forgetting that Charles was but seventeen and remembering only that there was a trace of insanity in his family, she set her face against the affair, and though she died the next summer, circumstances were on her side. Blakesware was closed to her grandchildren and, if that were not enough, Charles' hours of work were so long, his salary so small, and his holidays so few, that the episode with Ann was doomed.

Charles took his disappointment hard. Stealing away from London, he paid a visit to the "winding wood" which once "shrouded

Ann's beauties," wandered about lonely and disconsolate through scenes glorified by her "maiden purity" and their "innocent loves," and, on returning home, still "sore galled" by broken hopes, relapsed into dangerous brooding. But no romantic is inarticulate long. Charles sought balm for his soul in writing sonnets on his lost love and dispatching copies to his schoolday friend and hero, Coleridge, whose sympathy was certain.

In the autumn of 1794 the future author of the "Ancient Mariner" descended upon London and Charles, bringing with him a "heart yet bleeding" from a similar love affair and a tongue of such honeyed eloquence as glorified their midnight vigils at the Salutation Tavern and banished every dismal memory. But alack! the enchanter had to depart at last whereupon "I felt," said Charles, "a dismal void in my heart; I found myself cut off at one and the same time from two most dear to me."

Within a year the depth of Charles' boyish passion and the emotional instability of the Lambs were confirmed, for Charles spent six weeks in a madhouse at Hoxton. "It may convince you," he wrote to Coleridge, "of my regards for you when I tell you my head ran upon you in my madness, as much almost as on *another Person,* who I am inclined to think was the more immediate cause of my temporary frenzy." Who might "another Person" be but his Hertfordshire beauty, the fair-haired Ann Simmons?

If the traces of Charles' passion were a bruised heart and a mental breakdown, they were swept away in the tragic storm that befell his family. In September, 1796, Mary Lamb, in a fit of insanity, wounded her father and killed her mother, precipitating changes in Charles' life whose full extent even he was never to know. Overnight the boy became a man. With sense and courage he reestablished the household for his father and his aged aunt, found a temporary refuge for Mary, and then turned appraising eyes on the love episode whose outcome he had deplored so bitterly. How like a sentimental schoolgirl he had acted! What unmanly self-pity he had indulged in! How trivial and remote it all seemed now in the face of the tragedy which had desolated his hearth! Stung with shame and disgust at his weakness he acted decisively, burning all his verses and "a little journal of my foolish passion which I had a long time kept," and writing to Coleridge:

"Thank God, the folly has left me forever. I am wedded to the fortunes of my sister and my poor old father."

The fires burned low but the embers were long in dying. Ann Simmons was in his mind when he wrote his "Old Familiar Faces" early in 1798, for the third stanza clearly refers to her:

> I loved a love once, fairest among women.
> Closed are her doors on me, I must not see her—
> All, all are gone, the old familiar faces.

Ann Simmons married a pawnbroker named Bartram and Lamb in later years sometimes loitered along the streets in the hope of catching a glimpse of her face. We hear of her once more long afterward: she was then a widow residing in Fitzroy Street with her three daughters.

Charles' second love affair was shadowy, so shadowy that it reduces itself to two references in his letters and a single poem.

On the last day of December, 1796, Charles with his aged dependents, his father and his Aunt Hetty, moved to Pentonville on the outskirts of London. His years there were drab and unhappy. For it was in Pentonville that Aunt Hetty died in February, 1797, that old John Lamb followed two years later, and that Mary after finally rejoining Charles—to their mutual delight—was taken "ill" again within a few months and had to seek once more the dismal refuge of the Islington madhouse. "My heart is quite sunk," wrote Charles to Coleridge, "and I don't know where to look for relief. Mary will get better again; but her constantly being liable to such relapses is dreadful; nor is it the least of our evils that her case and all our story is so well known around us. We are in a manner *marked*." In his self-consciousness and resentment Charles sought another refuge, this time back in London where six weeks later Mary was well enough to join him.

His joy at being immersed in the metropolis again overflowed in a letter to Manning. "Streets, streets, streets, markets, theatres, churches, Covent Garden, shops sparkling with pretty faces of industrious milliners, neat sempstresses, ladies cheapening, gentlemen behind counters lying, authors in the street with spectacles, lamps lit at night, pastry-cooks' and silver-smiths' shops, beautiful

Quakers of Pentonville, noise of coaches, drowsy cry of mechanic watchmen at night, with bucks reeling home drunk; if you happen to wake at midnight, cries of Fire and Stop Thief; inns of court, with their learned air, and halls, and butterflies, just like Cambridge colleges; old book-stalls, Jeremy Taylors, Burtons on Melancholy, and Religio Medicis on every stall. These are thy pleasures, O London with-the-many-sins."

In this Babylonian litany, transformed by Charles' joy into a paean of praise, appeared a name destined to an immortality quite its own. It was the "beautiful Quaker of Pentonville" whose presence, all-too-rarely glimpsed in that unloved suburb, had been as dawn to his darkness and whose image rose above the myriad allurements of the great city with a rare charm, a radiant and half-mocking serenity.

The "beautiful Quaker" was Hester Savory, with sweet mouth and eyes as dark as a gipsy's. She was younger than Lamb, the daughter of a goldsmith in the Strand, and she lived in Pentonville with her brother and sisters during Charles' exile. About two years after his departure she was married and within eight months —while yet not twenty-six—she died. Charles was touched. He wrote to Manning: "I send you some verses I have made on the death of a young Quaker you may have heard me speak of as being in love with for some years while I lived in Pentonville, though I have never spoken to her in my life. She died about a month since."

> When maidens such as Hester die
> Their place ye may not well supply,
> Though ye among a thousand try,
>   With vain endeavour.
>
> A month or more hath she been dead,
> Yet cannot I by force be led
> To think upon the wormy bed,
>   And her together.
>
> A springy motion in her gait,
> A rising step, did indicate
> Of pride and joy no common rate,
>   That flush'd her spirit.

I know not by what name beside
I shall it call:—if 'twas not pride,
It was a joy to that allied,
   She did inherit.

Her parents held the Quaker rule,
Which doth the human feeling cool,
But she was trained in Nature's school,
   Nature had blest her.

A waking eye, a prying mind,
A heart that stirs, is hard to bind,
A hawk's keen sight ye cannot blind,
   Ye could not Hester.

My sprightly neighbour, gone before
To that unknown and silent shore,
Shall we not meet as heretofore,
   Some summer morning,

When from thy cheerful eyes a ray
Hath struck a bliss upon the day,
A bliss that would no go away,
   A sweet forewarning?

Perhaps, as Charles said, he had never spoken to Hester Savory in his life. But she spoke to him, and eloquently too, not with words but with her joyousness and grace and he answered by endowing one of the sweetest English poems with her bright spirit.

Lamb loved the theatre. In the days of his near poverty he and Mary gladly toiled up the narrow stairs to the top gallery to applaud Mathews, Kemble, Liston, or Mrs. Jordan, as they turned their talents to the creation of new parts or a fresh interpretation of old ones. Sometimes Lamb contributed his impressions to a periodical, usually Leigh Hunt's *Examiner,* and surely no dramatic criticism has ever equalled his for whimsical charm and for the penetration which inspired Hunt to name him "the profoundest critic now living."

Admiring talent and honoring sincerity, Lamb detested the "Delilahs of the stage" who sought to win their audiences by coquetry rather than fine work, and in the summer of 1813 he published a brief but sweeping condemnation. One actress, however, he held exempt. "The very absence of this fault in her and her judicious attention to her part, with little or no reference to the spectators, is one cause why her varied excellencies, though they are beginning to be perceived, have yet found their way more slowly to the approbation of the public, than they have deserved." The actress of Lamb's praise was twenty-three (fifteen years his junior) and Irish born, her full name was Frances Maria Kelly, and she was destined to become the foremost comedienne of her time and the object of the final love affair of Lamb's life.

During the years that followed Lamb continued to pay open tribute to the genius and charm of his favorite actress until at last, on his own half-humorous admission, he was accused of flattery. The charge, of course, was false, but an unmade charge was true: Charles was in love with Fanny Kelly. At the India House (he tells Wordsworth), perched on his high stool, gravely casting up sums in his ledgers, he reserves "in some corner of my mind some darling thoughts all my own—faint memory of some favorite passage in a Book—or the tone of an absent friend's voice—a snatch of Miss Burrell's singing—a gleam of Fanny Kelly's divine plain face."

Fanny Kelly's *divine plain face!* The unforgettable phrase, inspired by love and understanding, is perfect. Fanny Kelly was not beautiful, but her broad low forehead, her blue eyes, her generous mouth (with upturned corners), her smile so radiant that it seemed to "completely *sun* her countenance," gave one a sense of goodness, reserves of power, and intelligence transfigured by spirit.

Sometimes, perhaps in those moments when Charles gazed with unseeing eyes on his account books, the undercurrent of his "darling thoughts" was transformed into the only music for which he had an ear, scraps of rhyme crept doubtfully along the ledger margins, and one day, months after, a sonnet saw the light.

To Miss Kelly

You are not, Kelly, of the common strain,
That stoop their pride and female honor down
To please that many-headed beast *the town,*

And vend their lavish smiles and tricks for gain;
By fortune thrown amid the actor's train,
You keep your native dignity of thought;
The plaudits that attend you come unsought,
As tributes due unto your natural vein.
Your tears have passion in them, and a grace
Of genuine freshness, which our hearts avow;
Your smiles are winds whose ways we cannot trace,
That vanish and return we know not how—
And please the better from a pensive face,
And thoughtful eye, and a reflecting brow.

There, publicly, spoke the critic and poet. Soon he was to pay her public tribute as critic and lover.

When Miss Kelly appeared the following year as Rachel in *The Jovial Crew*, Lamb published in the *Examiner* the most unique dramatic review ever written which, to the initiate, meant that Fanny Kelly had scored a new success, and to Fanny Kelly, that Lamb adored her. Listen: "The Princess of Mumpers, and Lady Paramount of beggarly counterfeit accents, was *she* that played *Rachel*. Her gabbling lachrymose petitions; her tones, such as we have heard by the side of old woods, when *an irresistible face* has come peeping on one on a sudden; with her full black locks, and a *voice*—how shall we describe it?—*a voice that was by nature meant to convey nothing but truth and goodness,* but warped by circumstance into an assurance that she is telling us a lie—that catching twitch of the thievish irreproveable finger —those ballad-singers' notes, so vulgar, yet so unvulgar—that assurance, so like impudence, and yet so many countless leagues removed from it—her jeers, *which we had rather stand, than be caressed with other ladies' compliments,* a summer's day long— *her face, with a wild out-of-door's grace upon it*—'What a lass that were,' said a stranger who sat beside us, 'to go a gypseying through the world with.'"

Fanny Kelly must have caught her breath when she read those final phrases. What had been vaguely implied before was spoken out now and proved little less than a public declaration. What would that "susceptible stranger," that incorrigible Charles Lamb, do next? In little more than a fortnight she knew.

20 July, 1819.

Dear Miss Kelly,—We had the pleasure, *pain* I might better call it, of seeing you last night in the new Play. It was a most consummate piece of Acting, but what a task for you to undergo! at a time when your heart is sore from real sorrow; it has given rise to a train of thinking, which I cannot suppress.

Would to God you were released from this way of life; that you could bring your mind to consent to take your lot with us, and throw off for ever the whole burden of your Profession. I neither expect or wish you to take notice of this which I am writing, in your present over occupied & hurried state.—But to think of it at your leisure. I have quite income enough, if that were all, to justify for me making such a proposal, with what I may call even a handsome provision for my survivor. What you possess of your own would naturally be appropriated to those, for whose sakes chiefly you have made so many hard sacrifices. I am not so foolish as not to know that I am a most unworthy match for such a one as you, but you have for years been a principal object in my mind. In many a sweet assumed character I have learned to love you, but simply as F. M. Kelly I love you better than them all. Can you quit these shadows of existence, & come & be a reality to us? can you leave off harassing yourself to please a thankless multitude, who know nothing of you, & begin at last to live to yourself & your friends?

As plainly & frankly as I have seen you give or refuse assent in some feigned scene, so frankly do me the justice to answer me. It is impossible I should feel injured or aggrieved by your telling me at once, that the proposal does not suit you. It is impossible that I should ever think of molesting you with idle importunity and persecution after your mind [is] once firmly spoken—but happier, far happier, could I have leave to hope a time might come, when our friends might be your friends; our interests yours; our book-knowledge, if in that inconsiderable particular we have any little advantage, might impart something to you, which you would every day have it in your power ten thousand fold to repay by the added cheerfulness and joy which you could not fail to bring as a dowry into whatever family should have the honor and happiness of receiving *you*, the most welcome accession that could be made to it.

In haste, but with entire respect & deepest affection, I subscribe myself

C. LAMB.

That beautiful love-letter could have come from no hands but Charles'. Other men would have been passionate or urgent or lofty or self-abasing or sentimental but Charles was gravely, almost wistfully tender. No lover ever lent to words the overtones of a deeper reverence for his beloved while preserving a manlier sense of his own dignity. Miss Kelly replied at once, by messenger; perhaps she felt unwilling to intrust so intimate a missive to the mails.

Henrietta Street, July 20th, 1819.

An early & deeply rooted attachment has fixed my heart on one from whom no worldly prospect can well induce me to withdraw it but while I thus *frankly* & decidedly decline your proposal, believe me, I am not insensible to the high honour which the preference of such a mind as yours confers upon me—let me, however, hope that all thought upon this subject will end with this letter, & that you will henceforth encourage no other sentiment towards me than esteem in my private character and a continuance of that approbation of my humble talents which you have already expressed so much & so often to my advantage and gratification.

Believe me I feel proud to acknowledge myself

Your obliged friend
F. M. KELLY.

Charles replied on the instant. He could not know that what kept Fanny Kelly from him was not her alleged attachment to another but fear of insanity, the Damoclean sword which menaced the Lambs. All he knew was that within the space from dawn to sunset his dream had taken shape only to perish and that at all costs he must play the man.

July 20th, 1819.

Dear Miss Kelly,—*Your injunctions shall be obeyed to a tittle.* I feel myself in a lackadaisical no-how-ish kind of a humour. I believe it is the rain, or something. I had thought to have written seriously, but I fancy I succeed best in epistles of mere fun; puns & *that* nonsense. You will be good friends with us, will you not? let what has past "break no bones" between us.[1] You will not refuse us them next time we send for them?

Yours very truly,
C. L.

Do you observe the delicacy of not signing my full name?
N.B. Do not paste that last letter of mine into your Book.

[1] Bones were ivory discs which entitled the holder to free admission to the theatre. Even in his dark hour Lamb could not resist a pun.

Within a fortnight of that day of broken hopes Charles saw Fanny Kelly in "The Hypocrite" and wrote thus of her in the *Examiner:* "She is in truth not framed to tease or torment even in jest, but to utter a hearty *Yes* or *No;* to yield or refuse assent with a noble sincerity. We have not the pleasure of being acquainted with her, [Charles loved these little ruses, especially where, as here, they let him play with edged tools to no one's hurt] but we have been told that she carries the same cordial manners into private life."

Charles Lamb was a miracle of tact. Who else could have gone on without embarrassment accepting Fanny Kelly's gifts of complimentary tickets, reviewing the plays in which she had leading roles, meeting her socially at friends' houses, and even welcoming her to his own?

To Charles, Thursday evenings at home were a delight, for within his low-ceiled sitting-room with its torn furniture, Hogarth engravings in black frames, and well-thumbed folios, a group of friends foregathered for whist and talk, capped with supper of cold meats and porter. The porter was good, the lamb and beef excellent (Mary saw to that), and the talk the most brilliant, diverse, and, on occasion, the most profound in London. It warmed Charles' heart and loosened his witty tongue to behold such a conjunction of stars ablaze within his tiny domestic firmament. There at various times shone Wordsworth, Coleridge, Hazlitt, Southey, Leigh Hunt, Basil Montagu, man of affairs, James Burney, retired old sea-dog, Kenney, the play-wright, Ayrton, the composer, and two brilliant figures of stageland, Liston and Kemble. Sometimes after the play—sweetest moment in many a month—Fanny Kelly joined the company, bringing a glow to Charles' fine eyes and a touch of color to his sallow cheeks. A sense of fragrance, of radiant vitality, came with her into the crowded old-fashioned rooms and when, the evening spent, she took her leave, they must have seemed to Charles as empty as his heart.

Charles' dream, denied fulfilment, retreated to the sanctuary of his fancy to be cherished there until, assuming a shadowy existence of its own, it took a new form, an exquisite substance in that perfect thing, "Dream Children," published in the *London Magazine* of January, 1822. Therein, you remember, Charles tells how his little ones crept about him, John and Alice, to hear the story of their grandmother Field and her great house with its ancient splendor. That done, they "prayed me to tell them some stories about their pretty dead mother. Then I told how for seven long years in hope sometimes, sometimes in despair, yet persisting ever, I courted the fair Alice W—n; and, as much as children could understand, I explained to them what coyness, and difficulty, and denial meant in maidens—when suddenly, turning to Alice, the soul of the first Alice looked out at her eyes with such a reality of re-presentment, that I became in doubt which of them stood there before me, or whose bright hair that was; and while I stood gazing, both the children gradually grew fainter to my view, receding, and still receding till nothing at last but two mournful features were seen in the uttermost distance, which, without speech, strangely impressed upon me the effects of speech. 'We are not of Alice, nor of thee, nor are we children at all. We are nothing; less than nothing, and dreams. We are only what might have been, and must wait upon the tedious shores of Lethe millions of ages before we have existence, and a name." To the world which read that was proved the charm of Lamb's prose and his graceful fancy, but to the woman he had offered his heart was revealed the pathos of an infinite longing.

Three years slipped by bringing Charles to his fiftieth birthday and his longed-for emancipation from the "d—d India House for ever." But physical decay followed in the train of that release, and the nine difficult years that remained took their unrelenting toll. A nervous breakdown aggravated by insomnia left him definitely an old man, thin to emaciation and with deeply furrowed cheeks. Restlessness plagued him, driving him from London to Enfield, from Enfield back to London, from London to Edmonton, weary of new faces, ever hungering for the beloved old ones. When he crept into the great city now and then it was to find the houses there like "empty caskets" and to return "to my hole like a cat in my corner."

The friendship between the Lambs and Fanny Kelly knew no change. In whatever company they were it was she to whom Charles' thoughts turned, to whose words he gave deferent attention, in whose presence care vanished and his flagging spirits revived. In his mood an irreverent jester to others, to her he was incurably reverent. When the Lambs turned their steps to suburban exile her visits followed them, always "dearly welcome" as became a friend laden with wanted gifts: gay warmth of heart, the brightness that illumined speech and presence, laughter that brought glad memories, news from the stage world Charles had always loved. Sometimes she regaled him with bits from her new parts or with high moments from old ones, achieving the transformations with an ease and swiftness that never failed to enchant him. Sometimes the simplest things diverted him as when, sitting on his little porch and yielding to his pleas, she pledged him in a bumper of punch, or when she brought to this incorrigible city lover an armful of wild flowers, or again when she confessed with a gravity whimsical as his own to a "passion" for little frogs.

But even Fanny Kelly's radiant presence could not light the oncoming darkness forever. Premonitions were not wanting. Lamb's brilliant and crotchety friend Hazlitt, three years his junior, with whom no one else could get on, died with only his son and Charles at his bedside, and in July, 1834, Coleridge followed, his "fifty years old friend without a dissension," leaving him desolate. Five months later, December 22, while out for a walk, Lamb suffered a severe fall. He was taken home and tenderly cared for, but the shadow of death was on him, his mind often wandered, and on the 27th, murmuring the names of old friends, he passed placidly as into sleep.

What memories, one wonders, of that strange tragi-comedy, his life, crossed Lamb's mind in those last days? What joys did he relive, what sorrows, what regrets? What place in those mysterious reveries did she keep who inspired—and shattered—his sweetest dreams?

Perhaps, with the clairvoyance of the dying, he counted the years, twenty of them, since she first occupied the place in his heart that no one else ever filled; perhaps he recalled that night at Covent Garden long ago when some madman whom no one knew fired a pistol at her, missing by a happy miracle but leaving his heart cold with a fear that even death could not bring again: it was then that she became the center of his dreams, giving a new dearness to his fireside, a fresh impulse to his pen, creating, in some curious way, a sense of music all about as if he heard the laughter of children, *his* children, and their footfalls in a nursery hallowed by her presence. . . . Did he tell himself, the dying Charles, that all that had remained a dream, producing nothing more substantial than a paper for the *London Magazine*—and an ache at his heart which he had hidden but never stilled? If so, he must have recalled in answer the blessed things she had brought him—friendship candid as a man's but tender as only a woman's could be, low laughter like music and a voice that awoke a strange joy in his heart, a sense —outlasting so much else—of May-time and the cheerful dawn. . . . What did the future hold for her, this "perfect woman, nobly planned" whose divine plain face other men had adored with no better fortune than his own? . . .

The year after Lamb's death Fanny Kelly retired from the stage and established a dramatic school which met with success for a long period. But fortune changed and ill days dawned though none ever set upon her defeated will or darkened courage. A great part of her savings was swept away and the years came on apace. Late in 1882, in response to a memorial signed by most of the leading actors, artists, and authors of the time, Gladstone awarded her a royal grant of £150. Within a week she died, aged ninety-two. By the terms of a will executed in 1830 her heir proved to be a middle-aged woman known as Mary Ellen Greville.

These things of course Lamb could not know. What he might have known but did not was that Fanny Kelly had entered into a liaison some nine years after his offer of marriage and was the mother of an only daughter who was five at the time of his death. The child grew up to be an untalented and unprepossessing spinster. She bore the name of Mary Ellen Greville.

The Vagaries of De Quincey

OF ALL THE ENGLISH ROMANTICS THE MOST ELUSIVE AND PARADOXI-cal personality was that of the little man with the childlike blue eyes set in a face yellow as old ivory and wrinkled as a Chinese idol's, the tale of whose adventures with opium made him famous overnight. He was compounded of abstract wisdom and concrete follies, of an iron will which could turn weak as water, of a logic which worked everywhere except in his personal world, of tenderness and sentiment which triumphed over everything but his vast —and unconscious—egocentrism.

De Quincey was chronically uneasy; he could always discover reasons (often convincing to himself alone) why he should go from hither to yon. At sixteen he was so full of misery (his mother called it rebelliousness) that he "eloped" from the Manchester Grammar School and betook himself to Wales where he tramped about for the summer and early fall. Suddenly, though without funds, he decided to push on to London, *terra incognita* to him, achieving there what he called "freedom" but living an aimless life, adrift among wretched lodging-houses, second-hand bookshops, and the haunts of money-lenders. As a happy climax to four purgatorial months there came a reconciliation with his family and, after an interlude of study, Oxford at eighteen. But again, at the very moment when his course was over and he faced his final examinations, he was on the wing and Oxford saw him no more.

In 1809 he took up his bachelor residence at Dove Cottage (succeeding the Wordsworths) but his restless spirit gave him no peace. We have his own word for it that he was away a quarter of the time and when back at home he was always planning to start off again "next week" or "next month." It was only when marriage and children imposed heavy financial burdens upon him, that at thirty-five for the first time in his life he had to think of settling down and earning a living.

He became perforce a creature of books and notes, a slave of the pen, but until within the shadow of the grave he never really settled down. He remained what he always had been, a human shuttle, running from Grasmere to Edinburgh, from Edinburgh to Grasmere, from Grasmere to London, from London to Grasmere, then back to London again, sometimes for weeks, sometimes for months, and once for two years. Then he turned his thoughts north again and shuttled back and forth between Grasmere and Edinburgh with excursions (and plentiful alarms) to Glasgow, and minor shuttlings between Edinburgh and its seven-mile-distant suburb Lasswade, varied by endless shuttling between hiding-places and lodgings within the capital itself. It was a perpetual and bewildering odyssey. It so bewildered that simple country-woman, his wife, that after a dozen years of an existence in which De Quincey flitted home only to flit away again, leaving her with scant or highly colored information as to his plans and whereabouts, she broke down under the strain of poverty, loneliness, and the care of seven children and threatened to commit suicide. With the aid of Dorothy Wordsworth the tragedy was averted but nothing could conceal the fact that a life bound up with De Quincey's could be neither serene nor secure for long.

For fundamentally, and quite apart from the effects of opium, De Quincey was helpless in practical affairs. His logic and good sense faltered in the world of realities. He dreamed of doing something great for the amelioration of mankind, of devising a system of political economy which would "expose the rottenness of all other systems" and "leave itself standing on their ruins." He wrote learnedly about the Roman Caesars and the destructive economic forces within their Empire, but with a five-pound note in his pocket he deemed himself penniless because forgetful of the fact that it was legal tender. Indeed he had no sense of money; he

lent when common prudence required him to save, he borrowed
with a seeming conviction that some dream he entertained would
surely come true and resolve all his debts. In 1825 his wife's
mother, Mrs. John Simpson, inherited an estate so deeply involved
that only desperate efforts could save it. Thereupon De Quincey
concocted a plan so worthy of his ingenuity and so perfect as a
device that, had it worked, the estate would not only have been
saved to the Simpsons but become an inheritance for the De
Quinceys in perpetuity. A mortgage was raised in the name of
John Simpson and the title of the estate transferred to De Quincey
who thus became a landed proprietor and possessor of £500 by a
stroke of the pen. Here was a legal miracle: everybody gained and
nobody lost—for the moment. He was so elated at achieving a
surcease of debt and a landed proprietorship that he boasted of
his "lustrous ambrosial bread" and the "celestial earthiness" of his
potatoes, and came down to reality only when he discovered the
tragic truth that semiannual interest had to be paid on both his
loan and the mortgage! Of course he had forgotten that, of course
he failed to meet the interest, of course the mortgage was fore-
closed, and of course when the estate went under the hammer it
found him completely oblivious: he had already taken refuge from
this financial debacle in the world of dreams.

Fate took revenge for such helplessness in practical affairs, as
she usually does, by plunging him into a financial purgatory which
began shortly after his marriage and ceased only a few years before
his death. He became a chronic borrower, getting advances from
his publishers on half-done articles or on proposed volumes, seeking loans from his sister, his Anglo-Indian uncle, and most of all
from his mother, with a persistency which kept that good lady's
purse light and her heart heavy. Like a weary swimmer in a stormy
sea whom each succeeding wave threatens to engulf, he struggled
on desperately, knowing a moment's relief as he rode the crest but
sick with despair as he descended into a new and deeper trough.

During his long residence in Scotland he was often so hard beset
that he fled to Holyrood, a legal sanctuary for "notorious bank-
rupts," where he and his fellow "Abbey lairds" lived like rabbits
in a warren. "Holyroodhouse" was not without its own laws. Its
denizens could incur debts while in residence, be sued for them
in the local Bailie's court, and be duly imprisoned as in the outer

world.[1] It goes without saying that De Quincey, about whom "debts sprang up like weeds in a garden," was constantly in the toils.

His sojourns in Holyrood cancelled no debts contracted outside and we can only conjecture by what miracle he now and then gained temporary immunity in the city. But in or out he had no peace. What with importunate landlords, grocers, booksellers, and servants, he was frequently "at the last gasp," and when even Holyrood grew too hot to hold him he took to skulking about Edinburgh. But an unfriendly Fate dogged his steps, relenting once for a little space to let the tormented man enjoy a blessed interlude with the three daughters of a deceased friend. There is something pathetic and naive about his account of it: "From all care, forethought, or expense, I was entirely liberated. I had the luxuries of elegant female society, polished conversation, music, and all those delicate attentions which flow so naturally and so delightfully from female hands. . . . I knew, I said, that it was *too* happy to last." And so it proved: the minions of the law discovered his retreat. "On Sunday night therefore I took a sorrowful leave of my three fair friends: and, except to *them,* I have confided the secret of my new abode to no human creature."

De Quincey's landladies were numerous not only because he rented one lodging after another to escape his creditors but because he often engaged several simultaneously! Usually he forgot to announce his departure or to pay his rent and expressed surprise and even indignation when one of his erstwhile rooms was held for him for weeks or months and payment eventually demanded. All his days he had a passion for making voluminous notes, and wherever he lodged he was soon buried under an accumulation so "vast, far above portability," that he was fain to turn the key on it and seek fresh quarters. These papers assumed in his eyes an importance so immense, so mysterious, that the threat of an irate landlady to seize them for rent threw him into a panic.

His sharpest torture from this source came about in a curious— though in De Quincey's Alice-in-Wonderland world a *natural*— way. One Sunday, when midnight caught him outside his Holy-

[1] They could cross the deadline into Edinburgh without danger of arrest between midnight Saturday and midnight Sunday. A moment's tardiness could be tragic!

rood sanctuary and so left him open to arrest, a kindly woman named Mrs. McIndoe gave him quarters "for the night"; typically, he clung to them three years. The inevitable happened. He accumulated a mass of notes, fell behind in his rent, and from within his barred door not only resisted all attempts to oust him but met all requests for payment with letters bristling with excuses, promises, pleas, and finally recriminations, all couched in stately and rhythmic phrases. Mr. McIndoe, though endowed with a less regal vocabulary and less exquisite ear, met the epistolary challenge in kind, and this extraordinary verbal duel between landlord and tenant under the same roof went on for nearly a year.

To De Quincey his landlord was "this very importunate person" who "has latterly betrayed a strong spirit of extortion," a spirit to which, he adds with a touch of the naive grandiloquence that lends color to the comedy, "I have neither wholly yielded, nor showed that resolute opposition which I should have done under more favourable circumstances." Mr. McIndoe's style, on his side, though indulging in an oblique approach, was not without dignity: "How can Mr. De Quincey suppose for one moment that he is to remain in his house to support an extravagant family while Mr. McIndoe is imputed with receiving all the money he requires? Mr. McIndoe therefore requests that Mr. De Quincey shall remove tonight for he is resolved that no further communication shall take place between them on this subject and that before 10 o'clock so as to prevent any unnecessary steps being taken." But despite this plea the stalemate continued, each contestant nursing a martyr complex and getting, for all we know, a subconscious thrill from crossing swords with a foeman worthy of his steel. However that may be, it seems that as surely as De Quincey feared to leave lest McIndoe seize his papers so surely McIndoe on his side feared to let him leave lest his chance of payment should go glimmering. As De Quincey put it, "This is terrific," but by some miracle (of whose nature, as usual with this odd little man, we are in the dark) the hard-pressed tenant escaped from the McIndoe domicile "without sacrificing his MSS" and fled to Glasgow.

For the next decade the shadow of McIndoe darkened his days. At last in 1855 (four years before his own demise) De Quincey recorded the death by drink of his erstwhile foe, naming him "that hideous man who for years has persecuted me with claims of the most fantastic kind," and plainly convinced that in his untoward end poetic justice had been vindicated.

But in Glasgow a similar drama was enacted, the Youilles playing the roles of the McIndoes, and De Quincey running so true to form that, after a sojourn there of twenty-seven months, he escaped to Edinburgh only by leaving behind a mass of books and papers as surety. Were the Youilles ever paid? On that as on various other points in De Quincey's life the record is silent.

Back in Edinburgh there were other creditors besides the McIndoes who did not slumber during the absence of their elusive creditor. Late one night two bailiffs got him in their clutches releasing him only when a friend intervened and paid the sum required. "Unideaed wretches!" cried the naive little man, "I tried them on every subject under heaven, but they did not seem to have a thought in their minds unconnected with their base and brutal profession!"

Of all nineteenth century men of letters De Quincey was most given to intricate sentences and *sesquipedalia verba*. Even his business notes were of the same pattern as his formal articles and he talked as he wrote, in rhythmic, sinuous clauses which seemed to have been formulated with infinite care in advance and unfolded as naturally as flowers. When a guest in John Wilson's house he gave the cook daily instructions as to his diet in such terms as these: "Owing to dyspepsia afflicting my system, and the possibility of any additional disarrangement of the stomach taking place, consequences incalculably distressing would arise, so much so indeed as to increase nervous irritation, and prevent me from attending to matters of overwhelming importance, if you do not remember to cut the mutton in a diagonal rather than in a longitudinal form." Threat the cook, her mouth agape and her patience gone, would remark, "Weel, I never heard the like o' that in a' my born days; the bodie has an awfu' sicht o' words." It was reported that a maidservant left the family alleging that she was "feared of Mr. De Quincey, he used such awfu'-like language" and that another declared, "Ah, Mr. De Quincey, you are a great man, a very great man; *no* body can understand you."

He had a habit of "dropping in" on friends for an hour's chat and of remaining weeks on end. Curious things always happened. He would lock himself in his room for days, directing the maid to leave his meals at his door but frequently forgetting to touch them. He would let the water overflow his wash-bowl while he stood gazing at the impending catastrophe paralysed and perplexed, unable to turn off the faucet. If his host gave a dinner in his honor the diminutive guest (in neat but threadbare clothes whose component parts failed to match) might be discovered sidling up to a fellow-guest just introduced, raising his childlike blue eyes to his face, and in the softest of tones inquiring, "Dr. N——, can you lend me tuppence"? Or his host might come upon him in an unguarded moment busily scrubbing whatever bank-notes he possessed or vigorously polishing his coins in an outburst of impatience with dirt. Once De Quincey found in his bedroom an array of half-empty medicine bottles belonging to an earlier occupant, the sick brother of his host. Emily De Quincey told the story long after: "My father, left alone, began to examine them. . . . Surely, he thought to himself, it would be hard if one of these mixtures did not suit him. Surely no one would grudge him the heel-taps of a lot of old medicine bottles. Having read and marked the labels, he forthwith proceeded to inwardly digest the contents of the bottles. Soon, however, his conscience began to prick him. Had he not taken a great liberty? Perhaps his host wished to try their effect upon himself, or his wife did. Perhaps they were to be kept as a tender reminiscence of the absent brother. The next morning he descended to the breakfast-table, and made his apologies to his host for having abused his hospitality." His apology, to his astonishment, was greeted with a burst of laughter which ceased however at the thought of the possible dire consequences of his act. But De Quincey allayed all fears. The medicines, he announced gravely, had had a very beneficial effect!

Like all denizens of a dream-world of their own making De Quincey was a hero-worshiper of what he would call "the purest water." Twice he flung himself at the feet of idols; twice he discovered that the feet were of clay; twice, with an air of cool detachment, he took revenge for his disillusionment.

As early as 1802 he was quoting from Wordsworth ("I only in all Europe") and the next year, obeying an impulse, he wrote the poet a letter. After remarking upon "the transcendency of his genius" which "makes all applause fall beneath it," he "humbly sues" for his friendship and concludes by declaring that he is so "full of admiration" for his "mental excellence" and of "reverential love" for his "moral character" that he is ready "to sacrifice even his life" to promote the poet's "interest and happiness." That was pretty strong even for a romantic lad of seventeen, but Wordsworth, sensing his sincerity, wrote a cordial reply and laid the foundation for a meeting which occurred four years later. The delay was due to De Quincey's overwhelming sense of deference mingled perhaps with a subconscious fear lest his idol prove somewhat less than divine. Twice he approached the poet's domicile visible across Coniston Lake in its setting of yew trees; twice, overcome by panic, he turned and departed. When, finally, in the company of Mrs. Coleridge, he stood at the threshold of that sacred portal, he was aghast at the thought "that this little cottage was tenanted by that man whom, of all the men from the beginning of time, I most fervently desired to see." He trembled as "never before or since at the approaching presence of any creature that is born of woman. . . . I heard a step, a voice, and, like a flash of lightning, I saw the figure emerge of a tallish man, who held out his hand, and saluted me with the most cordial expressions of welcome."

Four years after this first meeting, De Quincey, at Wordsworth's invitation, was installed as one of the family, while Dorothy Wordsworth described the "sweetness in his looks, especially about the eyes, which soon overcame the oddness of your first feeling at the sight of so little a man." He remained there three months, then went to London to see Wordsworth's pamphlet *The Convention of Cintra* through the press, slaving away with an industry so meticulous, interspersed by delays so inopportune, that he began to get on the poet's nerves. Impatience crept into Wordsworth's letters and finally so irked De Quincey that he revealed vexation in his turn; and though all ended amicably with the publication of the pamphlet, a rift had appeared in the lute, the day of blind worship was over, and De Quincey's mind was no longer closed to the suspicion that his idol was not a superman.

For a time there was no overt breach. When Wordsworth gave up Dove Cottage for Allan Bank, he secured it for De Quincey as a permanent residence and it was Dorothy Wordsworth who saw to its proper furnishing. But De Quincey's irregular relations with the youthful Margaret Simpson, even though they culminated in marriage, offended the Wordsworths who showed their disapproval by holding socially aloof. Perhaps this disapproval was sharpened by the very intimacy which had long existed between De Quincey and the poet's household; perhaps De Quincey's resentment was deepened, paradoxically enough, by his own awareness of the injustice he had done to a girl ten years his junior. Outwardly relations continued amicable but the early bonds of affection and understanding were worn thin. The old intimacy was at an end. Of course De Quincey's critical sense was too fine to miss genius and all his life he proclaimed Wordsworth one of the greatest of English poets; but when in later days he publicly recorded his ten years' adoration of the great man, it must have been with a wry smile at the extravagant idealism of his youth.

To Coleridge scarcely less than to Wordsworth De Quincey bent his knee, first recognizing "the ray of a new morning" when he read "The Ancient Mariner" as an Oxford undergraduate. "I am in transports of love and admiration for him and begin to think him the greatest man that has ever appeared." He was eager to meet him, so eager that he thought of pursuing him to Malta but luckily restrained the impulse, and at last in 1807, a few months before encountering Wordsworth, he had his heart's desire. For three hours he listened to a mighty monologue, an "eloquent dissertation, certainly the most novel, the most finely illustrated, and traversing the most spacious fields of thought that it was possible to conceive." That same night Coleridge confessed himself an opium addict, a tragic example of what De Quincey might come to if he ever toyed with the drug. De Quincey kept his own indulgence secret, but was so moved by the "sad spectacle of a man whose majestic powers were already besieged by decay" and who was harassed by pecuniary difficulties, that he made the poet-philosopher an anonymous gift of £300 (perhaps $4000 in present-day value) from the patrimony which had come to him the preceding year, at twenty-one. It was typical of De Quincey to perform this impulsively generous act and of Coleridge to accept the gift as a *loan;* and it was part of the irony growing out of the character of each, that fourteen years later the donor was compelled to request the recipient for repayment, and that the recipient, shamefaced, was forced to confess himself unable to comply.

Meanwhile De Quincey the neophyte eagerly made himself useful to Coleridge, escorting his wife and children from Bristol to Keswick, cheering the melancholy poet-philosopher when in London, and securing him certain material for his lectures at the Royal Institution. On his side Coleridge, in a slough of despond from illness, opium, and his unhappy marriage, confessed to this friend of twenty-two his "moral cowardice of moral pain" and invited frank criticism "of anything I may submit to you." To become thus a confidant of the great Coleridge was a dazzling part for a hero-worshiping youth not yet out of college, and his quite human vanity found it sweet. But alas! Coleridge, whose critical sense for men as well as books was as acute as De Quincey's own, had found him out and was confiding to a friend that his worshiper and benefactor was "anxious yet dilatory, at once systematic and labyrinthine," whose "natural tediousness" might readily become "a great plague." When he adds that he once "saw an instance of Mr. De Quincey's marvellous slowness in writing a note to a pamphlet, the sum and meaning of which I had dictated in better and more orderly sentences in five minutes," we are amused not only to find one archprocrastinator impatient with another but to foresee their inevitable—and mutual—disillusionment.

Of the idol's discovery of the idolater's weaknesses De Quincey knew nothing but he was soon busy making such counter-discoveries of his own as carried him even deeper than Coleridge's self-revelations. He became convinced that Coleridge pretended to a richer knowledge than he actually possessed and that he was not above plagiarism. He felt resentment that Coleridge, whose equipment he deemed inferior to his own, should have come to be considered the authoritative exponent of German philosophy in England, and it gave him a pang of jealousy to see, in contrast with his own single-handed struggle against poverty, the generous aid so freely extended to this weakling. Finally he came to plume himself (in his role of Opium-Eater whose *Confessions* were a literary sensation) on triumphing over the drug to a degree which his rival addict lacked sufficient will to match. Thus in his recollections of Coleridge which appeared after the poet's death in 1834, he spoke of his "mysterious plagiarisms," his domestic unhappiness, and his personal weaknesses with a candor which infuriated the Wordsworths no less than the surviving Coleridges, and moved Southey to declare that De Quincey deserved a whipping. . . . Thus in coldness and resentment the glory of his twin idolatries died away.

Murders fascinated De Quincey. As a lad he devoured novels of mystery, murder, ghosts, and highwaymen, and in later life his interest in fiction never went much further. When editor of *The Westmorland Gazette* he often withheld important news to make room for murder trials or for killings unusually ghastly or mysterious, and many of his studies (such as *The Caesars*) reveal his preoccupation with deeds of blood. Paradoxically enough he was gentle and soft-spoken, almost sentimentally considerate of animals, children, and women, and a detester of violence in every form. Again, paradoxically, his only important work to fall within the category of humor is the series of papers which deal with his obsession, and treat selected instances gathered from history, literature, and current newspapers. The result was *Murder Considered as one of the Fine Arts,* of its kind a triumph of ironic humor, but at moments so grotesque, so sardonic, so macabre, that many readers, proclaiming it as mirthless as a death's-head, give it up in disgust.

For children this connoisseur in murder had an abiding reverence and an almost passionate tenderness. An egocentric to the core he looked back upon his own childhood with glances of tender sympathy, and painted a revealing picture of the unforgettable wounds which death can inflict on the hearts of children. The Wordsworth nursery fell in love with this diminutive young man with the soft voice and gentle ways who invented such captivating games and stories and who when absent wrote them delightful letters. His favorite was little Kate Wordsworth, a plain but fascinating child, whose "radiant spirit of joyousness" made him her slave. The news of her death at three reached him in London and was like a knife-thrust to his heart. "Ah pretty, pretty love," he wrote in agony, "would God I might have seen thy face and kissed thy dear lips again," and on his return to Grasmere he spent many a night at her grave.

De Quincey had eight children of his own; the oldest, William, was "the crown and glory" of his life whose death at eighteen was the bitterest blow Fate ever dealt him. From that hour (like Wordsworth on the loss of little Kate) De Quincey was numbered forever after among those "who weep in secret for the vanished faces of their household." He loved all his children tenderly, they found it a "dignity and delight" to sit up with him late, cutting the pages of his new books and enjoying the pictures, and it was their innocent faces greeting him when he awakened from the horror of his opium nightmares that moved him to tears.

A born romantic, De Quincey stood at the heart of his own universe. Though unaware that his primary interest in life was himself and ready to deny the charge—in sentences of rhythmic beauty and eloquence—he confessed the fact by his sins of omission. The literature of self-excuse, extensive though it is, offers nothing more ingeniously conceived, consistently maintained, meticulously argued, or pervertedly logical than his epistolary *apologia pro vitâ suâ*. He covered reams of paper with personal and dietary small-beer, enraged his publishers by sending them verbose excuses instead of promised articles, thought with bitter ingratitude of his dead mother whose resources he had tapped for years but whose business sense he resented, and was guilty of injustice to his children in ways that would have been ludicrous had they not been so nearly tragic.

While his debts kept him dodging about Edinburgh, "a man forbid," pursued by "the emissaries of his creditors," he kept contact with home through two of his children, Florence and Fred, not yet in their teens. At all hours of day and night they skulked about the purlieus of the city, awaiting the appearance of their elusive sire, until through long and unhappy association the backs of Canongate and George IV Bridge became nightmares haunted by fearful and mysterious footsteps. It was these children whom he charged to interview importunate beggars and report the findings on which he might give them aid more sadly needed at home; it was they he expected to throw the astute bailiffs who pursued him off the scent, and if they failed it was they whose carelessness he blamed. He would not disclose to them his next hiding-place, he declared, "for they have too little presence of mind and too little discretion."

His amazing failure to sense the tragedy of all this is ironically darkened by his sentimental sympathy for the troubles of various women, often bibulous, deceitful, or dishonest, who crossed his path. He persistently declined receipts for rent paid—a precaution urged by bitter experience—as "contrary to his principles where a lady was concerned," refused a lower rate offered by one landlady because she was "a woman of excellent heart who had met with serious misfortunes," although his own family faced starvation at the time, and, to cap the climax, he guaranteed another's payment to her landlord of four years' back rent. Long afterwards his daughter Florence, recalling these incredible follies, excused him only on the ground that opium and debt had driven him temporarily insane.

But it all came to an end at last. When marriage and death had scattered his other children De Quincey's competent daughter Emily remained to be his housekeeper, fiscal secretary, and good angel-at-large. His debts in all their intricacies were eventually settled, his finances efficiently managed, his home transformed into a pleasant asylum, where he could pack his study with books and such endless notes that the bath tub was permanently commandeered for the excess, and where his evenings could be made delightful with the music he loved.

All his friends passed on before him, Lamb, Coleridge, Southey, Wilson, and even the long-lived Wordsworth. The glittering stars of the later Romantic firmament, Byron, Shelley, and Keats, had risen and set long since; an entire new galaxy had come within men's ken, Carlyle, Newman, Macaulay, Ruskin, Dickens, and Thackeray, compared to whom the withered little Opium-Eater seemed like a relic of a mighty but ancient day, another Tithonus, denied youth but cheating death.

In his last illness he was "wonderfully sweet and gentle," the word "love" was often on his lips, and his mind, wandering, seemed to know in some remote but gracious place the faces of those long dead who had been dear to him in life. After a night of heavy sleep he lifted his arms and called "Sister," perhaps to her whose death had left him desolate in childhood, and as dawn broke he, too, passed into the Morning. It was the 8th of December, 1859.

Hazlitt's Dual Fate

IN THE LITTLE BURIAL GROUND OF ST. ANNE'S, SOHO, STANDS A modest stone to the memory of the man whom Lamb loved, Stevenson worshiped as a master, and Saintsbury proclaimed the greatest of English critics. It bears the inscription:

> On the northern side of this ground lie the remains of
> William Hazlitt, Painter, Critic, Essayist,
> Born at Maidstone, April 10, 1778,
> Died at Soho, September 18, 1830.

With typical and passionate intensity Hazlitt craved two things. One of these was granted in a measure so rich that few men of his day equaled him; the other was dangled before his eager eyes like a glittering toy before a child, but each time he clutched it, as the sweetest prize of life, it turned to ashes in his hands.

If Frustration claim its Goddess no less than Achievement, the twain must have met at Hazlitt's cradle and covenanted, as handmaids of Fate, to share his life between them. The Goddess of Achievement granted him the literary gift, the joy of the things on which it fed (books, pictures, plays, the "face of nature," the foibles and talents of men), and recognition as a writer of genius. The Goddess of Frustration denied him the joy of social intercourse, abiding friendships, and, as the crown of his desires, the blessedness which love brings, the peace of the fireside, the dear delights of home.

The sister Goddesses, the one benignant, the other malign, must have met again at his death-bed, for poetic justice would have it so. The dying Hazlitt weighed the fruitage of his years, his successes against his failures, the gift granted against the gift denied, and put to himself the tacit questions: "How shall I appraise my life, as a blessing or a curse, as success or failure, as misery or happiness?" The figures in the darkening chamber who kept silent vigil, his son and Charles Lamb, heard his answer and recorded it for posterity.

Hazlitt's father, the Reverend William Hazlitt, was a nonconformist minister of Irish birth, who met Ben Franklin, was moved to sympathy for the "rebellious" colonists, emigrated to America (where he lectured at what is now the University of Pennsylvania), and established the first Unitarian Church in Boston, returning to England after three years to accept a living at Wem. William, then aged nine, was destined for the ministry but forsook the idea after two years' study, and settled down at home to what must have seemed a drone's existence, doing nothing more gainful than devouring books, scribbling endlessly, and taking twenty-mile hikes across the country. What he thought of himself during this period he recorded in after years: "I was dumb, inarticulate, like a worm by the roadside."

One day a plump young man of twenty-five with superb brow, full red lips, small nose, and unaggressive chin called at the Hazlitt parsonage and William met him. That meeting transformed Hazlitt's life. The stranger was Samuel Taylor Coleridge, preacher for the nonce, soon to write "The Ancient Mariner" and enter upon his amazing literary career, who became to Hazlitt, in that magic hour and the glorious ones that followed, guide, philosopher, friend, and idol. It was he who let the light in upon Hazlitt's darkness; in answer the chrysalis struggled into freedom and spread its glittering wings to the sun. Hazlitt never forgot what he owed to Coleridge and in after years immortalized his gratitude in one of the finest essays ever written, "My First Acquaintance with Poets."

Hazlitt did not find himself at once. He took up painting but abandoned it for philosophy, turned next to social science, then to biography, and even devised a grammar for the use of schools. Finally in desperation—for he now had a wife and child to support

—he "threw himself upon London" and like Johnson before and Dickens after him became a parliamentary reporter. With this as a start he turned to dramatic criticism. Then, broadening his field, he wrote original articles which attracted attention by their sparkling incisive style and independent judgment, and won him a hearing in the *Champion,* the *Times,* and Leigh Hunt's *Examiner.* He ventured upon a lecture course on Shakespeare, was encouraged by the applause of the discriminating to publish the series in book form, and feeling firmly established at last, proceeded to pour out a stream of essays on men, books, pictures, plays, and a thousand-and-one fascinating things which ceased only with his death. "I have written no commonplace," he once said, proudly, "nor a line that licks the dust," and Stevenson, his avowed disciple, wrote, "We moderns think ourselves pretty fine but what one of us can write like Hazlitt?"

It was his custom to rise late and immediately address himself to the essay in hand. Clad in bed-gown and slippers and fortified by French rolls and countless cups of strong tea he worked steadily till four in the afternoon. So perfectly disciplined was his mind that each sentence moved steadily forward, carrying his thought with it and pulsing with life. There were no hesitancies, ambiguities, circumlocutions; no spineless clauses, no padding. From under his pen the long white sheets emerged clean and errorless, ready for the printer.

Everything he had encountered in his early and enormous reading was ripe for use in his perfectly ordered memory, for it had been assimilated in the years when it was the food of endless reflection. He was a master of prose whose essays were eagerly read and generously paid for, not because they were objects of editorial favoritism but because they were of the stuff of genius.

His benign Divinity made good her promises: Hazlitt became one of the great literary figures of his day.

But Hazlitt's malign Goddess had not forgotten him. Oversensitive, suspicious, hot-tempered, and sharp-tongued, he went to extremes of candor and was surprised and embittered at his victims' resentment. One by one he fell out with his friends, Coleridge, Wordsworth, Southey, and even for a time the amiable Lamb. He flaunted his political views and aired his pet antagonisms on all occasions, proclaimed England's archenemy, Napoleon, "the saviour of Europe," and brought down on his head in return a storm of abuse from Tory periodicals which assailed him as "an acknowledged scamp" and a "fetid, blear-eyed pug."

Hazlitt was no coward and he gave as good as he received. But the abuse of his foes and the alienation of his friends embittered his loneliness and sharpened his craving for the one thing he thought necessary to make him happy. What that was we are startlingly reminded in his essays by revelations of a longing for affection almost too poignant to be borne. Is it possible that this man, so self-sufficient, should "all his life have wanted one thing and wanting that have wanted everything?" Is it this same Hazlitt, so engrossed in things of the mind, who writes: "My soul has remained in its original bondage, dark, obscure, with longings infinite and unsatisfied; my heart, shut up in the prison-house of this rude clay, has never found nor will it ever find, a heart to speak to"? I have, he confesses, "wasted my life in one long sigh" for a glimpse of "a gentle face turned gently upon mine." Therein lay his tragedy. To make this clear we must consider his first marriage.

Sarah Stoddart was a sentimental young woman who liked to see a fresh suitor at her feet each season, but was sure to discover when it came to the point that her feelings were not seriously engaged. These adventures had in her eyes the twofold merit of flattering her vanity while leaving her zest for further conquests unimpaired. Miss Stoddart shared her confidences with Charles and Mary Lamb, with the result that the romantic old maid and the whimsical old bachelor decided to make a match between the impressionable Miss Stoddart and the shy William Hazlitt. In May, 1810, the two were married, undisturbed by any premonition of the outcome.

The Hazlitts withdrew to a small property owned by the bride at Winterslow (on the edge of Salisbury Plain) whose name was later to be given to one of Hazlitt's finest volumes. This was Hazlitt's year of groping but the following one saw him established in London and beginning his career as a man of letters. From the first his beneficent Goddess smiled; tragically, as if in derision, her malign Sister countered with a frown. Success came but love vanished.

Hazlitt was cruelly disillusioned. He had always idealized love, "raising and magnifying its sweet power" until it seemed like a desecration for any but those "in whom his godhead shone outwardly to enter his court. This was my notion once," he wrote bitterly, "but it was one of the errors of my youth." He had dreamed of a love that would make golden amends for his vain struggles and hopes deferred, and would bestow upon him, dark, reticent, passionate, as he was, intellectual comradeship, affection, and sympathy born of understanding. In return he had expected to dedicate himself to love's service with the noble abandon of a Bayard to the claims of chivalry.

His awakening was tragic. He found himself bound to a selfish, unimaginative woman who was utterly unable to stimulate his mind, share his thoughts, or arouse his best impulses. He had "ventured into the courts of Love," to use his own phrase, only to find himself "rejected"; Shame and Disappointment awaited him in what he had believed to be the dwelling-place of Joy. In the wake of disillusionment came disgust and revolt, and by the end of twelve years of uncongenial married life they had swept him far from his moorings. Domestic peace was impossible and the Hazlitts separated.

In the late summer of 1820 Hazlitt took lodgings in a boarding-house presided over by a Mrs. Walker, a tailor's wife whose daughter, Sarah, buxom and pretty, acted as maid. It was not long before Sarah made the discovery that the slender, high-strung gentleman who wrote things (sometimes on long white sheets and occasionally on the walls) was in his room during the hours when the other lodgers were away at work. Casual good mornings soon became daily talks and friendliness warmed to intimacy, until the measure of Hazlitt's happiness was the length and frequency of Sarah Walker's visits. He began to watch for her coming as a lonely sleepless prisoner watches for the first ray of dawn. He told her of his writings, read her brilliant excerpts, and "beheld in the gentle face turned gently upon his" a sympathy and comprehension such as he had sought so long and so vainly. His hopes revived. Love, it seemed, was not to deny him her smiles forever. Gazing upon Sarah Walker he cried, "It is not too late if that face, pure, modest, downcast, tender, with angel sweetness gladdens the prospect of the future."

Love transformed him. "A purple light hovers round my head.

The flowers of Hope and Joy spring up in my mind." He burned with such new energy and fresh ambition that he resolved at all costs to insure the permanent presence of this radiant being by his side, to make certain that this Egeria, his comfort and his inspiration, should never forsake him.

His method of severing his marital ties reveals the psychology of the man in a flash. Seeking out his wife, he disclosed his infatuation for Sarah Walker and begged her to help him to a divorce. What Mrs. Hazlitt thought does not matter now. What matters is that she acceded to her husband's request, and as a divorce under English law was virtually impossible, agreed to advance his cause by securing a domicile in Edinburgh, the contemporary Reno. A kind of intoxication animated Hazlitt. He arranged everything, the journey of his wife and himself to Scotland, the required sojourn there, the services of attorneys, the submission of data, the untangling of legal red tape, and, intellectually alert as ever, the essays and lectures to which he intended to devote his months of exile from London—and Sarah Walker.

When at last the final bonds were legally cut and Mrs. Hazlitt was once more as a stranger, Hazlitt rushed back to London in a fever of longing. Now that the barriers were down, he could domesticate his divinity, could lead Egeria to his fireside, and in her radiant presence recover the joy which his first marriage had left so desolatingly unfulfilled. He stood, however, all unwittingly, on the threshold of a bitter awakening. He had forgotten his malign Goddess but she had not forgotten him. On the contrary, she had already played him false and ironically enough had made him the instrument of his own undoing. To any eyes but his Sarah Walker would have seemed what she actually was, pretty but only in a commonplace way, ill-educated, self-seeking, and hopelessly dull. It was his own yearning that deemed her desirable, his incurable romanticism that so fatally transformed the chambermaid into a nymph endowed with intelligence, beauty, and the power to inspire. During his absence in Scotland she had written him occasional letters, concealing, however, two facts of cardinal importance: she found it impossible to exist on the intellectual plane which was his familiar habitat and which he thought to share with her, and she discovered in an adorer of her own class satisfactions neither too remote nor too unrealistic for her taste.

Ignorant of this and fancying her feelings to be as passionate as his own, Hazlitt expected to be welcomed with open arms and radiant looks. When to his amazement he found his erstwhile divinity "cold and sullen," he flung discretion to the winds and stormed about the shabby Walker *ménage* white with rage and disappointment, bitterly accusing Sarah of betraying him. With the passing of that mood he made a pitiful effort to reawaken what he supposed to be the girl's former affection, but finding that futile he yielded himself to an engulfing self-pity which submerged for a time every vestige of restraint and good sense.

Abandoning the Walker house he sought lodgings elsewhere, only to find himself pouring the wretched tale of his infatuation and "betrayal" into the ear of every boarding-house mistress he interviewed, and at last, as a climax to folly, he retailed the ill-starred episode in a little book entitled *Liber Amoris, or the New Pygmalion*. What a shame it was ever written! Generations have snickered over it as a boarding-house idyl written by a great man in an hour of madness. And so it is, and for that very reason deserves something less ignoble than scorn. When all is said, the pity and tragedy of Hazlitt's madness are the pity and tragedy of his heartbreak at having for the second time sought Eden and found a desert.

Eventually Hazlitt got to his feet again and carried on. Things which he always cared for were mercifully still his, and books, nature, pictures, and the theatre became again for a time at least "the Ultima Thule of his wandering desires." But while they supplied him material for brilliant, vivid, and thought-provoking essays, readily marketed, the inner fires of the man were not quenched and the "one thing he wanted to make him happy" still lured and plagued him. The years were swift, the shadows lengthening, his health becoming dubious, and as he looked over his shoulder at life he named it "a contract of pleasure unfulfilled, a promise of happiness rescinded." Lonely, isolated, the prey of tantalizing memories, he still craved someone to convert the bitter of his days to sweet, to share his counsels, and to praise his work. Was his heart to be like a withered garden shaking its dry stalks in the wind? Was Frustration to vanquish him after all?

While traveling in a stage-coach one day in the spring of 1824 Hazlitt chanced to meet a lady about whom little is known even

now. She was a widow named Isabella Bridgwater, a "very pleasant
and lady-like person," who had read Hazlitt's work and admired
it greatly. It was not Hazlitt's vanity nor Mrs. Bridgwater's £300
a year that led him to his third venture within domains forbid,
but his thirst for the cup already twice dashed from his lips.
Hazlitt no longer expected the kind of affection which once could
have uplifted him to kinship with the stars (the hour for that had
passed), but a tamer, less fiery emotion, in which the place of
ecstasy was taken by sympathy, understanding, and serene faith.
A brief courtship was begun, followed by marriage and, in the
autumn, a thirteen months' sojourn on the continent.

That was a happy interlude. The malign Goddess seemed to be
slumbering or even to have rescinded her curse. The Hazlitts
returned to London, and during the following months Mrs. Hazlitt's good qualities and the improvement in her husband's looks
and temper were subjects of comment among their friends. At
last, in the autumn of his life, Hazlitt appeared to be happy, and
affection and serenity dwelt at his hearth. The impossible had
happened!

Suddenly, however, and from an undreamed of quarter, the
blow fell. For a long time Hazlitt had nourished the thought of
writing a monumental life of his idol Napoleon, and on resolving
to make a start, he set out for Paris in search of fresh material
accompanied by his wife and his sixteen year old son. Young
Hazlitt, who was the only living child of the union with Sarah
Stoddart and who had been at school in England during his
father's most difficult years, no sooner learned the details of his
mother's story than he became her partisan and harbored bitter
resentment against the woman he deemed an interloper. Exactly
what happened in the weeks that followed is not known, but there
is good reason to believe that the lad's animosity made the situation impossible, that Mrs. Hazlitt felt obliged to offer her husband a final choice between her society and his son's, and that
as a result she left him forever. Thus ended his last bid for happiness. For the third time "the one thing necessary" was denied him;
the Goddess of Frustration overwhelmed him in defeat. Embittered, humiliated, but stoically silent, Hazlitt returned to England,
burying himself in his work and raising his hand against her no
more.

He completed his *Napoleon* but his days were numbered. A chronic disorder of the stomach laid him low and he weakened steadily. His benign Goddess, however, did not forsake him: when plays became impossible because he could no longer leave his room, he still found solace in books, pictures, and essay writing. Propped up with pillows, he continued to wield his pen within the shadow of death with all his old-time brilliancy and incisiveness, publishing in the *New Monthly Magazine* for August, 1830, one of the finest—as it is one of the most pathetic—things he ever wrote, "The Sick Chamber." He begins: "What a difference between this subject and my last [the theatre]! Yet from the crowded theatre to the sick chamber, from the noise, the glare, the keen delight, to the loneliness, the darkness, the dulness, and the pain there is but one step." Poor Hazlitt! The texture of his life, the warp and woof of all his years of manhood, are implied in that sentence.

With that last essay Hazlitt's wasted fingers laid aside his pen forever.

Beside his bed two figures kept vigil, his son and Charles Lamb. It was they who recorded his answer to Destiny given as the dying man weighed the bitter of his years against the sweet, achievement against frustration, the victories of the intellect against the defeats of the heart. His verdict? "Well," he said, "I have had a happy life." Those were his last words.

Jane Carlyle, Recording Angel

WHEN THOMAS CARLYLE WAS TWENTY-FIVE YEARS OLD HE MET, AS everybody knows, a piquant, *chic* little lady of nineteen named Jane Baillie Welsh. Her black ringlets, bright eyes, brilliant smile, and keen wit ensnared the none too susceptible Thomas at the very outset. Jane was the daughter of a physician, Thomas the son of a stone mason. In the eyes of Jane Welsh this raw-boned youth with the tousled brown hair, fighting chin, and Scotch burr on his tongue, was socially her inferior and she let him know it. For five years the affair was on the knees of the Gods and then Jane capitulated, willingly enough, even in the face of her mother's coldness and her relatives' disapproval. She had come to consider Carlyle a genius and may have believed that her own literary gift would flourish in the sunlight of his; maybe too she dreamed of the day when London would be at his feet (and hers) and she would preside over a *salon* that would dazzle all eyes. In that high hour Jane Baillie Welsh would be brilliantly justified in the person of "the incomparable Mrs. Carlyle."

It was Stevenson who voiced the discovery that to marry was to domesticate the Recording Angel, and in Thomas Carlyle's personal experience that was to prove as gospel. Thomas loved Jane's radiant eyes and her caustic tongue (when turned on others) but he had no intention in the world of trying to write merely "popular" books (considering that as "selling himself to the Devil") or of seeking any road to fame—much as he craved it—

except the one of his own choosing, dolorous though that might
be. He gave up Edinburgh for a farm at Craigenputtock, spending
seven years there, reading mightily, taking long walks, sinking
into frequent silences, writing essays, and wrestling valiantly with
what was to be his masterpiece, *Sartor Resartus*. Jane hated those
years and came to detest the memory of them, even after she and
Thomas, giving up Craigenputtock, adventured upon London,
determined to stake everything on one stroke. The two years
that followed taxed his industry and her Scotch frugality, but out
of his incessant grumbling and travail of body, mind, and spirit
came the *French Revolution* and fame.

After this brilliant and successful assault on the chief citadel of
literary Britain, Carlyle ascended into the high places of renown
and authority whence he delivered Jovian utterances as became a
"prophet" of his generation. The incense was heaped high at his
shrine. He was an honored guest at the tables of the aristocracy;
his celebrity in America sent streams of "undaunted Yankees" to
his door; Emerson treated him with the deference due an oracle;
when he opened his lips at a dinner party all but the boldest fell
silent. To his house at No. 5 Cheyne Row, Chelsea, came the
great *literati* of his day; Browning, Tennyson, Dickens, and
Thackeray were happy to be named his friends; such men as
Ruskin and Froude were proud to be called his disciples; and
such famous foreigners as the French Cavaignac and the Italian
Mazzini paid him the homage due to one of the wisest of his day.
Carlyle had come into his own. Verily here was a "prophet"
indeed.

In one pair of eyes however Thomas Carlyle did not cease to
be a mere man. On one pair of ears his evening-long monologues
palled. In one mind his megaphonic rhetoric, his threats of
Tophet, and his entire arsenal of "unutterabilities" inspired only
partial conviction and no terror. The gaze of one observer remained undazzled and declined to regard Thomas's Scotch home-
spun as the mantle of Elijah. In a word Thomas was not a hero
to Jane.

The Recording Angel at No. 5 Cheyne Row had a keen eye,
a biting tongue, and a voluminous correspondence. What she
did, how she cleaned house "with a great washing of blankets,"
why she discharged a maid, what visitors descended upon her

husband, how devastatingly she suffered from neuralgia and
Thomas from dyspepsia, what a famous poet looked like, are
only a few of the intimate matters which fill letters so brilliant,
vivid, and witty that they challenge even those of the incomparable Lady Mary Montagu. In them Jane glances at Thomas
frequently, sometimes in writing to certain of her intimates,
sometimes in letters to him written with a saucy directness that
must have been at once his bane and his delight. The result is
perfect: he is brought before us in a series of close-ups that make
him more real than a dozen biographies.

Among the qualities which Carlyle ascribed to heroic men was
the power to keep silent. "Silence is golden," he announced in
Sartor Resartus; "it is, indeed, of eternity." But in personal practice he scorned it, driving Jane frantic by interminable monologues to visitors while she vainly tried to get in a word on her
own account. On one occasion she broke in, got the reins into
her own hands, and raced on breathlessly about the mysteries of
making bread. At first Thomas was perplexed, then impatient.
"My dear," he interrupted at last, "what can Mr. X. possibly
care about bread making?" "Well," retorted Jane, "you've gone
on for two hours on the Irish question; why shouldn't I have a
word about what interests *me?*"

Thomas never maintained silence on the innumerable occasions when the servants roused his ire, and his invectives never
failed to be masterly and colorful. Like most men when ill, he
aided his recovery by grumbling mightily and quite forgot his
own aphorism that "silence was of eternity." One lovely autumn
Jane's restful days at Lady Sandwich's Lodge in Windsor Forest
are wrecked by lumbago which came, she writes, "not into my
back but into Mr. C's; which made the difference so far as the
whole comfort of my life was concerned! For it was the very first
day of being here that Mr. C. saw fit to spread his pocket-handker-
chief on the grass, just after a heavy shower, and sit down on it!
for an hour and more in spite of all my remonstrances!! The
lumbago following in the course of nature, there hasn't been a
day that I felt sure of staying over the next, and of not being
snatched away, like Proserpine, as I was from the Grange last
winter! For what avail the 'beauties of nature,' the 'ease with

dignity' of a great house, even the Hero Worship accorded one, against the lumbago? Nothing, it would seem! less than nothing! Lumbago, my dear . . . admits of but one consolation—of but one happiness! viz.: perfect liberty to be as ugly and stupid and disagreeable as ever one likes! And that consolation, that happiness, that liberty, reserves itself for the domestic hearth!"

Mazzini said it all when he shrewdly observed that Thomas "loved silence somewhat platonically," and Jane found the witticism too clever to keep to herself. She passed it on to sympathetic friends and to Thomas himself who probably chuckled over it— but failed to mend his ways.

Writing was an agony to Carlyle as it was to Newman. In whatever book he was engaged on he "lives, moves, and has his being," says Jane, adding dolefully: "Oh dear me, if all book writers took up the business as he does, fidgeting and flurrying about all the while like a hen in the distraction of laying its first egg, and writing down every word as with his heart's blood—what a world of printed nonsense would be spared to a long-suffering public!"

After the lull which followed the completion of one work Thomas betook him to distant parts for a rest, to return in due time and begin to amass new and ominous piles of books, pamphlets, maps, and ancient engravings. His writhings and groanings begin again. Jane knows the symptoms. She writes: "For my husband, he is as usual, never healthy, never absolutely ill; protesting against 'things in general' with the old emphasis; with an increased vehemence just at present, being in the agonies of getting under way with another book. He has had it in his head for a good while to write a *Life of Cromwell,* and has been sitting for months back in a mass of great dingy folios, the very look of which is like to give me locked-jaw."

Carlyle's immersion in his *Cromwell* does not give Jane "locked-jaw" but so bad an attack of nerves that she devoutly wishes it were "at the bottom of *something* where I might hear less about it. . . . Carlyle manages to bring it up, in season and out of season, till I begin to weary of him (the Protector), great man though he was. But as everything comes to an end with patience, he will probably get himself written at last, and printed, and published;

and then my husband will return to a consciousness of his daily life, and I shall have peace from the turmoil of the Commonwealth."

While in the throes of composition ("getting delivered of my black electricities and consuming fires," Carlyle called it) he required silence from every other thing, animate and inanimate, in the immediate neighborhood. Howling dogs, "crowing, cackling, shrieking roosters," screaming parrots, and girls playing the piano drove him to despair—and to plugging his ears with cotton. He indited epistles to the neighbors, couched (by a miraculous exercise of self-command) in diplomatic language, pleading for noiseless mornings at least. The result, alack! was an imperfect realization of his hopes, whereupon he "informed heaven and earth in a peremptory manner that 'there he could neither think nor live.' " Soon he made a discovery: "The roof on the house could be made all that a living author of irritable nerves could desire: silent as a tomb, lighted from above." The idea appealed to Thomas, and Jane, who had put the finishing touches to the house only a fortnight before, writes despairingly: "I find myself in the thick of a new 'mess': the carpets, which I had nailed down so well with my own hands, tumbled up again, dirt, lime, whitewash, oil, paint, hard at work as before, and a prospect of new cleanings, new sewings, new arrangements stretching away into eternity for anything I see!" As for Thomas: "At the sight of the uproar he had raised he was all but wringing his hands and tearing his hair." Jane was exhausted to tears but virtuously "held her peace as an example to her husband." At length order was restored; plumbers, plasterers, carpenters, masons, and paper-hangers departed, and "this new hubbub" was over. "But when my husband proceeded to occupy his new study, he found that devil a bit he could write in it any more than beside the piano, 'it was all so strange to him'! . . . He has been ever since shifting around from one room to another, like a sort of domestic wandering Jew!" Jane does not conceal her grievance; she has worked like a slave— and for nothing. "The hands of me are blackened and coarsified," she wails, and what with "discomfort and Cinderella hours" she is "physically ill." But she will have her revenge: "I shall get my hands kept clean and put into mitts for a time as soon as I have patched together a carpet for the new bedroom—*and will lie on the sofa, by heaven, for two weeks and read French novels!"*

Carlyle was given to peppering his pages with vague but high-sounding terms which his worshipers invested with infinite meaning but at which the iconoclastic Jane could on occasion shrug derisively. She writes Miss Barnes: "Pray come to tea with me tomorrow evening at seven, if my husband's particular friends 'the Destinies' *alias* 'the Upper Powers,' *alias* 'the immortal Gods' (your father says you read Mr. C., so you will understand me), don't interfere to keep you away." When in bantering mood Jane holds up to mirth the oddities of Thomas, she refers to him as "His Wisdom," and when she expects him home, she vows she will lock him up from inopportune visitors until (shades of *Sartor Resartus!*) they two have had "a quiet, comfortable talk about Time and Space."

Usually for a period in the summer the Carlyles got away from London, but only after much "dubiety" (as Thomas would say) on his part as to whether he would go at all, and *whither,* and *when,* while, perhaps, he keeps his portmanteau half packed for weeks during his frantic "hithering and thithering," with Jane's plans waiting perforce on his. Sometimes Jane accompanies him and on other occasions she seizes the blessed opportunity for a separate holiday. But at a word from Carlyle that he is returning to No. 5 Cheyne Row, Jane packs up and rushes back before him to clean and air the house and put everything to rights. Readjustment provided problems of its own. "Figure this: (Scene—a room where everything is enveloped in dark London fog. For air to breathe, a sort of liquid soot! Breakfast on the table—'adulterated water'!) Mr. C. at one end of the table, looking remarkably bilious; Mrs. C. at the other, looking half dead! Mr. C. 'My dear, I have to inform you that my bed is full of bugs, or fleas, or some sort of animals that crawl over me all night.' "

Jane was always at his beck and call but sometimes failed to be amiable about it. She became through the years a kind of shock-absorber, standing between him and the stupidities of servants, the inconveniences of unwanted callers (particularly Yankee ones), the demands of jury duty, and even the mistakes of the tax-assessors. Naturally enough Thomas took alarm at the remotest prospect of her leaving him alone, and if she managed that unusual feat she was certain to have her holiday spoiled. Once she executed a master-stroke. Her servants were used to the routine of the house and the ways of its master, her friend Geraldine Jewsbury was taking a holiday, and Jane, trying the experiment of leaving Thomas alone, accompanied her. The two women stayed at Ramsgate, "one of the most accessible seaside places," says Jane, "where I was within call, as it were, if anything went wrong at home." Woe worth the day! "If Mr. C. were like other men," she writes, "he might be left to the care [of the servants] without fear of consequences. But he is much more like a spoiled baby than like other men. . . . The letter that came from him every morning was like the letter of a Babe in the Wood, who would be found buried with dead leaves by the robins if I didn't look to it." So back Jane goes to Cheyne Row and the disconsolate Thomas, nursing the hope that she may slip away again in a few days for another fortnight. "But I found him so out of sorts on my return that I gave it up, with inward protest and appeal to posterity."

It must be recorded, in the face of this, that Jane is not always so adverse from returning home or Carlyle so helpless without her. One of his end-of-the-summer letters must have recounted unusual goings-on by the sedate Thomas for it elicited the following from Jane, restored to amiability by a rest, *sola:* "Oh, my dear, my dear! you give me the idea of a sensible Christian man making himself a spinning dervish. Oh, 'depend upon't, the slower thou ridest, the faster thou'lt get,' etc. These dinings 'before sunset,' teas, 'about ten'—don't I know what comes of all that, and that what comes of it is 'eventually,' 'rale mental agony in your inside'? hardly to be assuaged by blue pill and castor oil. . . . If I hadn't been coming home at any rate, your last letter would have determined me to come, just to put a spoke in your wheel. . . . If you hadn't had a counter-pull on you in the direction of order, and regularity, and moderation, and all that stupid sort of thing, where would you have been by this time? Tell me that!"

Carlyle's accounts are not always on the wrong side of the ledger. When Jane is forty-one he astonishes her with a birthday gift, the first but not the last she receives. "Only think," she writes, "of my husband having given me a little present! he who never

attends to such nonsense as birthdays, and who dislikes nothing
in the world so much as going into a shop to buy anything, even
his own trousers and coats; so that, to the consternation of cockney
tailors, I am obliged to go about them. Well, he actually risked
himself in a jeweller's shop, and bought me a nice smelling bottle!
I cannot tell you how *wae* his little gift made me, as well as glad;
it was the first thing of the kind he ever gave me in his life. In
great matters he is always kind and considerate; but these little
attentions, which we women attach so much importance to, he
was never in the habit of rendering to anyone."

Carlyle is tender in his bungling way and, when Jane suffers
from one of her devastating headaches, he does his best at the
impossible task of alleviating the pain. He rests "a heavy hand
on the top of my head and keeps it there in perfect silence for
several seconds, so that, although I could scream with nervous
agony, I sit like a martyr, smiling with joy at such a proof of profound pity from him." One day, while out walking, she wrenched
her foot badly and "once at home on a chair, I couldn't touch the
ground with it on any account. Mr. C. had to carry me to bed,
at the imminent risk of knocking my head off against the lintels.
So I wouldn't be carried by him anymore, my head being of more
consequence to me than my foot." Poor Thomas, literary lion and
prophet of his age! In the role of nurse he becomes a very bungler
like the meanest of his sex!

To Carlyle the world was made up largely of blockheads, and
he was not disposed to make an exception even of the men and
women who attended his lectures. One of his friends fears he may
say "Gentlemen and Ladies" instead of "Ladies and Gentlemen,"
but Jane, who knows him best, is in terror lest he blurt out,
"Fool-creatures come here for diversion." When Carlyle survived
his first two appearances Jane bubbled over in a letter to his old
mother, to whom "Tom" was as the apple of her eye: "Our second
lecture 'transpired' yesterday, and with surprising success—liter-
ally surprising—for he was imputing the profound attention with
which the audience listened to an awful sympathising expectation
on their part of a momentary break-down, when all at once they
broke into loud plaudits, and he thought they must have gone
clean out of their wits! . . . The short and the long of it was, he
had neglected to take a pill the day before, had neglected to get

himself a ride and was out of spirits at the beginning: even I, who consider myself an unprejudiced judge, did not think he was talking his best, or anything like his best; the 'splendids'; 'devilish fines,' 'most trues,' and all that which I heard heartily ejaculated on all sides, showed that it was a sort of mercy in him to come with his bowels in a state of derangement, since, if his faculties had had full play, the people must have been all sent home in a state of excitement bordering on frenzy!"

The precise nature of the pill which Jane, between satire and comedy, records Thomas as having forgotten to take (so fortunately for his audience!) is not recorded, but Jane, with whom the household aches and ailments were a subject of endless mirth, is more explicit about one, which, thanks to Thomas's "false refinement," was "introduced into her interior by mistake." She writes: "I had been wretchedly bilious for some days and sent him to Alsop's for my blue pills—he also being in the practice of getting pills there—of *five grains*—which he swallows from time to time 'in werra desperation' and in fellowship with an ocean of castor oil. The pills came and I swallowed one; merely wondering why they had sent me only *three* instead of my customary *dozen*— but ten minutes after, when I became deadly sick, I understood at once how it was." Carlyle frankly admitted it was quite likely there had been a mistake. "When he went into the shop a gentleman was with Alsop and he *did not like* to say *send the blue pills* for Mrs. Carlyle, but said instead, send the blue pills *for our house*. Alsop, of course, had preferred the *masculine gender* as grammatically bound to do—and . . . all yesterday I was sick enough as you may fancy." And how about the culprit, whose "false delicacy" caused the mischief? Says Jane, with icy irony: "Carlyle comforted himself and tried to comfort me, by suggesting that 'it might possibly do me *a great deal of good* in the long run!' "

Perfect Peace and Jane have scarcely a bowing acquaintance. Something new comes up perilously often to raise (in Jane's phrase) "considerable of a row." Once Thomas fails to find a pamphlet, whereupon he storms about it as "one of those books seen for a moment—laid out of his hand, and then swept *irrecoverably* into the general chaos of this house." (Of course Jane discovers it after a moment's search, just where he had left it.)

Once it is a stream of visitors, some of whom stay to tea and then on till nearly midnight, while Thomas is ill and she has to entertain alone and complete a harrowing day by "putting a mustard blister on the man's throat and putting him to bed." "The man," she records later, surprised her by waking up in the morning "miraculously mended." Again "the man" (Thomas, of course) has shirts to be mended, "accursed flannel ones," Jane declares; and then Helen, first adjudged a jewel of a servant, betrays bibulous proclivities which decline to be exorcised until at last "the man" (who figures this time as "the head of the mystic school") aided by "a delicate female" (none other than Jane) succeeds in getting "the maddened creature" to bed at three in the morning!

Jane was the original Carlylean; it was she who first detected Carlyle's amazing gifts and pronounced his masterpiece *Sartor* a "work of genius," an opinion shared by only three other people in the world, the American, Emerson, the Irishman, Father O'Shea, and—Thomas himself. When Carlyle later was famous and flattered poor Jane grew jealous, the "female" devotees of the "prophet" especially arousing her ire. "You cannot fancy," she writes, "what way he is making with the fair intellects! There is Harriet Martineau presents him with her ear-trumpet with a pretty blushing air of coquetry, which would almost convince me out of belief of her identity! And Mrs. Pierce Butler bolts in upon his studies, out of the atmosphere as it were, in riding-habit, cap and whip (but no shadow of a horse, only a carriage, the whip, I suppose, being to whip the cushions with, for the purpose of keeping her hand in practice)—my inexperienced Scotch domestic remaining entirely in a nonplus whether she had let in 'a leddy or a gentleman'! And then there is a young American beauty—such a beauty! 'snow and rose-bloom' throughout, not as to clothes merely, but complexion also; large and soft, and without one idea, you would say, to rub upon another! And this charming creature publicly declares herself his 'ardent admirer' and I heard her with my own ears call out quite passionately at parting with him, 'Oh, Mr. Carlyle, I want to see you to talk a long long time about— *Sartor!! Sartor*, of all things in this world! What could such a young lady have got to say about *Sartor*, can you imagine? And Mrs. Marsh, the moving authoress of the *Old Man's Tales*, reads *Sartor* when she is ill in bed; from which one thing at least may be clearly inferred, that her illness is not of the head. In short, my dear friend, the irregular author of *Sartor* appears to me at this moment in a perilous position, inasmuch as (with the innocence of a sucking dove to outward appearance) he is leading honorable women, not a few, entirely off their feet. And who can say he will keep his own? [Poor Jane! You had no cause—save an imaginary one—to be anxious on that score!] After all, in sober earnest, is it not curious that my husband's writings should be only completely understood and adequately appreciated by women and mad people? I do not very well know what to infer from that fact."

Jane's memory tricked her for the moment. Earlier in the same letter she had drawn her inference—an unflattering one to the unconscious Thomas in all truth: "Let no woman who values peace of soul dream of marrying an author." In many another letter Jane was to make a similar observation, and the whole world has had opportunity to read what she intended solely for the sympathetic eyes of a few intimates. The world has taken all this and much else "in sober earnest," has believed Jane desperately unhappy, and has proceeded to place the blame. One half lays it on Thomas's shoulders, the other half on Jane's own. The "tertium quid" refuses to take sides, sees ample proof that each loved the other devotedly, knows that intense personalities inevitably clash, and, when all is said, agrees with Jane's own shrewd observation: "When one has married a man of genius, one must take the consequences."

A Gallant Lady

OUR ULTRACONSERVATIVES ARE WONT TO LAMENT THAT FEMININE aggressiveness is a present-day evil. They speak with hushed reverence and a deep regret of the times when "feminism" was unknown and women were unspoiled by cocktails, politics, profanity, and ideas. But alas for the eulogists of the good old days! There have always been aggressive women: witness Zenobia, Hypatia, Cleopatra (no pretty *ingénue,* says Ferrero, but big, homely, and mannish), Queen Elizabeth, Catherine the Second, Lady Hester Stanhope, and—model of efficiency—Florence Nightingale, who upset the comfortable myth that Victorian women were too "delicate" to face reality. And then there was Lady Mary Wortley Montagu.

Born in 1689, Lady Mary Pierrepont was the daughter of an Earl, and although she loved Ovid, talked politics, and was witty enough to be a Celt, she upset the calculations of most philosophers by being amazingly pretty as well. Her father, Lord Dorchester, who was a member of the famous Kit-Cat Club, sent for her one night (she was only eight) to convince his boon companions that she was clever and beautiful enough to be entered among their toasts. In the midst of that brilliant assemblage the little maid was quite at home, now caressed by a statesman, now petted by a poet, now in the arms of a great soldier, all of whom swore that in wit and beauty she was the peer of any lady in England.

Of course Lady Mary was vain, but less of her beauty than of her wit and her knowledge of Greek, Latin, French, and Italian. With a not undiplomatic deference she used to credit Mr. Edward Wortley Montagu, whom she afterwards married, with being her chief intellectual guide, though Wortley's intellectual distinction resided solely in the fact that Steele dedicated to him the second volume of the *Tatler*. Mentally ponderous and methodical, Montagu somehow attracted the clever bluestocking (he was thirty-one and she twenty) who cultivated his sister Anne as the readiest means of opening a breach in his heart. But alack! the good Anne died prematurely and Lady Mary, deprived of this friendly screen, was fain to write her future lord direct. With disarming candor she says, "Give me leave to say that I know how to make a man of sense happy," adding, "I don't enjoin you to burn this letter. I know you will. 'Tis the first I ever writ to one of your sex and," artfully tantalizing, "shall be the last. . . . I resolve against all correspondence of the kind; my resolutions are seldom made and never broken." This particular resolution was more honored in the breach than the observance, for Lady Mary was to achieve fame as one of the most voluminous—and most clever—letter writers of all time.

Despite this Shavian love-making Montagu's heart continued to hang fire. When at last he put the question, new difficulties arose whereupon he decided to drop the whole affair. He reckoned, however, without Lady Mary. Realizing that if one way to a man's heart lies through his stomach, a more direct route lies through his vanity, she wrote to assure him of her approval of his decision, concluding, *"I shall never forget you have a better understanding than myself."* Could diplomacy at its highest say more? What wonder that Montagu's resolution wavered! Verily here was an Egeria whose discernment he might well requite with his name! At this, the psychological moment, Fate intervened and, by evoking a suitor whom Lord Dorchester would constrain her to wed, slipped Lady Mary a trump-card. The difficulty was allowed to become a spur to the sluggish Montagu's intent, an elopement was arranged (one wonders if Mary first suggested it!) and by the time Montagu had caught his breath it all was over and he had been installed for life as Lady Mary's husband.

Not for naught was Lady Mary (in Sentimental Tommy's

phrase) a "magerful" woman. She had aggressiveness, an ambition, and a sense of worldly values which (to old-fashioned notions) would have belonged more properly to her spouse. When in the country with her infant son, her eager thoughts follow her husband to London and she urges him to seek a place in the Cabinet, concluding with a shrewd practicality worthy of Lord Chesterfield: "No modest man ever did or ever will make his fortune. . . . The Ministry is like a play at Court; there's a little door to get in, and a great crowd without, shoving and thrusting who shall be foremost. . . . Your modest man stands behind in the crowd, is shoved about by everybody, his clothes tore, almost squeezed to death, and sees a thousand get in before him that don't make so good a figure as himself." Montagu was wise enough to have the courage of his wife's convictions and was justified by an appointment as Commissioner of the Treasury.

At Court the beautiful and piquant Mary attracted the eye of the King, but his phlegmatic Germanized Court soon proved insufferably dull, and it was a joyous day (August, 1716) when she set out with her husband on a diplomatic mission to Turkey. Her journey thither was slow but fascinating. She found the Germans quarrelling endlessly over the question of precedence and the title of Excellency, and gaily recounted the story of "two coaches, meeting in a narrow street at night; the ladies in them not being able to adjust the ceremonial of which should go back, sat there with equal gallantry till two in the morning." When she is regaled in winter with oranges and "perfectly delicious" bananas she discovers that the Germans owe them to "lengthening their summer" by the use of stoves. "This leads one to consider our obstinacy in shaking with cold six months in the year, rather than make use of stoves, which are certainly one of the greatest conveniences of life. . . . If ever I return, in defiance of the fashion, you shall certainly see one in my chamber."

Lady Mary's letters from Turkey to her friends were so keen, witty, and illuminating that copies went the rounds from one fortunate reader to another and won her a reputation among the *élite* of England and eventually of western Europe. She was so impressed by the Turkish bath that she sent home a lengthy (and piquant) account of it, and so intrigued by the Turkish garb for women that she donned it, bifurcated skirts and all. With a typical—and not unmalicious—desire to chasten the complacency of her countrymen, she exposed their ignorance of Turkish life and made unflattering comparisons between their manners and morals and those of the East.

But the most important letter Lady Mary wrote from Turkey— or anywhere else—was the one which contained the following passage: "The smallpox, so fatal and so general among us, is here entirely harmless by the invention of *ingrafting,* which is the term they give it. . . . An old woman comes with a nutshell full of the matter of the best sort of smallpox . . . immediately rips open the vein that you offer her with a large needle (which gives you no more pain than a common scratch), and puts into the vein as much venom as can lie upon the head of her needle." The Turks were not without vanity of their own for many "choose to have the inoculations in the legs, or that part of the arm that is concealed."

Lady Mary's interest was not merely casual. Smallpox in England was a scourge from which she had herself suffered in 1715, with some damage to a fine complexion and to eyes which Pope and Gay had considered beautiful. When on the recall of Montagu (April, 1718) she arrived in England with her son, her eight months' old daughter, and her disgruntled lord, she took immediate measures to introduce "ingrafting." Objections came to a head at once and what Horace Walpole called "the great preservative" was assailed as "a heathen rite" in the very quarters where the readiest support should have been offered. But Lady Mary was not cast down. On the contrary this was her hour and she knew it. To be in the public eye (except for a shameful or ridiculous reason), to sponsor a great cause, to know herself a generation ahead of her time—all this flattered her justifiable vanity, and as she hated ignorance and stupidity, she met the opposition they inspired with gay confidence. She carried on her humane mission with such faith and energy that three victories of ascending importance presaged her eventual triumph: first, a handful of progressive physicians espoused the cause; next, successful experiments were made on seven condemned criminals; and finally, royalty itself submitted its blue veins to the ingrafting needle. Thereupon the erstwhile "heathen rite," now blessed by fashion, was hailed as lengthening life—and saving complexions—and Lady Mary's struggle was over.

The twenty years of Lady Mary's stay in England after her return from Turkey had few dull moments. She was born for social life, loved parties, dinners, routs, and "almost perpetual concerts," had a keen ear for gossip and a ready tongue for relaying it, and found a delectable satisfaction in knowing that she awoke admiration in clever men and jealousy in commonplace women. Steele, Congreve, Sir Robert Walpole, Colonel Selwyn, and Pope openly admired her; the King welcomed her at court; she could "make" an affair by her presence or ruin it by her absence; not to have the entrée to her house was to confess oneself unknown. Such power was sweet but dangerous, as the worldly-wise lady knew well enough, but the sweetness was worth the danger. After all, to a philosophic mind (and Lady Mary regarded hers as a philosophic mind) jealousy was a compliment, rivalries were a protection against ennui, and in any case both were inevitable.

Lady Mary's wit was edged with Gallic malice. She thought too highly of it to let it grow dull in idleness, and her skilful use of it with tongue and pen (in screed, verse, and letter), while delighting her intimates, filled her actual victims with bitterness and her possible ones with apprehension. Thus the number of her social foes increased, eager to learn of flies in her ointment, hoping for the dawn of a day of reckoning.

There were flies in Lady Mary's ointment, chief of all her son. More than once Lady Mary has to record that "that young rake, my son, took to his heels t'other day" or that he is "gone knight-erranting, God knows where." Ironically enough his inclinations were away from smart society: on one occasion after a search of months he was discovered selling fish at Blackwall; on another, he turned up as a common sailor at Oporto; his crowning absurdity was to marry at twenty a woman of low birth and several years his senior. His escapades, his mother laments, make him "the talk of the whole nation," and so affect her temper that she seriously considers "crossing the water to try what effect a new heaven and a new earth will have upon my spirit." Not the least of her woes was the unkindness of Fate which bestowed the parental good looks on her incorrigible son rather than on her common-sensed daughter.

There were other flies in her ointment. The year 1720 offers a parallel to 1929. Speculation went mad; from prince to peasant every finger was in the South Sea pie. In it Sir Robert Walpole made a fortune and the Duke of Portland lost one. Even Pope received "tips" and passed them on to his intimates. Read this:

> To Lady Mary Montagu
> Madam,
>
> I was made acquainted, late last night, that I might depend upon it as a certain gain to buy the South Sea Stock at the present price, which will certainly rise in some weeks or less. I can be as sure of this as the nature of any such thing will allow, from the first and best hands, and therefore have despatched the bearer with all speed to you.
>
> I am sincerely, dear Madam,
>
> > Your most faithful servant,
> > A. Pope.

Lady Mary, not immune to the general infection, took the "tips," won, lost, won, and lost again, carrying down with her in the inevitable crash a French admirer (and cocky little poetaster) named Rémond, whose meager funds she had, with generous indiscretion, taken to invest. Lady Mary's losses were heavy and she lived in constant dread lest her husband discover them. All this was bad enough, but M. Rémond capped the desolating climax by losing his head and threatening to "expose" her unless she immediately made good his losses. For a moment she was panic-stricken. She did not resent piquant stories either as narrator or subject, but there was a limit, and she shuddered at open charges involving, however unfairly, her honesty and possibly even her virtue. Though dismayed she kept her head and, putting on a brave front, warned her persecutor not to dare show his face in London. "I solemnly swear that if all the credit or money that I have in the world can do it, either for friendship or hire, I shall not fail to have him used as he deserves." In the end her pluck scored a victory. Threats, cajolery, persuasion, and the surrender of such of Rémond's money as remained in her keeping, secured the return of her letters to him, induced his silence, and took him forever out of her life.

There was still another fly in Lady Mary's ointment. M. Rémond was not the only one among her adorers whose idolatry turned to hate. Her new foe, however, could not be bought off, cajoled, or intimidated, and his thrusts went to her heart like a dagger. Pope, extraordinary of mind and grotesque of body, had long affected the role of passionate admirer of Lady Mary, and on her return from Constantinople coaxed her and her husband to take a villa at Twickenham near his own. Both poet and blue-stocking were self-deceivers. She was flattered to be offered the homage of a great man of letters; he was flattered to be thought an intimate of a celebrated social leader. What turned their honey to gall? Nobody knows for certain, but the shrewdest explanation pictures the rickety little man in a hectic moment on his knees to the society queen, and the society queen moved to an outburst of mocking laughter at his ardor. That was enough, for Pope was as proud and as venomous as Lucifer. To him in his fury war was war, there were no rules, and a woman had no more rights than a Grub street dunce.

In meeting his attack Lady Mary was neither cowardly nor dull: she enlisted the aid of more than one pen as brilliant as her own and she had her witty say before the socially elect of London. But the warped little poet was too much for her. His piquant insinuations, his damaging allusions, his obscene personalities, half-veiled but unmistakable and expressed in dazzling couplets, became the talk of the town. Again and again he returned to the attack, transfixing "Sappho" (as he called her) with his poisoned shafts and leaving her social rivals—and victims—hysterical with delight. Lady Mary, though not oversensitive, must have winced under Pope's vitriolic thrusts, but outwardly, despite her anxieties and humiliations, she kept her morale unshaken, her verve un-dimmed, her mask of gay unconcern unlowered. She retained a frank delight in racy stories, retailed them with a show of her old spirit, and continued to write fascinating letters.

It is with peculiar gusto that she recounts the following incident in which we discover the ancestry of modern practitioners of the hunger-strike. At a certain "debate in the House of Lords it was unanimously resolved there should be no crowd of unnecessary auditors; consequently the fair sex were excluded and the gallery destined to the sole use of the House of Commons. Notwithstanding which determination, a tribe of Dames resolved to show on this occasion that neither men nor laws could resist them. . . . They presented themselves at the door at nine o'clock in the morning, where Sir William Saunderson respectfully informed them the Chancellor had made an order against their admittance. The Duchess of Queensbury, as head of the squadron, pished at the ill-breeding of a mere lawyer, and desired him to let them upstairs privately. After some modest refusals, he swore by G— he would not let them in. Her grace, with a noble warmth, answered, by G— they would come in in spite of the Chancellor and the whole House. This being reported, the Peers resolved to starve them out; an order was made that the doors should not be opened till they had raised their siege. These Amazons . . . stood there till five in the afternoon, without sustenance, every now and then playing volleys of thumps, kicks, and raps against the door. When the Lords were not to be conquered by this, the two Duchesses . . . commanded a dead silence of half an hour; and the Chancellor, who thought this a certain proof of their absence, gave order for the opening of the door; upon which they all rushed in, pushed aside their competitors, and placed themselves in the front rows of the gallery . . . and during the debate gave applause, and showed marks of dislike, not only by smiles and winks but noisy laughs and apparent contempts."

In the summer of 1739 Lady Mary abandoned England for the Continent, just why, nobody knows. Doubtless many things conspired to turn her thoughts to the relief of "strange faces, other minds." She was fifty years old and had seen death busy among her friends. Her husband, whom all the world knew to be her inferior in intelligence and feeling, took his revenge by studiously ignoring her.

Her daughter had first disregarded parental disapproval of her suitor, the Marquis of Bute, and then climaxed her undutiful behavior by eloping with him. Her son was likely to turn up at untoward moments and rejoice her foes by acting like a cad, a beast, or a fool. And then that little devil Pope, "the portentous cub who never forgave," whose eight years' malevolence had finally ceased, might at any moment slip his leash again. Is it surprising that the attractions of home, society, and England vanished?

Lady Mary's stay abroad extended over twenty years—almost the rest of her life. She spent some time at Venice, Rome, and Naples, at Genoa, Turin, and Avignon, and finally settled with some permanency at Lovere. It was during these two decades that she wrote the letters which comprise the greater part of her works, and as she was a cultivated and shrewd observer she had much to say and, blessed with leisure, took pains to say it well.

Some of her letters went to women friends, some to her husband, but most to her daughter, the Marchioness of Bute, whose indiscretion in marrying a future prime minister Lady Mary wisely learned to forgive. Like Mme. de Sévigné writing to her daughter—Lady Mary was never forgetful of the parallel—it was to Lady Bute that she wrote with most obvious satisfaction. "Keep my letters," she warned. "They will be as good as Mme. de Sévigné's forty years hence."

She met a score of notables abroad, among them the Old Pretender, the great soldier, Prince Eugene of Savoy, and Cardinal Guerini, whose request for a copy of her works (she had never printed a line and felt he misunderstood her refusal) brought her near "crying for vexation." Horace Walpole came upon her in Florence and, detesting her as he did, wrote home about "her dress, her avarice, and her impudence," helping by this ill-natured chatter to win a hearing for such tid-bits as this, with which the not unamiable poet Gray regaled his friend, James Brown:

> I must tell you a little story about Lady Mary wch I heard lately. upon her travels (to save charges), she got a passage in the Mediterranean, on board a Man of War, I think it was Commodore Barnet. when he had landed her safe she told him, she knew she was not to offer him money, but intreated him to accept of a ring in memory of her, w^{ch} (as she pressed him) he accepted: it was a very large emerald. some time after, a friend of his taking notice of its beauty, he told him, how he came by it: the Man smiled, & desired him to shew it to a Jeweller. he did so; it was unset before him, and proved a Paste worth 40 Shillings.

Whatever Lady Mary's weaknesses she dazzled visitors with her talk, and for further diversion played whist at penny points and devoured boxfuls of novels sent from England by Lady Bute. The works of her cousin, Henry Fielding (who returned her admiration) she enjoyed keenly and she paid the anonymous *Roderick Random* the compliment of thinking it good enough to be his. Richardson, however, she "heartily despised" but, like Macaulay at a later day, she confessed to being "such an old fool as to weep over Clarissa Harlowe. . . . You will call all this trash, trumpery, etc.," she writes to her daughter, but adds wisely, "I thank God, I can find playthings for my age."

As she grew older neither tongue nor pen lost its edge or often failed to record wisdom. Thus when Lady Bute, worldly-wise at twenty-nine, fell to moralizing on the changes she had seen all about her since her girlhood, Lady Mary shrewdly replies: "I have never in all my various travels seen but two sorts of people, and those very like one another; I mean men and women, who always have been, and ever will be, the same. . . . I remember when I returned from Turkey, meeting with the same affectation of youth among my acquaintance that you now mention amongst yours, and I do not doubt but your daughter will find the same twenty years hence among hers."

Some of her observations cling to the memory. Of children she warns: "Breed them free from prejudices; those contracted in the nursery often influence the whole life after." "Ignorance is as much a fountain of vice as idleness, and indeed generally produces it." "No entertainment is so cheap as reading, nor any pleasure so lasting." And with a touch of pardonable acidity: "Valuable books are almost as rare as valuable men." Like Carlyle a century later she held human intelligence in low esteem. He considered ninety per cent. of the world blockheads; Lady Mary, somewhat more conservative, declared, "He and she fools certainly constitute three-fourths of my acquaintance."

Lady Mary's intellectual interests could never obscure her practicality. She "went in for" poultry, bees, and silkworms, managed her domestic matters shrewdly, and was able to boast that "all things prospered under her care." Happy in an augmented income she followed an almost conventual regularity of life, rising at six, busying herself about her garden and her farm in the morning, indulging in a siesta in the afternoon with whist or picquet later (usually with some friendly priests of the neighborhood), and in the cool of the evening enjoying a row along the river. As proof

that her practicality had a typically feminine side, she cajoled the
Governor of Lovere to act for her at an auction, and as "nobody
would bid against him" she secured a coveted old palace "at a
scandalous bargain."

In the course of her twenty years' absence on the continent Lady
Mary became in England less a reality than a tradition. That was
to be expected. But actually it was one of her points of distinction
that she refused to dwell in the past and found the present fascinating. She was no praiser of dead yesterdays and, instead of
lamenting that the times were out of joint, she congratulated her
granddaughter "on being born in an age so much enlightened."
For girls to be brought up so remote from life that, married at
twenty-five, "they are commonly as ignorant as they were at five,"
seemed tragically wrong. Nature, she insisted, did not place
women in "an inferior rank to men": they deserve an education
which should, she held, include arithmetic, history, geography,
philosophy, language, drawing, and sewing, of which last it is as
"scandalous to be ignorant" as for a man "not to know how to
use a sword." She constantly preached the worthy use of leisure
"especially for women," who otherwise "commonly fall into va-
pours or something worse." They should not be completely de-
pendent on their husbands but should have the right, within
reason, to live their own lives. Perhaps she was thinking of her
husband, now a sour old miser, who owed to her energy and ambition whatever career he had achieved. Doubtless it was the thought
of him, rather than any recollection of the advice of Walter Raleigh or of Sir John More, that moved her to write of matrimony:
"I will not say the virgin state is happier but it is undoubtedly
safer than any marriage. In a lottery, in which there are (at the
lowest computation) ten thousand blanks to a prize, it is the most
prudent choice not to venture." When she asserted that marriage
should be for a term of years with option of renewal—or, as she
wittily put it, "a repairing lease"—she was indulging a half-cynical
humor. In a serious mood toward the end of her days, she confessed
to envying the happiness of domestic life "where only true happiness exists."

It was not to her occasional cynicism but to her constant pluck
and good sense that Lady Mary owed the serenity of her Indian
Summer in Italy. At times, of course, she recalled as in a litany the

names of friends and foes who had passed into silence since her self-exile on the Continent, but on the whole her spirits were high and she tried to "maintain them by every art I can, being sensible of the terrible consequences of losing them."

It was only after her husband's death in England in 1761 (gossip, wrote Gray, fixed his wealth at between £800,000 and £1,000,000, an enormous sum for those days) that Lady Mary heeded the warnings of her threescore years and ten and decided to give up Italy for home. She returned to London, to be sneered at by Horry Walpole and to find herself a neglected relic of a vanished generation. But through it all she "kept her form." Disdainful of repining over past or present, she took a tiny furnished house in Hanover Square, entertaining such of the smart set as came out of respect or curiosity to see her, and occasionally gracing an assembly with her presence. Her mental vigor remained undimmed, her interest in public affairs lively, and, though her hands were tremulous, her letters to her friends were unceasing.

One secret she withheld from friends and family alike. It was a tragic secret but she had no wish to distress those she loved or to be the object of any one's pity. She was the victim of cancer. When it burst and her end was only a matter of days she wrote her last letter: it was to a friend in exile with whose political pardon she was much concerned, and it ended on a note too beautiful to be ignored, too sincere to be doubted: "My heart is always warm in your service."

On August 21, 1762, she passed away, unterrified by death, satisfied to have lived so long, a gallant lady to the end.

A Jacobean Chatterbox

IT IS NOT GIVEN TO EVERY MAN TO SEE A SCION OF ROYALTY AT CLOSE range, to recount his exploits when making love, and record how, forgetful of his royal dignity, he scaled a garden wall to catch a glimpse of the high-born lady of his choice. It happened in that land of Romance, Spain, and the city of many a cavalier's song, Madrid. The season, the summer; the year, 1623. That canniest of Scots, James I, was on the English throne, and his son, Charles, the handsome and luckless lad who was afterwards to lose his head in the Puritan Revolution, was in the market for a bride. The diplomatic wiseacres thought they had solved the problem; wherefore Charles, accompanied by the brilliant rake Buckingham, journeyed to Spain, and the negotiations for the hand of the Infanta were on.

In Madrid at the time was an Englishman of twenty-nine whose ears were always open for gossip and who retailed it to innumerable correspondents in the chattiest letters in the world. Little did the young Prince of Wales suspect that even the adoring glances which he cast upon the Infanta would be handed on to immortality by this observant chatterbox, James Howell. "I have seen the Prince," he tattles, "have his eyes immovably fixed upon the Infanta half an hour together in a thoughtful, speculative posture, which," continues the bachelor-philosopher gravely, "sure would needs be tedious, unless affection did sweeten it; it was no handsome comparison of Olivares, that he watched her as a cat doth a mouse. Not long since the Prince, understanding that the

Infanta was used to go some mornings to the Casa de Campo, a summer house the King hath on the other side of the river, to gather May dew, he did rise betimes and went thither. . . . [He was] let into the house and into the garden, but the Infanta was in the orchard, and there being a high partition wall between and the door doubly bolted, the Prince got on the top of the wall and sprang down a great height, and so made towards her; but she, spying him first of all the rest, gave a shriek, and ran back. The old marquis that was then her guardian came towards the Prince and fell on his knees, conjuring His Highness to retire, in regard he hazarded his head if he admitted any to her company. So the door was opened, and he came out under that wall over which he had got in." How that solemn old owl, King James, would have blinked his disapproval, had this tale of filial indiscretion met his eye! When Howell adds, "I have seen Prince Charles watch a long hour together in a close coach in the open street to see the Infanta as she went abroad," one might recall a homely observation of Olivares that a "watched kettle never boils" and understand why the match with the Infanta fell through. Even royalty must have squirmed under the inquisitive eye of Madrid— and James Howell.

One of a large Welsh family, Howell was born in 1594 and took his degree at Oxford at the age of nineteen. He then became steward in a glass manufactory, was later sent to study the business on the Continent, and passed through Holland, France, Spain, and Italy, acquiring the language of each country with surprising facility like his contemporary traveler Tobie Matthew. The warrant from the Council permitting him to travel forbade visits either to Rome or to St. Omar lest perchance the wiles of the Scarlet Woman should prove too much for his faith. This very contagion, however, greeted him on his return home in 1622, when he forsook business and was appointed tutor to the sons of the Catholic Lord Savage. Abandoning this post soon after, he remained for some years in touch with public affairs as secretary to men in high place, member of semi-diplomatic missions, parliamentarian, and, one suspects, man about town. He was a friend of the poet Carew, an intimate of Ben Jonson, and a regular correspondent of Sir Kenelm Digby and Lord Herbert of Cherbury. He knew the ill-fated Buckingham and the no less ill-fated Strafford and indeed seems to have had a genius for acquiring blue-blooded acquaintances—and for retailing gossip.

He tried his hand at verse, long since forgotten, and dabbled in politics to the extent of writing a political allegory and some tracts, an act of temerity which perhaps helped to make him a marked man. Marked he certainly was, though we know not whether for his debts or for his loyalty to King Charles, who no longer scaled garden walls for a glimpse of a Spanish beauty but, wed to a French Princess and seated on the throne of his fathers, found himself a storm-centre, betrayed by friends, hounded by enemies, driven to the wall, and forced to fight for his crown. The swelling storm caught our fascinating chatterbox in its vortex just as it caught Sir Tobie Matthew. But Sir Tobie fled the Kingdom in the nick of time while Howell was arrested, deprived of his private papers, and flung into the Fleet Prison. There, despite his various remonstrances to the autocratic Parliament, he was compelled to remain for eight years. For such a serene soul as Howell however

> Stone walls do not a prison make
> Nor iron bars a cage.

He refused to be crushed by ill fortune but found a refuge in composing numerous pamphlets (who bothers about them now?) and endless letters addressed to old friends, which are an abiding delight to later generations. They are not filled with importunities, or complaints against fate, or with details of the hardships of prison life, but with fascinating odds and ends picked up during joyous journeying on the Continent. Now he chatters about the rise of the Netherlands, now of the origin of the tobacco habit, now of the history of religions, and now about the Copernican system. Many of these missives were essays in miniature rather than letters, but he wrote them with unfailing zest, brightening them with countless human touches and good stories garnered in his travels—seventeenth century drummers' yarns which, if they point no moral, adorn many a good tale.

"A German gentleman," he tells us, "speaking one day to an Italian, said that the German tongue was the language of Paradise.

" 'Sure,' said the Italian (alluding to its roughness), 'then it was the tongue that God Almighty chid Adam in.'

" 'It may be so,' replied the German, 'but the devil tempted Eve in Italian before.' "

With even greater gusto, quite understandable in a bachelor, he relates the story of a henpecked husband who, when threatened by an apparition of the devil, declined to show concern "because," said he, "I have married his kinswoman." Who that loves Browning can forget that it is Howell who tells (in one of his delightful letters from the Fleet) the tale of the "pied-coated piper of Hamelen" and the bewitched children, which our honest chatterbox protests he would not relate, "were there not some ground of truth for it." Of course he was gullible—what would happen to the stock in trade of a chatterbox who wasn't? Yet who but a barren rascal would challenge such colorful discoveries as that perjurers in Bithynia betray themselves if they bathe in the waters of a certain river?

Like most bachelors he is fond of moralizing on matrimony and he essays now and then to admonish his intimates with the air of a Solomon. In such a role he writes to an old friend regarding his heir: "I have observed that he is too much given to his study and self society, especially to converse with dead men, I mean books. Were I worthy to give you advice, I could wish he were well married, and it may wean him from that bookish and thoughtful humour. Women were created for the comfort of men, and I have known that to some they have proved the best helleborum against melancholy." What Howell's own helleborum was—for he never married—we can only surmise; perhaps it was his unshakable complacency. One of his letters discusses the problem (unsettled until the advent of equal suffrage!), whether women are inferior to men. With a magnanimity far in advance of his sex Howell confesses: "I believe there are as many female saints in Heaven as male, unless you make me adhere to the opinion that women must be all masculine before they are capable to be made angels of." That was a shrewd thrust, James Howell, God save the mark!

It is when writing from prison in April, 1645, that Howell is moved to answer that question most flattering to a bachelor's vanity, why he does not marry. He will not wed for money, he avers, for while his purse is lean, yet "my genius prompts me that I was born under a planet not to die in a lazaretto." And he adds with tantalizing self-depreciation: "I have upon occasion of a sudden distemper, sometimes a madman, sometimes a fool, sometimes a melancholy old fellow to deal with: I mean myself, for I have the humours within me that belong to all three: therefore who will cast herself away upon such a one? Besides I came tumbling out into the world a poor cadet, a true cosmopolite, not born to land, lease, house or office. It is true I have purchased since a small spot of ground upon Parnassus which I hold in fee of the Muses, and I have endeavored to till it as well as I could though I confess it hath yielded me little fruit hitherto. And what woman would be so mad as to take that only for her jointure?"

In an earlier but no less delightful note he muses over various types of women with true bachelor detachment. "I confess," he writes solemnly, "such is the nature of love, and which is worse, the nature of women is such, that like shadows the more you follow them the faster they fly from you. It is all very well to lay siege to a beauty's heart, but," he adds, with that practical sense in which the cynical may discover the ultimate explanation of his bachelorhood, "if you cannot win the fort, retire handsomely, for there is as much honor to be won at a handsome retreat as at a hot onset, it being the difficultest piece of war."

Like us of today, he found his times sadly out of joint: "To take all the nations in a lump," he writes to the Earl of Dorset in 1646, "I think God Almighty hath a quarrel lately with all mankind and given the reins to the ill spirit to compass the whole earth, for within these twelve years there have been the strangest revolutions and horridest things happen, not only in Europe, but all the world over, that have befallen mankind, I dare boldly say, since Adam fell, in so short a revolution of time. It seems the whole earth is off the hinges." An apprehension which now, as then, does not go unshared.

Most of the letters written in the Fleet lack the spontaneity and zest of his earlier epistles. But they have the Howellian savor none the less and helped our irrepressible chatterbox to escape melancholia and writer's cramp.

Of course he was freed at last and of course he did the usual things: he dedicated a pamphlet to Cromwell, he heralded the Stuart restoration with loud rejoicings, and he begged the generous Charles II for a sinecure. What was not a matter of course was that he actually received a gift of £200 from the King (February, 1661), and an appointment at £100 a year as historiographer of England. The slings and arrows of outrageous fortune assailed him no more and the brief round of days which still remained brought him the contentment of deserved and slippered ease. Five years later he was dead, having left directions, genial egotist as he was, that a tomb should be erected over him duly adorned with a Latin inscription.

Today our favorite newspaper regales us at breakfast with the latest happenings at home and abroad gathered by highly paid specialists and spiced by pictures and intriguing head-lines. But the itching ear and eager eye of seventeenth century England had no such recourse. Lucky the friends of the indefatigable Howell, to whom were vouchsafed the choicest tidbits of news in a relation vivid, satisfying, deliciously intimate. Here is the story of the death of the handsome and dissolute Buckingham who had accompanied Prince Charles to Spain on his wooing and had wormed his way into the favor of two kings:

Upon Saturday last . . . the Duke did rise up in a well-disposed humour out of his bed, and cut a caper or two; and being ready, and having been under the barber's hands (where the murderer had thought to have done the deed, for he was leaning upon the window all the while), he went to breakfast, attended by a great company of commanders, where Monsieur Soubize came unto him, and whispered him in the ear that Rochelle was relieved; the Duke seemed to slight the news, which made some think that Soubize went away discontented. After breakfast the Duke going out, Colonel Fryer stept before him, and stopping him upon some business, one Lieutenant Felton being behind, made a thrust with a common tenpenny knife over Fryer's arm at the Duke, which lighted so fatally, that he slit his heart in two, leaving the knife sticking in the body. The Duke took out the knife and threw it away, and laying his hand on his sword, and drawing it half out, said, "The villain hath killed me" . . . so reeling against a chimney, he fell down dead. The Duchess being with child, hearing the noise below, came in her nightgears from her bedchamber, which was in an upper room, to a kind of rail, and thence beheld him weltering in his own blood. Felton had lost his hat in the crowd, wherein there was a paper sewed, wherein he declared that the reason which moved him to this act was no grudge of his own, though he had been far behind for his pay, and had been put by his captain's place twice, but in regard he thought the Duke an enemy to the State . . . therefore what he did was for the public good of his country. Yet he got clearly down, and so might have gone to his horse, which was tied to a hedge hard by; but he was so amazed that he missed his way, and so struck into the pastry, where, though the cry went that some Frenchman had done it, he, thinking the word was Felton, boldly confessed it was he that had done the deed, and so he was in their hands.

Jack Stamford would have run at him, but he was kept off by Mr. Nicholas; so being carried up to a tower, Captain Mince tore off his spurs, and asking how he durst attempt such an act, making him believe the Duke was not dead, he answered boldly that he knew he was dispatched, for it was not he but the hand of heaven that gave the stroke, and though his whole body have been covered over with armour of proof, he could not have avoided it. Captain Charles Price went post presently to the King four miles off, who being at prayers on his knees when it was told him, yet he never stirred, nor was he disturbed a whit till all Divine service was done.

This was the relation as far as my memory could bear, in my Lord of Rutland's letter, who willed me to remember him unto your ladyship, and tell you that he was going to comfort your niece (the duchess) as fast as he could. . . . So I humbly take my leave and rest your ladyship's most dutiful servant, J. H.

Fortunate Countess of Sunderland who got the news in this epistolary masterpiece! What could be finer than those intimate touches—the Duke on arising "cutting a caper or two"; the murderer leaning upon the window as he watches his victim under the barber's hands; the wounded favorite plucking the penknife from his heart and reeling against the chimney as he fell dead; the murderer in a daze missing his way; the King hearing the tragic news at prayers but maintaining an iron self-command.

It is not at all surprising that Thackeray loved James Howell. True he did not canonize him as he did Charles Lamb, but he kept the *Epistles* ever at his bedside with the genial egotists Elia and Montaigne, to bring balm to his midnight pillow. Verily, that were gallant company to keep; the genial James knew no courtlier when he was numbered among the quick.

Once he declared that he had "purchased a small spot of ground upon Parnassus" and "tilled it devotedly." But his efforts were vain. It was not in his verses but in his delectable letters that he has reaped a posthumous and rich reward.

A Forbear of Addison

THE COURT OF JAMES I, THE "WISEST FOOL IN CHRISTENDOM," WAS A hotbed of profligacy and dishonor. Scandalous intimacies were not only permitted but actually connived at, sacred things were made a mocking and a byword at midnight orgies, drunkenness among women as well as men went open and unrebuked, and the revelries at Whitehall became so gross as to evoke the fiery denunciation of Mrs. Hutchinson. The court was honeycombed with political as well as social vice; peculation, bribery, plots and counterplots were rife; and men who were untroubled by any sense of decency and who did not flinch from deeds of shame found it a short step from selling bishoprics, committing perjury, and destroying a woman's honor to the plotting of murder itself.

Whatever grace had cloaked the immoralities of Elizabeth's court was wanting to that of James, who was too mean-spirited to command the reverence which had surrounded the Tudors despite their faults. Conceited to the last degree, utterly lacking in personal dignity, coarse of speech, a buffoon and a pedant, a gabbler and a double-dealer, this canny, odd-looking son of the beautiful Mary Queen of Scots entrusted his personal judgment and the guidance of his councils to one favorite after another, and in no instance did he select for his dubious affection a man distinguished for character or intelligence. Beauty of person was the primary qualification; without that the smile of favor was never given.

One day in the year of grace 1606, at a tilting match, James

chanced to see a handsome blond youth suffer a fall which broke
his leg. His ready sympathies were excited. He instructed the
royal physician to attend the injured lad, kept in close touch
with him during convalescence, and celebrated his recovery by
making him a royal page. From that hour "Robin" Carr's fortunes
were assured. Though not conspicuous for either learning or
brains, his name and shapely person became all too well known
in the royal circle, where his influence steadily grew until he dictated virtually all court appointments. Not only was he handsome
but he could handle a horse dexterously, tell a good story, laugh
loudly at the King's jests and—item of high importance—he had
been born north of the Tweed, a stroke of luck which left him
with the northern burr still upon his tongue despite several
formative years in France.

The role of King's favorite was full of dangers. He was the
object of every courtier's jealousy and of countless cabals; his
lightest word was distorted; his character was blackened; his
motives were questioned; his most trifling acts were misconstrued;
his very jests were given a sinister import. All this was clear
enough to the new favorite and grew even more apparent as his
star ascended and Master Robin Carr became Viscount Rochester.
The incense of adulation was sweet in his nostrils but it did not
blind him to the fact that he had need of more than an equable
temper, charming manners, and striking good looks. What he
required was a secretary who would handle his correspondence
with intelligence and dispatch; keep an ear to the ground for the
mutterings of impending storms; estimate his master's acquaintances with unblinking eyes, and classify the vicious and the adroit,
the stupid and the usable, the jackals, the serpents, the foxes,
the doves. Besides, Master Secretary should be stimulating and
clever, should be a repository for my lord's secrets, both personal
and political, should be able to create the illusion of my lord's
intelligence and, whatever might betide, should be unfailingly
discreet. In this, his great need, the luck of Viscount Rochester,
Robin Carr that was, did not desert him. A man who seemed
perfectly fitted for the difficult part was ready to his hand.

Thomas Overbury, born in 1581, was a squire's son who had
made a brilliant course at Oxford and taken his degree at seventeen. For a time he had his residence in the Middle Temple, and

though he dabbled in the law his chief interests were in literature and public affairs. He made the Grand Tour, missing none of the elegance of France and Italy and seriously studying the political conditions he encountered. Polished, keen, with an admirable sense in political matters, Overbury gained a reputation as a wit, became an intimate of Ben Jonson, and, through the interest of Sir Robert Cecil, secured a footing at court.

Carr and Overbury were well met; the gifts of the one perfectly supplemented those of the other.

Overbury enjoyed his position immensely. If, as secretary of a King's favorite, he had certain duties to perform, he had numerous privileges as that favorite's friend; and the adulation bestowed on him, his conscious superiority (which he was at no pains to conceal), and the knowledge that he enjoyed the confidence of the most powerful subject in the kingdom, all added to the joy of living. Besides, he learned much that was socially piquant and politically vital from Rochester (who had it in turn from the King himself) and who did his Secretary the doubtful honor of making him the repository of dangerous secrets. Such knowledge tickled Overbury's vanity as in his turn it had tickled Rochester's, although to a mind as active as Overbury's it tended to sour his worldly wisdom into a premature cynicism. He saw, as few others had the opportunity to see, the double-dealing and hypocrisy of those that dwell in the houses of Kings, and he had glimpses of secret dishonor committed in high places and concealed by unblushing effrontery or dexterous bribery. He came to learn how far the Spanish, the French, and the Scottish factions at court dared to carry their intrigues, and what a precious set of rogues they were that surrounded James and played high stakes for the control of the kingdom. No doubt he smiled cynically as Rochester, detailing the amusements of the King's intimates, described a mock baptism administered by courtiers in vestment and stole, whose crowning jest was achieved when the "infant" in swaddling clothes and gorgeous mantle proved to be a suckling pig.

Among the most able—and shameless—of the professional courtiers of the time the Earl of Northampton was conspicuous. He had been rewarded with an earldom for abandoning the Catholic faith, and increasing years blunted neither his ambition nor his craft. As he cast about for a means of further advancing his fortunes he saw none so promising as an alliance with my lord of Rochester, and once this thought possessed him he hit upon a method of accomplishing it which was ripe for use and, though fraught with danger, offered the chance of complete success.

Northampton's grandniece, the beautiful Frances Howard, daughter of the Earl of Suffolk, had been brilliantly married at thirteen to the Earl of Essex, scarcely a year her senior, who had thereupon been packed off alone to the Continent to continue his education. The atmosphere of the court, heavy with corruption, was not the place in which so lightly guarded and precarious a virtue as the young bride's was likely to flourish; and when the crafty Northampton brought about the meeting between his niece, Milady of Essex, and the handsome royal favorite, Milady, though only eighteen, had already been stigmatized as "the Moabitish woman."

It required iron restraint to resist the beauty of Frances Howard, and Rochester was not a man of iron restraint. Besides, the girl unmistakably liked him and made little effort to conceal her feelings. Rochester, thus flattered, was swiftly responsive and in his ardor neither suspected that the shrewd Earl of Northampton had put the girl in his way nor dallied with the chilling thought that her husband might at any moment return from the Continent to claim her.

And what of young Thomas Overbury? How did he, keen and ironic, look upon this affair between Milady and his master, at which the court soon began to prick up its ears and open wide its eyes? At first he was amused, perhaps a bit cynically, and so far entered into the spirit of what he deemed a mere flirtation that he composed the letters and sonnets with which (bearing Rochester's name) the "assault" against Milady's heart was carried on. Gradually, however, as he came to realize that Rochester's interest in the Countess was ripening to infatuation, he took alarm.

Overbury was not heroic. He felt no moral revulsion at the liaison in which his master was involved. It was his fortune to be conceited, sharp tongued, and, above all, ambitious, and he felt that the success of his ambition depended on Rochester. He was convinced that this affair with Lady Essex boded no good to

Rochester, on whom the anger of the powerful Essex family seemed certain to fall, and at the same time he feared in the siren's ascendency over the favorite the death-knell of his own influence. He told himself that he must resist her growing power, being quite too blind, with all his cleverness, to see that in a duel between the sinister beauty of eighteen and himself, with Rochester as the stake, the weakness of Rochester, the passion of Milady, and the schemes of Northampton conspired with the social corruption in which they lived to adjudge the victory before the contest was well begun.

Northampton, backed by his nephew Suffolk, father of Milady, was delighted with the progress of the scheme for snaring Rochester, a scheme of which the youthful participants were ignorant but which their mutual infatuation brought to the threshold of success. To crown his hopes of binding Rochester securely to his side Northampton must marry him to Milady—a consummation possible only if her husband, the youthful Earl of Essex, were removed from the path. To accomplish this he devised a bold plan—nothing less than to have the Essex marriage nullified by a Commission appointed by the King. The plan could not be concealed for long and of course reached Overbury's ears. Knowing the influence of the clique involved he could not doubt its success, and he was too keen not to foresee his hold on Rochester lost, his own influence gone forever, his career ended.

Resentment overcame good sense; his tongue, never honeyed, dropped venom. Flinging tact to the winds, he assailed his patron's folly and the Countess' character with an insistence which at first evoked Rochester's impatience, then his resentment, and finally his hatred. One evening at Whitehall the two came to violent words. Rochester on returning late to his chambers encountered Overbury and on inquiring, "How now, are you up yet?" was greeted with the angry retort: "Nay, why are you abroad at this time of night? Will you never leave the company of that loose woman? And seeing that you do so neglect my advice, I desire that tomorrow morning we may part; and that you will let me have that portion which is due to me; and then I will leave you free to yourself, to stand on your own legs."

That was an unfortunate outburst for Overbury. All unwitting though he was, he was a doomed man from that hour. The infatuated Rochester was not the man to conceal from his mistress his Secretary's bitter disapproval of their intimacy, and she, at the mention of whose name even courtiers smiled and women raised questioning brows, swore to be rid of Master Secretary and his sardonic tongue.

She proved as good as her word.

In the beginning it is probable that Northampton and certain that Rochester shared and advanced her plans, for otherwise the King's concurrence (whether innocent or knowing is still a question) would not have been secured and she would have been balked at the very outset. Throughout the dark events that followed, hers seems to have been the instigating villainy to the end, and the snares she laid for the doomed man were managed with inexhaustible skill.

As the first step in his ruin Overbury was offered a diplomatic post on the Continent which, for reasons best known to himself, he preferred to decline. But his fate was on the knees of the gods and he went blindly forth to meet it. Putting his trust in Rochester he sought his counsel and was told to refuse the appointment. That advice proved fatal; Overbury followed it only to find himself the centre of a storm whose fury overwhelmed him. He was accused by the Royal Cabinet of contempt for the King's wishes, was summarily arrested, and cast into the Tower.

All this happened with such bizarre suddenness that Overbury was stunned. The supposed confidant of a royal favorite, the object of a court's envy, a turn of the wheel had flung him from his high estate to the level of a felon. That a plot was afoot to ruin him, in which Rochester and probably the King were involved, never entered his dreams, and he turned in this hour of dismay to the one man whose lightest word could have saved him just as surely as it had contributed to his undoing. It did not occur to him that his resentment of Rochester's affair with Milady of Essex had been divulged to her by Rochester himself, and in his blindness he wrote the favorite a stirring letter, man-fashion, reminding him of their intimacy and begging his influence for his release. But this appeal brought no reply. Again the wretched prisoner, still unable to conjecture what dark intrigue was seeking his ruin, besought the favorite's aid and again his letter went unheeded.

The days dragged by and poor Master Secretary, upon whom but yesterday the reflected light from a throne had cast a halo, languished in prison, wondering pitifully why and whence came the bolt that had singled him out and stricken him low. Before a month had passed his pride was broken and, in a fresh appeal to Rochester, in whom, strangely enough, he still had confidence, he cried passionately: "Lose no hour to declare your resolution that God forsake you if ever you forsake me for any hope or fear."

As the months wore on the torture of spirit and the rigors of confinement began to tell on his health, and his letters to his friends were full of his fevers and his loathing of food. Some suspicion of the source of the sinister designs against him must have awakened, for he writes to the despicable Northampton through whom he craves pardon of his niece, Milady of Essex. As if Fate had decreed that he should drink the cup of humiliation to the dregs, he confesses that he "may have spoken of her with less respect than was fit," but denies that he has ever impugned her honor; adding, "If I might be only freed from her ill-will for time to come, there shall be no man readier to respect and honor her than myself." But this, like all his other appeals to those in high places, brought only silence for answer, a silence that taunted, terrified, and finally broke him.

His thoughts constantly returned to Rochester. Others owed him little, but Rochester owed him much; and yet this very Rochester, whose brains he had been, answered his appeals with silence like the rest or with specious explanations of inaction. Whatever Overbury's suspicions may have been as to the identity of his foes and their intentions, he appears never to have conjectured the worst of fates; and yet it was the worst of fates that was to befall him. "I dare pronounce of Sir Thomas Overbury," whispered the canny Henry Wotton to his intimates, "that he shall return no more to this stage."

While the plans for nullifying the Essex marriage progressed, thanks to Northampton, Rochester, and their ally the King, the Countess was busy playing her private hand. Undaunted by obstacles, she drew into her scheme to destroy Overbury a coterie of profligates and poisoners, and even succeeded in having the Lieutenant of the Tower removed and a creature in her own pay appointed in his stead. When the grim setting was thus arranged the drama proceeded to its tragic *dénouement*. Poisons were introduced in Overbury's food, but the hapless prisoner, though weakening daily, seemed to the impatient Countess to bear a charmed life. To tempt his jaded appetite dainties were served him, heavy with arsenic, and the deadly reactions were carefully noted by her creatures and reported on.

Meanwhile the wretched prisoner, in his agony of body and mind, sought aid from foes he still deemed friends; and it is not good to think of the indifference or derision which met the pitiful pleas of an innocent man. He begins to fear he may not live to be released. "I was let blood," he says in one of his letters, "Wednesday ten o'clock; to the Friday morning my heat slackens not; my thirstiness the same, the same loathing of meat, having eat not a bite since Thursday sennight to this hour."

Five months of anguish passed and the hand of death lay heavy upon him. Hopeless now and with the prescience of coming doom, he realized at last that Rochester had played him false. With the energy of despair he roused himself to a final effort and flung at the cowardly favorite an indictment which must have stirred even that mean soul to the depths. He reminds him of his unfounded reputation for intelligence and his successes at court, threatens him with a public trial, and pictures him in silken raiment philandering with Lady Essex, "won by my letters," while making no effort to secure his friend's release. He has committed to paper, he declares, "under eight seals," the story of their mutual relations so that all the world may learn of Rochester's perfidy; and it is with the last words he ever penned that he brings his denunciation to a close. "So then," he warns with bitter vehemence, "if you will deal thus wickedly with me, I have provided that, whether I die or live, your name shall never die nor you cease to be the most odious man alive."

At last the end came. A poisoned clyster was administered to the dying wretch and when September 15, 1613, drew to its close the Moabitish woman had accomplished her purpose. The emaciated body, stained with blotches from the poisons, was flung into a hasty grave in the chapel of the Tower. Then silence. . . .

Over the passing of Master Secretary no tears were shed. King and court were weary of his sharp tongue and "the stiff carriage of his fortune," and were disposed to ask no questions. As for

Rochester, he breathed a sigh of relief that his passion for the beautiful Lady Essex would be rebuked no more and that dangerous and unhallowed secrets were sealed forever within the newly made grave in the Tower.

Fate smiled broadly upon the favorite. He was raised to the earldom of Somerset; the marriage of the Countess of Essex, thanks to the King's influence, was declared null; and on the day after Christmas, Milady and the favorite were wed with unparalleled splendor under the King's eye and amid the smiles of the Muses of Campion, Ben Jonson, and Donne.

For a dazzling hour Somerset stood upon the pinnacle of success, observed of all observers, the brilliant centre of the court. From the infatuated James he secured for the asking the houses and lands torn from the luckless Raleigh, and he passed his days in a magnificence which rivaled royalty itself.

But avenging Fate, though she seemed to smile upon him, was already unsheathing her dagger. . . .

Two years passed since Overbury's death and then, with an unexpectedness which stunned the court, the blow fell.

An apothecary's boy babbled of poisons, of a lady of high degree, of errands to the Tower, and of a prisoner there, named— he knew not what. But that was enough, and in a flash all ears were open and all tongues unloosed and everybody was recalling Overbury until the court rang with his name and "the deep damnation of his taking-off." Then the King, after slobbering on Somerset's cheek and protesting his undying love, threw him over for a new favorite, Villiers, and swore that the murderers of Overbury should be punished "as he hoped for salvation." Therewith, summoning such equanimity as he might, he awaited the course of Justice. And Justice acted with inexorable precision.

The sordid tragedy was probed to the core and the crew of lesser assassins were hurried off to Tyburn. The Countess of Somerset (she was only twenty-two and of matchless beauty) was hailed to the bar of Westminster Hall (May 24, 1616) and in a voice low with fear confessed her part in the murder and pleaded with the Peers for mercy. At ten o'clock on the following morning Somerset himself was brought to trial. The King, in terror lest his former favorite, under the strain of a protracted trial, might betray the dubious secrets of their earlier intimacy or even accuse him of a hand in the crime, secretly admonished the accused Earl to confess the murder "and leave some place for my mercy to work on." But Somerset stubbornly refused.

With pallid face and sunken eyes he faced his peers at Westminster Hall (packed by the prurient and with seats at an exorbitant price) dressed in black satin but adorned with all the orders showered upon him by his doting master, and with iron composure bore up hour after hour under the assaults of his erstwhile friend, Francis Bacon, the Attorney-General, in charge of the prosecution. Darkness had fallen and torches were aflare in the great hall when at last Somerset was permitted to address the court, and to most of his peers his proofs of innocence seemed as fantastic as the grotesque shadows among which he stood. . . . He was found guilty with his wife and sentenced to be hanged.

But in the end both the Earl and his Lady cheated the gallows: she was pardoned, his sentence was commuted, but both were confined to the Tower. When in January, 1622, at the King's intervention they won a certain measure of freedom, it was to find that most of their enormous estates had been confiscated and that Somerset, whose conviction had made his name a byword in the ballads of the streets, had fallen into oblivion.[1]

Overbury died at thirty-two. His was a busy life, for courtiers have little time to seek a literary reputation. He dabbled a bit in verse ("The Wife" is a charming poem) and wrote observations on his travels; but best of all he gave us a handful of "characters" which won him a place in the history of English literature and brought him into the tradition fathered by Theophrastus the Greek and (in a later generation than Overbury's own) distinguished by the talent of the French La Bruyère.

"A character," Overbury tells us, "is a picture (real or personal), quaintly drawn, in various colours, all of them heightened by one shadowing." It is not focussed sharply enough to present the individual, although at times, as when Overbury pictures the "Courtier," the "Glory-hunter," and the "Flatterer," you feel that he has his eyes fixed on definite figures among the satellites of the King. You would probably not be far wrong in supposing that he had Somerset in mind when he wrote of the "Courtier": "He

[1] It is said that Somerset never exchanged a word with his wife from the hour of his conviction. She died August 23, 1632. He survived her thirteen years.

knows no man that is not generally known. His wit, like the marigold, openeth like the sun, and therefore he riseth not before ten of the clock. He puts more confidence in his words than meaning, and more in his pronunciation than his words. He follows nothing but inconstancy, admires nothing but beauty, honors nothing but fortune, loves nothing." All his delineations are concise, keen, often brilliant and touched by an ironic humor. They were not intended for anything more serious than the amusement of his friends, and when written were handed about in manuscript, laughed over, praised, and perhaps now and then regarded as daringly suggestive of some prototype at court.

There was more than a touch of the mordant about Overbury's pen no less than about his tongue, and he strikes at the vices and follies of his day sharply. Read his "Elder Brother," his "Covetous Man," and his "Ordinary Widow," whose tears secure her a new husband, and you will feel the presence of a satire which a century later was to tip the pen of Dean Swift with vitriol.

Overbury's surroundings were unwholesome, but even in the stifling air of the court his thoughts could wander to the daisied fields of a sunlit countryside, where he pictures "a fair and happy milk-maid, who makes her hand hard with labor and her heart soft with pity," and whose highest hope is that "she may die in the springtime, to have store of flowers stuck upon her winding sheet." There is the fragrance of spring in this which is to drift on to the gardens of the poet Herrick.

Purity won Overbury's homage, and his pictures of the good widow and the true wife show how vastly higher were his ideals of virtue than those of the court in which his lot was cast.

Though Overbury's characters were probably written in 1608 they were not published until a year after his tragic death. Within a few months the book ran through no less than five editions and before 1673 it was reprinted twenty times, for the seventeenth century proved to be the heyday of the character. Hall, Earle, Breton, Stephens, and many another helped to satisfy the demand for the *genre,* and a veritable flood of characters poured from the press.

The character however was not destined to strike root of itself and flourish for long. It tended to affect other types and to become merged in them. It influenced the drama in the direction of precision and aptness of delineation. It influenced history, teaching Clarendon the art of portraiture and making his great *History of the Rebellion* live in the figures of Falkland, Cromwell, Rupert, and the rest who backed the fortunes of King or Parliament. But most important of all it influenced Addison, a hundred years after Overbury, and through him the English novel.

Sir Andrew Freeport, Captain Sentry, Will Honeycomb, and even Sir Roger de Coverley might easily have been characters in any other hands than those of the adroit Addison. But Addison, refining upon Overbury, shaped them with such particularizing and transforming touches that their dormant pulses awoke to life.

Walter Raleigh, in his study of the English novel, has cleverly indicated the connection between Addison and Overbury and the advance which character drawing in fiction owes to the creator of Sir Roger, by selecting various traits ascribed to the good old knight in the *Spectator* and weaving them in the Overbury manner into a typical "character" which might be called "An Old Country Squire."

An Old Country Squire is a thing that was a fine gentleman three reigns ago, and is now a mere Justice of the Peace. He is of the opinion that none but men of fine parts deserve to be hanged; yet he will pretend to wisdom in his own shire, where he can explain the game laws, and determine a knotty point in the law, after grave deliberation, with the opinion "that there is much might be said on both sides of the question." At the Assize Courts, to keep up his credit in the county, he will whisper in the judge's ear, "That he is glad his lordship has met with so much good weather in his circuit." He is much given to sport, but loves his neighbour's game better than his own; he will go three miles to spare his own partridges, and when the farmer's sons open the gates for him a-hunting he requites them with a nod and an inquiry after their fathers and uncles. In church he is landlord to the whole congregation, and will suffer nobody to sleep in it besides himself. In town all his talk is of how he killed eight fat hogs at Christmas, and has sent a string of hogs' puddings with a pack of cards to every poor family in the parish. When he dies he leaves for mourning, to every man in the parish a great frieze coat, and to every woman a black riding-hood, because it was a cold day when he made his will.

Macaulay went so far as to say that if "Addison had written a novel on an extensive plan, it would have been superior to any we possess." But Addison did not write a novel after all. What he did was to refine upon the art of Overbury and, by his powers of observation, humanized by compassion and indulgent laughter, transform the generic character into a living likeness, leaving it to more competent hands than his own (Macaulay notwithstanding) to provide a formal plot. It is when we undertake to trace the development of the novel that we realize its obligations to the great "Spectator" and his debt in turn to his well-nigh forgotten forbear. And we pause long enough, even in this hurried generation, to yield to the memory of the brilliant and hapless Overbury a word of tribute.

The Eternal Problem

War and More's Utopia

AT THE AGE OF THIRTY-SEVEN, WITH HIS PEN POISED ON THE FIRST
page of *Utopia,* Thomas More viewed his world—the world that
was England and the world that was Europe—as a Christian and
as a humanitarian and what he saw troubled him profoundly.
As a Christian he was revolted by the spectacle of kings whose
megalomania, greed, and rivalries bred war and imperiled the
unity of Christendom, a thing priceless as a bond of understanding among nations and as a barrier against the vast inroads of the
Turks. Already Rhodes and Belgrade had fallen into their hands
and they were soon to destroy the flower of the Hungarian army
at Mohacz.

These fractricidal rivalries could not go on forever and there
were interludes of peace supported by the most solemn pledges.
But when an advantage was to be gained no covenant was too
sacred to be violated, no excuse too frivolous to be alleged, by men
who called themselves worshipers of the Prince of Peace.

If these violations of truth and of the just claims of peace were
repellent to More the believer in the unity of Christian Europe,
their social consequences appalled More the humanitarian. For
the contemporary scene at home and abroad revealed the endless
evils begotten by war:

> The military expenditure, the money and the time wasted for
> instruments and means of offence to the neglect of all social
> improvements, unsettled habits, trains of idle serving-men re-

enacting in the streets the interminable brawls of the Montagues and Capulets, broken and disabled soldiers turning to theft, and filling Alsatia for lack of employment, labor disarranged, husbandry broken up, villages and hamlets depopulated to feed sheep, agricultural laborers turned adrift, but forbidden to stray, and driven home from tithing to tithing by the lash, to starve; no poorhouses, no hospitals, though the sweating sickness raged through the land, but the poor left to perish as paupers by the side of the ditches, filling the air with fever and pestilence, houses never swept or ventilated, choked with rotten thatch above and unchanged rushes within, streets reeking with offal and filthy puddles, no adequate supply of water for cleanliness or health, penal laws stringently enforced, more stringently as the evils grew greater, crime and its punishment struggling for the upper hand, justice proud of its executions, and wondering that theft multiplied faster than the gibbet.[1]

What held More's eyes captive in this ghastly picture was "the common sort" of people in their vast misery, victims of the devastating plague of war, and doomed to a living hell from which they vainly sought escape. As More looked upon them his heart swelled with compassion, he remembered that whether friends or foes they were sons of God, and he found himself beset by dreams of a new kind of life which would be worthy of that high heritage.

After years of scrutiny and study the fruit of meditation became ripe in his mind. How could he share it with the leaders of European thought, the men who could not hope to perform a miracle of regeneration but whose influence might reach, however slowly, the consciousness of princes and awaken in them the hope of a better day and the will to hasten its advent. Wearing neither crown nor miter he could command no vast auditory nor inaugurate a crusade, for his object was not the delivery of Jerusalem from the tyranny of the infidel but the delivery of men's souls from the tyranny of their passions. What he had was a ready quill, mastery of the *lingua franca* of scholars, a bit of leisure, and ideas which seethed within his mind and would allow him no peace until he gave them utterance. So he wrote *Utopia*—a little book but a great classic—endowing it with the colors of his many-sided mind, his seriousness, his love of paradox, his humor, his whim-

[1] Brewer: *Reign of Henry VIII*, Vol. I, p. 291 ff.

sicality, his idealism, and finally, his profound belief in the power of the human reason.

In *Utopia* [2] More pictures "the good life" as he imagines it in operation among a people possessing no supernatural gifts but only the natural reason, through whose means they have attained the four cardinal virtues which Plato had set down as the foundation of his Republic—Wisdom, Fortitude, Temperance, and Justice. Thus covetousness, the taproot of More's nightmare, war, devourer of all fair things, is curbed and, through the willing adoption of a community of goods, incitements to it are destroyed. More (and the Utopians) does not desiderate peace because he sympathizes with those who detest discipline and love ease or shrink from necessary sacrifices, but because war with its violence and bloodshed is the way of beasts and not the way of beings endowed with reason, and because the social, spiritual, and intellectual enrichment which he dreams of as the possession of all Christians everywhere is possible only in peace.

Under this reign of reason, such customs and laws prevail in Utopia and such advancement has been effected as are a reproof and an example to Europe. Towns are handsome and sanitary; a working-day is limited to six hours and found sufficient; there are time and inclination to cultivate the health of mind, spirit, and body. Penology is reformed, education universalized, tolerance guaranteed, and religion cultivated. Thus the Utopians achieve their ideal of "the good life," not a perfect ideal to be sure, but one so sane, just, and satisfying to the desires of the natural man that the citizen is considered disgraced who, in the end, does not "depart merrily and full of good hope to God."

Why does More fail to represent the Utopians as Christians? Why does he picture them as unendowed with the virtues of Faith, Hope, and Charity? In order to hold his contemporaries up to shame. Christianity had adjured all true believers to conquer their vices but with what scant success More—and all the

[2] *Utopia*, written in Latin and first published at Louvain, did not appear in English till both More and Henry VIII. were in their graves. Had it come to the king's attention in More's lifetime he might have regarded it as the harmless fantasy of a brilliant scholar. Had he studied it carefully he would have considered its author one of the most dangerous men in Europe.

world—knew.[3] Faith, Hope, and Charity, the great Christian virtues, were so commonly professed and so brazenly ignored by those in high places that only an unconquerable optimist like More could escape the temptation to despair. Throughout his book More's voice is audible like the whisper of conscience: "We Christian Europeans do so little; these Utopians, with only Reason to guide them, achieve so much!"

The Utopians' neighbors are not Christians nor do they share the Utopian philosophy, but certain of their practices are so vicious as to mirror perfectly those of Christian Europe and to provide More's keenest irony with a target. There are, he remarks, some "peculiarities" in the Utopian thinking: for instance, they enter into no leagues with their neighbors, reasoning that, if natural benevolence does not operate among peoples, words written down will have no force. Furthermore, the examples set by neighboring states are disheartening for no prince among them regards a covenant as sacred. In fact the Utopians have noticed, to their astonishment, that treaties increase rather than abolish the mutual suspicions of the signatories. Of course the Utopians might surround the signing of covenants with "more and holier ceremonies" were it not that in their observation those are the kind most readily broken! Their neighbors indeed have devised a technique which in private business would be universally condemned but which seems essential in framing treaties: words are so used and phrases so adroitly shaped that "the bands can never be so sure nor so strong but they will find some hole open to creep out at and to break both league and truth." Having been thus disillusioned the Utopians have been forced to conclude that there are two kinds of justice, one for the inferior sort of people, the other "a princely virtue" to which "nothing is unlawful that it lusteth after." If, More remarks with smooth but deadly irony, they saw how inviolable treaties are deemed to be in Europe "where the faith and religion of Christ reigneth" their prejudice against them would vanish!

These are not the only instances, More adds with mock inno-

[3] More would have appreciated Chesterton's retort to the gibe made after the first World War that religion had failed. "Failed," snapped Chesterton, "it has never been tried."

cence, of curious Utopian thinking: they cannot understand how "the space of a little hill or a river" should make men consider themselves born enemies. They detest bloodshed so much that they call the killing of animals "slaughter and murder," and if they must be slain assign the task to bondmen; they hold war in abhorrence "as a thing very beastly and yet to no kind of beasts in so much use as it is to man."

Feeling such detestation of war and regarding reason as superior to brawn the Utopians put faith in diplomacy. In their eyes the diplomatic service is of such extreme importance that men are not admitted to it as a reward for literary fame, as recognition of social claims or wealth—since these do not exist among them —or even because of distinguished service in a field which provides no particular preparation for diplomacy. They select for this vital service youths in whom they detect prudence, intelligence, and integrity and subject them to years of the most careful and extensive training. When thus selected and educated the Utopian ambassadors—"career men" in the best sense of the term —eschewing guile and deceit in accordance with Utopian principles, carry out their assignments with a success so striking and so frequent as to justify the faith reposed in them by the home government.

The Utopians are not sentimentalists; they dwell in no world of rosy dreams. Like More himself they look upon international relations realistically. They know that in the world as it is the basis of successful diplomacy is force, and that even skilful ambassadors may occasionally be doomed to failure. Their watchword is preparedness and they translate it into reality by daily military drill and by "exercising themselves in the discipline of war." At appointed times the women practice in the same fashion, just as their forbears did in Plato's Republic and as the custom was among the ancient Germans, Gauls, and Britons.

The phrases "peace at any price" and "too proud to fight" would be meaningless to the Utopians. Let us consider for what causes and under what conditions they will take up arms.

First of all the Utopians fight in defense of their own country. They do not wait until their foe is on the march but strike as soon as they are certain of his intention to invade their land, for it is a matter of tradition and basic policy to keep war away from their borders. Their attack is not a half-way but an "all-out" measure delivered swiftly and with all the power they can command. They make no secret of their determination to minimize their own losses in battle, and to achieve this purpose they engage mercenaries whom, while despising them for their willingness to shed blood for hire, they assign to the first assault of the enemy. Supporting the mercenaries are the Utopians' allies. Should the enemy penetrate the ranks of mercenaries and allies he is met by the Utopians themselves, each man of them accompanied by his wife, his children, and his kinsfolk, that "they whom nature chiefly moveth to mutual succor thus standing together may help one another." Since it is a disgrace for a husband to return home without his wife, or a wife without her husband, or a son without his father, it is not surprising that the Utopians fight "with great slaughter and bloodshed" to the last man if necessary. These practices, which are traditional when they are defending their own land, are followed with equal fidelity in whatever kind of war they undertake. Their detestation of war and confessed reluctance to enter it is the measure of the fierce courage and passionate energy with which they wage it when once begun. Sherman's maxim, "War is hell," and *"Blitzkrieg"* (minus its deliberate civilian horrors) would be entirely comprehensible to the Utopians.

A second *casus belli* recognized by the Utopians recalls the insistence of the Romans in their great days on the inviolability of their citizens abroad. If a Utopian in a foreign land be injured or killed, whether by a private force or by the people at large, the facts in the case are fully ascertained by the Utopian ambassadors and reported to the home government which then makes immediate demand that the offenders be yielded up for condign punishment—either death or slavery. If this demand is not promptly complied with the Utopians declare war.[4]

If the injury done is confined to goods or purse no drastic action is taken, for material losses of themselves mean little to a people who hold all property in common. Besides, what was lost "was at home plentiful and almost superfluous, else had it not been sent forth: therefore no man feeleth the loss." But where

[4] The principle implied here was followed by the Austrian government after Sarajevo and precipitated the first World War.

a like offense has been committed against the citizens of a friendly nation the Utopians bestir themselves. This is not because they feel more interest in their friends than in their own citizens but because the former, dealing in their own private goods, sustain direct personal losses which they can ill afford. What action do the Utopians take? Not a declaration of war, since that would involve a punishment out of all proportion to the losses sustained, but a demand for adequate financial satisfaction. Until that is given they "abstain from occupying with the [offending] nation," in other words they establish an economic boycott—a step advocated by President Roosevelt in 1937 against "aggressor nations" and invoked by the League of Nations against Italy during the Abyssinian war.

Despite the reluctance of the Utopians to have recourse to arms they do not reserve that fateful step for cases where the issues immediately concern themselves. Hence a third cause of war arises when a friendly people require aid to expel an invading army. Probably enlightened self-interest plays a part in such cases; on this point More is silent.

However that may be, it is not self-interest but "pity and compassion" which incites them to another type of war: war "to deliver from the yoke and bondage of tyranny some people that be oppressed." Clearly the Utopians, who are realistic enough to practice preparedness in a world full of dangerous neighbors, are idealistic enough to wage wars of intervention in the interest of friendly and of oppressed peoples and in each case without conditions.

So far we find the Utopians engaging in what are essentially defensive wars. They do not stop there, however, but join a friendly nation in prosecuting an offensive war under the stress of any one of three provocations: one is injuries not potential or impending but actually sustained. The precise nature of these injuries More does not state but he implies their gravity when he says that on their face they appear to the cool and cautious Utopians to deserve to be "requited and revenged." A second provocation is aggressive and predatory raids of which spectacular examples, matching those known to More on the Scotch border and in Italy, have frequently occurred in present-day Europe since the rise of Hitler. A third provocation occurs when the merchants of a friendly nation, traveling in a foreign country, are victimized by her courts "under the color of justice," a crime made possible by the inequitableness of the laws or by the deliberate prostitution of their true meaning.

Even though one of these momentous provocations appears to be present, the Utopians, so great is their caution, so rooted their abhorrence of bloodshed, make no warlike move except under four conditions: their aid must be invoked; the injuries sustained must be fresh (More and the Utopians were acquainted with too many long-forgotten "grievances" which were duly exhumed, invested with specious importance, and put forward as a pretext for aggression); thirdly, the appellant's cause must be found just (More the diplomat no less than More the lawyer believed that the accuser should himself have "clean hands"); and finally the offender nation must refuse to make adequate restitution. If these conditions are present, the Utopians take up arms and in such a vigorous all-out fashion as "makes them rather than their friends seem to be the chief authors and makers of the war."

Of these causes the one which stirs them to fight "most mortally" is the victimization of their friends abroad through the abuse of law. This injury must be distinguished from one already mentioned—the robbing of the citizens of a friendly country when traveling abroad, which the Utopians punish not by force of arms but by an economic boycott. While in each case it is property not life which is involved the method of victimization is vitally different: in one the wrong is perpetrated by private persons or groups, in the other by the recognized agencies of legitimate government, those which enact the laws or those which interpret and apply them. To tolerate injuries from these sources is impossible to More (and to the Utopians) for as a lawyer, a future lord chancellor, and a passionate believer in the sanctity of justice, he knows that only in the even-handedness of law and the incorruptibility of the courts will it be possible to maintain the equitable treatment of pauper no less than prince, of foreigner not less than native, without which chaos will reign at home and abroad.

More emphasizes in signal fashion the enormity of this offense for he records the recent "cruel and mortal" war in which, solely on this issue, the Utopians backed with arms the Nephelogetes against the Alaopolitanes. He recalls that the war spread far and wide, involving "flourishing and wealthy peoples" on each side, until at last the Alaopolitanes were utterly defeated and summarily punished. "The Utopians," he remarks grimly, "fought not this war for themselves," and repeats that its cause was the infliction of wrong "under the pretense of right."

We come now to the final *casus belli* acknowledged by the Utopians, one involving a principle on which great jurists [5] have disagreed but which nations have followed for centuries, always for reasons allegedly beneficent but usually for conquest or exploitation. The Utopians take elaborate measures to prevent congestion in the various cities of their island but, if the number of inhabitants exceeds what seems a desirable maximum, the surplus population is sent to colonize "the waste and unoccupied ground" of a neighboring country. This sounds high-handed but the Utopians lay down justifying conditions: the natives have more land than they can cultivate; the colonists invite them to "join and dwell with them," easing the process and insuring a mutually advantageous way of living far superior to that which the natives followed before. What happens if the natives refuse to cooperate, if they "resist and rebel"? The Utopians "make war against them; for they count this the most just cause of war, when any people holdeth a piece of ground void and vacant to no good nor profitable use, keep other [people] from the use and possession of it, which notwithstanding by the law of nature ought thereof to be nourished and relieved."

Despite the almost universal abuse of this principle there is, as Chambers [6] points out, nothing inherently evil in it. Assuming, as seems reasonable, that the Utopian view is More's own and that he has in mind the epochal discoveries across the Atlantic, it is certain that he advocates neither conquest, an English colonial empire nor, least of all, the oppression of the natives. What stirs More's imagination are two other and more splendid dreams: as a Christian he envisions the vast tracts claimed for England in the New World inviting and rewarding the efforts of missionaries to

[5] Grotius supported, Puffendorf and Barbeyrac denied, the right claimed by the Utopians.

[6] *Thomas More*, p. 142.

win the natives to his faith and, as a humanitarian, providing a refuge for hordes of unemployed laborers, "poor silly wretched souls," dispossessed of their hovels and forced to steal or beg "whom no man will set to work, though they never so willingly offer themselves thereto." The Utopian colonists (and More), it must be remembered, accord the natives every advantage they themselves enjoy, including the rights of citizenship, and (as Chambers puts it), "If More is staking out a claim it is for the common body of Christendom."[7]

Once the Utopians resort to war they adopt without a moment's hesitation certain practices traditionalized among them. They surreptitiously cause placards to be displayed in conspicuous places throughout their enemies' country, offering immense rewards to those who will assassinate the prince and other specified leaders and promising a double reward if they are delivered alive. Pursuing this policy even further they offer similar rewards, together with freedom and the guarantee of life and security, to such enemy leaders as betray their country and espouse the Utopian cause. Sometimes these tactics are so successful that the enemy prince himself is betrayed and by one of his most trusted associates. Even though the Utopians fail to corrupt their foes by such means they impair their morale by sowing the seeds of fear and suspicion among them. (Rewards earned, be it added, they meticulously pay.)

If this practice should fail the resourceful Utopians have recourse to another: they arouse contention among their foes,[8] embroiling them in party rancor to the point where the prince's brother or some other rival may be put forward in his place. Should this scheme prove fruitless they stir up neighboring nations against them "under color of some old title of right such" (More adds wryly) "as kings do never lack."

These practices, from which the Utopians shrink with abhorrence in time of peace, they justify when they are forced to take up arms on the ground that their main business is to win the war, to visit the enemy with such exemplary punishment as will deter him from ever again offending, to minimize the slaughter

[7] *Thomas More*, p. 142.

[8] These procedures, now associated with the term "fifth column," were followed as More knew by Henry VIII. and his minister, Lord Dacre, against Scotland.

of their own citizens and equally (here is More's authentic voice) that of "the base and common sort of their enemies' people . . . knowing that they be driven to war against their wills by the furious madness of their princes and heads."

In the present world conflict, the use of torpedoes by submarines without warning to the doomed ships and the practice of sowing mines indiscriminately in enemy and even neutral waters, lend special interest to another procedure which in principle the Utopians ban in peace but which they adopt and justify in war. Within the embracing arms of an enormous bay stands their capital guarded by a citadel and garrison. The bay is full of dangerous rocks among which only the Utopians, relying on certain landmarks, know the way. Should an enemy fleet seek to attack their capital the Utopians "by turning, translating, and removing these marks" deliberately lure it to destruction.

If we follow the Utopians' thought we discover without surprise that they find no glory in victories won by much bloodshed like beasts, but "with wit and reason" like men. They have no compulsory enlistment for foreign service lest from reluctance or fear a man prove valueless or even chill the courage of his fellows. When, however, the borders of Utopia are threatened even the faint-hearted, if physically fit, must join the forces, fighting "whence he may not fly," either on shipboard or on the walls of a beleaguered city. Brief truces with the enemy are scrupulously kept even in the face of provocation—fresh proof of More's disgust for the practice among rulers of breaking their pledged word. The Utopians abstain from ravaging their enemies' country and burning their corn for—unfailingly prudent—"they know not but they may want it themselves." They hurt no unarmed men but spies and they neither plunder a captured city nor harm the inhabitants. Utopian logic dictates this humane treatment of non-combatants but an entirely different treatment of the armed forces: the members of the garrison of a captured city who opposed capitulation are put to the sword, the others are enslaved; out of their estates rewards are given to those who advocated surrender. Logical again, the Utopians exact no indemnities from their allies but only from the conquered people; prudent again, they set these aside for use should they be forced to undertake a future war.

If many of the Utopians' practices seem to a greater or less degree repellent to us, we must keep certain things in mind: the Utopians' rooted detestation of war as unworthy of reasonable beings because destructive and illogical; their efforts, honestly and tirelessly pursued, to avoid it by all means consistent with their conception of justice; their consequent conviction that *whenever they become involved in war they are completely blameless.* Granted these premises their logic is inescapable. They concentrate their energies on achieving a swift and complete victory with the minimum of human losses to themselves and, as pointed out above, to the masses—the burden-bearers—of the enemy people. Thus the Utopians would have smiled at the notion that any of their practices violated the rules of chivalry and ethics. "War," they would say, "is a bloody and tragic business, not a sporting event with accepted rules and an umpire to interpret and enforce them. The lives of ten thousand Utopians, even of a single Utopian (blameless, remember), is of vastly more importance than that of a royal war-maker and a handful of highly-placed advisers who sought their destruction. If by guile and without bloodshed we can bring about his dethronement or his death, if we lure his fleet to destruction or shatter the morale of his people or defeat his army by means of bribery or a war of nerves, reason bids us do it. Who but a fool, a betrayer of sound sense, would bandy words or discuss fine codes with a murderer beating at his gate? If our foes like not our reasoning let them look to it."

It remains to consider how far the Utopians' attitude toward war reflects the views of More.

Utopia, as already suggested, is not More's ideal commonwealth but such an approximation to it as may be achieved by men who live by reason and the four great natural virtues. After listening to Raphael Hythloday's story of this remote and fabulous commonwealth and his glowing approval of its laws and procedures, More remarks: "I cannot agree and consent to all things that he said" even though he is "without doubt a man singularly well learned and also in all worldly matters exactly and profoundly experienced."

Among the things to which More does not completely "agree and consent" are certain Utopian practices in time of war. We may for example be sure that he does not countenance the slaughter or enslavement of a captured garrison or attempts to secure the assassination of enemy kings and leaders. What he thinks of offering bribes for kidnaping them and keeping them in protective custody for the duration of the war or of luring an enemy fleet to its destruction may be open to debate. As to the causes of war recognized by the Utopians I see no reason to doubt that More agrees *under the conditions they prescribe.*

Of the great and enduring lessons he seeks to bring home to all thinking men, there can be no question, for he employs all his art to give them clarity and point: the interest of the state must be in the many not in the few; absolutism (dictatorship, if you prefer) must go; in international relations, passion and duplicity must be discrowned and reason and fair dealing take their place; peace with honor is blessedness, justice the only way to peace; war, the ancient, evil thing, is the foe of the only way of life worth living, of the only kind of advancement worth striving for. Men who live according to the ideals of Plato succeed in banishing that plague forever. How then shall they fail who are willing to live in the spirit of Christ?

DATE DUE

JUN 10 1969			